# Reflections on My Lives:

## An Adoptee's Story

**By David A. Umling**

Written by David A. Umling – 2000
Edited and updated – 2014

The author wishes to express his sincere appreciation to Karen Cresap, Victor Rezendes, Michael Morgan, Frank O'Hara, and my wife for their gracious assistance in editing this book.

The author also gratefully recognizes Anthony Velasquez for his artwork in creating the cover for this book.

Copies of this book may be obtained in Kindle format through Amazon.com.

Printed by Kindle Direct Publishing – Seattle, WA

Library of Congress Control Number - 2020909038

# About this book and its author:

Adoption touches so many lives that virtually everyone has an opinion about it. The knowledge that so many people willingly open their hearts and homes to accept an abandoned or orphaned child inspires great hope in the fundamental decency and generosity of humankind. As well it should. It is a truly wonderful gift of love to embrace a lost child and give him a secure home he would not otherwise have.

But is that really all adoption is or can be? Is it being conducted in a way that truly balances the basic needs and fundamental rights of the adoptee and both affected families? How does it really feel to have all knowledge of your roots and medical history locked away, and how does that affect the adoptee's cognitive development and self-image? How would it feel to look in the mirror and see a reflection with no context, depth, or connection? How does it feel to have your true identity divided between two different families—one that raised you and one that gave you life? How would you feel if you were forced to choose between the two, but made to feel illegitimate in both?

Drawing upon his own childhood and adult experiences, David tackles these difficult questions and explains how the bizarre circumstances surrounding his adoption affected him and inevitably drove him to seek out and find his biological roots. In the process, he teaches us how adoption and the veil of secrecy surrounding it, can affect an adoptee's self-image and sense of identity. His search, and the incredible truth he ultimately learns from it, teaches us that there is far more to the adoption process than is commonly understood. His story illuminates the hidden irregularities, loss and pain that underlie many adoptions and challenges our most basic and casual assumptions about the adoption process. In facing these truths and how they impacted his life, we learn why many adoptees feel that the adoption process should be improved to ensure that the inspirational promises of adoption can be realized by all.

David lives with his wife of 23 years, Barbara, and their 22-year-old son, Michael, in New Creek, West Virginia. From that home base they are working to complete their future retirement home in rural Pendleton County. David is the City Planner for the City of Cumberland, Maryland, a job he has held since 2007. Over his 27-year professional planning career, David has worked for regional planning agencies in New Hampshire, Vermont, Georgia, and Alabama, and he has also served as the Planning Director for LaGrange, Georgia, and Charles County, Maryland. He also served a 3-year term on the Mineral County, West Virginia Planning Commission from 2009 through 2012. David earned a Bachelor's Degree in Sociology and a Certificate in Applied Social Research from the University of Hartford, Connecticut in 1984, and a Master's Degree in City Planning from the University of California, Berkeley in 1986. In 2004, he received the Distinguished Leadership in Planning award from the Alabama Chapter of the American Planning Association. Having lived the first 18 years of his life on a small family dairy farm, David has been an outspoken advocate for rural communities and their special needs within the planning field.

# Dedication

This book is dedicated to the following important people in my life:

> To my adoptive family, who made this story possible;
> To the staff of the NH Dept. of Health & Human Services who, through their manipulative handling of my adoption case, made my story interesting;
> To my biological family, who made my life complete;
> To my wife and son, who make my life worth living;
> To my long-time friends, who helped give my life new meaning;
> To all of the good people, who helped me search; and
> To all other adoptees and birth families, who are searching for their missing souls.

May all adoptees and birth families ultimately achieve the peace of mind they so richly deserve. It is my sincere hope that my story will inspire you on and contribute to the efforts of those people seeking to open adoption records and restore the basic civil rights of adoptees everywhere. I also hope that by writing this story, my son will gain a better understanding and appreciation of our shared past and the struggles I faced in restoring it.

# Contents

Part I: Prologue ........................................................................................ 1
    Wednesday, February 14, 1962 .............................................................. 4
    Tuesday, February 20, 1962 ................................................................... 8
    Wednesday, April 25, 1962 .................................................................. 13
    Tuesday, May 1, 1962 ......................................................................... 19
Part II: A New Beginning ......................................................................... 23
    The Great Divide ................................................................................. 26
    The Prodigal Son ................................................................................. 32
    School of Hard Knocks ........................................................................ 38
    The First Search .................................................................................. 42
    Seventeen ............................................................................................ 48
Part III: One Flew Out of the Cuckoo's Nest ............................................ 63
    Rebirth ................................................................................................ 66
    The Yellow Brick Road ........................................................................ 72
    Learning to Love ................................................................................. 79
    Made in Vermont ................................................................................ 89
Part IV: My Final Epiphany ..................................................................... 97
    Fall from Grace ................................................................................... 99
    The Final Search ............................................................................... 109
    49 Hours ........................................................................................... 121
    First Contact ..................................................................................... 163
    The Rest of the Story? ....................................................................... 180
    Ultimatum ......................................................................................... 183
Part V: A New Chapter Begins ............................................................... 201
    Reunion and Beyond ......................................................................... 203
    Desperately Seeking Sabrina ............................................................. 211
    The Final Homecoming ..................................................................... 223
    Afterthoughts .................................................................................... 240

# Part I: Prologue

If you had met me on the street in 1997 and asked me to tell you something interesting about my life, my answer would have required few words. In fact, a hearty laugh would have been my most likely response. To me, it would be a rhetorical question. I never thought that anything about my life would have been of interest to anyone, not even me. I felt like such a worthless person for so much of my childhood that all I wanted to do was to hide from the world. As a child, I was convinced I was ugly, stupid, and socially awkward. So much so that I avoided being the person I really was inside. I always dreamed of being someone else—in fact, almost anyone else. I thought that if I assumed the interests and personality of the person I wanted to have as a friend, that person would like me. It never seemed to matter who *I* was or what *I* wanted to be. After all, who really cares about an ugly, stupid, and socially awkward person? That question seems especially legitimate to me today in a society where vanity is a growing obsession and beauty and popularity are so highly prized—regardless of how they are achieved.

It wasn't until I went away to college that my self-image began to change. I lived in a dormitory with a great bunch of guys, who I still think about today. They were all young, free, energetic, and ready to squeeze every ounce of vitality they could get out of life. Nothing could faze them or get them down—not even me. Gradually, over time, I began to discover that I was not as awful or stupid as I had thought. This awareness did not come easy. I had to argue about it with myself many times before I could be convinced. As the years passed and I learned to better understand myself, a new person began to emerge in me. That person was so different from the child I had been that it would be difficult for anyone to believe the two had ever shared the same body.

As I became more self-confident, questions about my dark and secret past began to haunt me. I refer not to my childhood, but to a time before my living memory. You see, I am an adoptee, and I once had, if only for a brief moment, another set of parents—perhaps a whole family. Who were they? Why was I given up for adoption? Did I look like them? Did I act like them? Were they still alive? What medical conditions might I have inherited from them? All of these questions ran through my mind from time to time. If you had no knowledge of your own parents or family, wouldn't you think about those questions too, even if only privately? I had known for years that I did not fit well into my adoptive family, but I needed to know about my biological family in order to understand why my childhood seemed like a failure, and how that failure continued to affect me. I wanted reassurance that the personality traits and characteristics that made me feel different from my adoptive family were not due to some character flaw in me; rather, I preferred to believe that my personality was just genetically inclined to be different. I often imagined that, somewhere out there, there was another family into which I would naturally fit. It seemed the only way I'd ever know for certain was to find them.

Like so many adoptees before me, I decided to search for my biological family. But what I never suspected was that my life would be completely changed again by the things I would learn along the way. Piece by painstaking piece, the circumstances surrounding my adoption began to unfold. My story seemed so complicated and bizarre that it became a fascinating soap opera to the people I worked with at that time. Now that many years have passed since most of my questions were answered, I believe the time has come for me to tell you my story. I have tried to be as honest and objective as I can be about the major events and influences that shaped my life, but I do recognize that mine is but one perception of the many involved. Nevertheless, I do believe there is great value in expressing how I experienced it, even if others may have perceived it differently.

I believe that few in my adoptive family will appreciate the documenting of my story, even though I have altered most of the names and places to help protect their identities. I also tried to explain the context and circumstances that motivated their actions, as well as the errors I made as a child in interpreting their actions and motivations, and how they may have contributed to our problems. Over the years, I learned that I bore some responsibility for the problems I and the rest of my adoptive family faced. That should come as no surprise. In fact, we were all at fault for the eventual fate of my adoptive family. The gradual evolution of our relationships, in turn, affected each of us differently and subtly shaped the people we became in ways that were almost invisible to those around us. That's what can happen when people bury deeply their true feelings and concerns and refuse to discuss them. However, upon greater personal reflection, I believe that hiding or ignoring the mistakes of the past will not ultimately help my adoptive family or others who may face similar problems within their own families. I hope that I am acting with courage in explaining it all now. If not, I may be guilty of making another embarrassing mistake.

I do feel that writing this story has eased my anxieties about the past and allowed me to plane away the sharpness of the anger and bitterness I have harbored over the years because of them. The benefit I have realized from writing this story—along with the passage of time and growing distance from my adoptive family—is that I can now separate the guilt, anguish, resentment, and frustrations I felt about my social relationships with the people who framed my childhood from my deep appreciation for and attachment to the surrounding environment in which I was raised and the core values I internalized from it. This understanding has had a profound influence on my growth and evolution as an adult. Throughout my professional career, I have nurtured a greater comfort with and deeper appreciation for our remaining traditional rural communities and the cultural heritage that framed my childhood environment. I have been drawn to those areas throughout my working career. Those treasured elements of my childhood were not the cause of my anger and resentment, but they became innocent, collateral casualties of it. My subsequent personal growth and gradual acceptance of my childhood heritage eventually influenced me to retire in a part of rural West Virginia that I understand to be a cultural and environmental twin to my childhood home. As my wife has explained to me and others, my attachment to our Pendleton County retirement home is understandable because it allows me to revive those aspects of my childhood upbringing that I truly appreciate without having to live with all the excess baggage. I certainly cannot explain it any better or more simply than that. Perhaps it is also my absolution.

To begin my story, I need to start with the events surrounding my birth and adoption. In many instances, I had to speculate about the attitudes, intentions, and motivations of others in order to provide some context or understanding for incidents about which I have no actual memory. Beyond that, I really can't be certain how much of the tale I have crafted about the events preceding my adoption really occurred. The tale is consistent with the facts I have learned and documented. But, then again, reality has always been a hard concept for me to comprehend. My perspective on it and perception of it change with each new detail I uncover and each new life I live. That's why I've always been fond of saying, "*Reality is a blank piece of canvas and truth is the picture you paint on it.*" All I know for certain is that the New Hampshire Department of Health and Human Services does not want to discuss my case, and they will probably never openly reveal what really happened. I can only tell you how I think my life unfolded, in the hope that it will help you understand that adoption is not always what the public perceives it to be. At least, it certainly wasn't in my case.

# *Wednesday, February 14, 1962*

Jacki scurried as quickly as she could into her aging, weather-beaten house and closed the door. She had just stepped outside to bring in the mail, but the stiff, raw sea breeze made it unbearably cold to be outdoors for more than a few seconds. The radio had said that the temperature was 30 degrees, but it certainly didn't feel that warm. Menacing, gray clouds and fog were rolling in off the Atlantic. *It's going to snow again soon,* she thought to herself, as she removed her coat and scarf and laid them over the back of the chair. She carefully settled back into the chair, massaging her knees. They always ached when the weather turned raw or stormy. At least, that was the reason she always told herself. Today was her birthday, and she had planned a shopping trip to celebrate, but the cold weather and her sore knees made her think twice about it. Besides, her best friend down the street was going to give birth at any time, and Jacki had agreed to drive her to the hospital.

Jacki lived in Mariner's Village, a modest, worn, working-class neighborhood near Pease Air Force Base in the coastal city of Portsmouth, NH. Most of the men who lived in the neighborhood had served in the military or worked at the base, like Jacki's husband. Everyone knew everyone else in Mariner's Village, and the wives and women who lived there were all part of one large support network. That's the way life is when you live on the margins of society. You never know when you might need help from a friend, so you'd better take care of them when you can. Jacki knew that, as did all her friends. It was the code of the community. In fact, it could have been its motto. Her best friend needed her, and she was determined to be there for her no matter how much her knees ached. That's what it meant to be a "best friend."

After a few minutes of careful massaging, Jacki's knees began to feel better, and she decided to open the mail. The phone rang as she opened the first envelope. She reached across the end table and picked up the receiver. The rest of the mail slipped off her lap and onto the floor. "Hello," she said as if she didn't know who was calling.

"Jacki, it's me, Mary. I think it's time. She's been having a lot of labor pains. She keeps saying she wants to get it over with. How soon can you get here?"

"I can be there in a few minutes. Is her suitcase packed?"

"Yeah, she's ready to go. I'm staying with the kids. I'll help her down the stairs when you get here."

"Okay, I'm on my way." Jacki hung up the phone and glanced up at the clock on the wall. It was 2:05 PM. She grabbed her scarf and coat and put them on again. A rush of cold air accosted her as she opened the door and gingerly descended the steps. The car was parked at the curb right in front of the house. She had been lucky to find a space in front of her house yesterday, so she had left it there just to be ready when the call came through. As she started the engine and drove down the street, she began to think about what was happening. Normally, Jacki would be happy to know that her best friend was having a baby (which she sensed would be a son) on her birthday. However, this birth would be different, and she knew it. Her friend would not be raising this child; she had already signed the adoption papers. It felt like a death in the family even though the child hadn't been born yet.

As Jacki turned onto Profile Avenue, she could see Mary leaning around the partially open front door. A small, worn suitcase was already sitting on the porch by the steps. She pulled up to the curb as close as she could get to the house, put the car in park, and leaned across the seat to open the passenger door. Mary was already helping their friend down the walkway as the car door swung open. The two women were walking comfortably, arm in arm, until they got halfway down the walkway. Suddenly, her friend stopped and slumped forward, obviously in pain. Fortunately, Mary caught her before she fell and braced her for a few seconds. Mary cautiously scanned the street, first to the left, then the right, as if checking for witnesses. Then they resumed their hurried approach to the car. As her friend carefully slid through the doorway, Mary dashed back up to the porch, picked up the suitcase, and carried it back to the car, tossing it into the back seat. Not a word was said as Jacki drove away and headed for Portsmouth General Hospital.

The silence was oppressive and overwhelming making it feel warmer in the car than it really was. The longer it lasted, the more it made the two-mile trip seem longer. It even made the muffled groans of the aging car seem loud, as it lumbered down the street. Her friend sat quietly, focused resolutely on the street ahead of them—as if looking, but not really seeing. Jacki wanted to turn the radio on just to have some background noise, but she couldn't bring herself to do it. At this point, even the act of turning on the radio would make it too obvious that they were avoiding a conversation. It almost seemed better to let it go and avoid doing anything that might make the situation any more uncomfortable than it already was. Still, Jacki couldn't avoid the nagging thought that she was helping her friend do something that was wrong. She saw how suspiciously Mary had acted while they scurried to the car, and she couldn't help but think that Mary must feel the same way.

The car approached the traffic light at Woodbury Avenue. As they waited for the light to change, Jacki looked both ways down the street. She used the red light as an opportunity to surreptitiously steal a glance of her friend beside her. Suddenly, their eyes met for only a second, and Jacki nervously turned away. Under normal conditions, her friend could smile and chuckle at the most desperate and awkward situations. But this time, she saw only a cold, blank stare. It was a look of despair and futility sculpted by forces beyond her control. It was not a look Jacki wanted to see on her friend. It just didn't belong on that youthful and innocent face.

"I know what you're thinking," Jacki's friend abruptly said, struggling against her conscience as the traffic light changed. "It's really what's best for the baby, you know. I can't afford to take care of him without taking away from the others. This way, the baby will have a chance to live a better life than I could ever give him." Her words seemed more rehearsed than genuine.

Jacki heard her statement, but could only mutter a reassuring, "I know" in response. They had discussed it all many times before. She wanted to say something else, but she knew that no one could change her friend's mind, once it was made up. After all, at an intuitive level, Jacki knew her friend was right. Choices were seldom available to those who lived in Mariner's Village. That was especially true for a woman with three young children, who was recently widowed, who had no formal education beyond the sixth grade, and who, as a teenager, became responsible for raising her ten brothers and sisters after their mother suffered a nervous breakdown. She knew everything her friend had been through over the years. They had grown up together. Jacki didn't want to say anything that would only make her life more difficult. Her life was hard enough as it was. Still, she also knew that her friend was a good mother, and it was hard for Jacki to blindly accept the idea that the unborn child would receive any better from the state. She just kept focused on the road and said nothing more until they finally reached the emergency entrance to the hospital. Jacki pulled up as close to the doors as she could.

As she turned off the ignition, Jacki consoled her friend. "Wait here a minute, and I'll go in and get some help," but before she could get out of the car, she heard the passenger door open.

"No!" came the defiant and resolute response. "I don't need anybody's help. I can do this myself."

Her friend was moving so fast towards the hospital doors, that Jacki knew she couldn't catch her, especially when her knees hurt. Her friend's physical strength was only matched by her emotional determination. *Maybe*, Jacki thought, *it's just her way of punishing herself for what she was about to do*. After all, personal character and integrity in Mariner's Village was not measured by your solution to a problem, as much as it was by the way you faced it. Instead, Jacki opened the back door of the car and retrieved the suitcase, then followed her friend into the hospital. When Jacki finally caught up to her, she was already at the admissions desk. Jacki just took a seat close to the desk and waited patiently, while she guarded the suitcase. There was nothing more she could do but wait.

The admissions clerk picked up the phone to page a nurse to bring a wheelchair. During that moment, Jacki saw her friend suddenly turn toward her. As she got up from the chair and approached the desk, Jacki thought she noticed the glint of a tear in the corner of her friend's eye, but she couldn't be sure. Maybe she just wanted to believe it was a tear. Crying in the face of adversity was never easy for the women of Mariner's Village.

Suddenly, out of the blue, her friend said in a calm, reassuring voice (as though it was Jacki who needed solace), "It's gonna be all right. He's going to come looking for me when he's in his thirties. You just wait and see."

Jacki wanted to believe her friend, if for no other reason than to reassure her that she was doing the right thing. They had been close for years, and the last thing Jacki wanted to do was disagree with her best friend when she needed her the most. Yet, Jacki could not dismiss her lingering fears of dread. She just couldn't fully accept that a child who had been given up for adoption would want to find its biological mother. *Maybe*, she lied to herself, *this Valentine's Day baby will be different*. Then she felt a tear form in the corner of her own eye.

# Tuesday, February 20, 1962

After only a few minutes of gentle rocking, the baby began to fall asleep. It had long since stopped crying, and its breathing was regular and heavy. Angela gently lowered the sleeping infant off her shoulder and cradled it tenderly in her arms as she continued rocking gently in the heavy, wooden rocker. The lights were off, but she could still see the little girl's subtle features in the early morning glow from the window. Angela adored the curly wisps of blonde hair that graced her head, her full lips, and her tiny pug nose that turned up slightly at the end. And when she looked at you, her deep blue eyes would melt your heart away. Angela loved the little girl. In fact, she loved all of the babies that came to her house even if she knew they wouldn't stay for long. It's just that sometimes, the really special ones stood out.

Angela rose slowly from the rocking chair and carried the baby to one of the bassinets in the far corner of the large nursery. She really wanted to just sit there and admire the little girl for a while longer, but she was expecting a visitor, and she didn't have the time. She carefully placed the little girl in the bassinet and covered her with a pink blanket. The hardwood floor creaked under her feet as she left the room, and Angela cringed. She didn't want to wake the other infant sleeping in the bassinet closest to the door. She closed the door gently leaving it slightly ajar and tiptoed gingerly down the stairs.

The television in the living room was on, and three other babies, ranging in age from one to three years, were sitting quietly in a large, wooden playpen, mesmerized by the images on the screen. As she checked to see that the children were okay, Angela, too, became captivated by the picture of a giant rocket rising off the launch pad above a furiously billowing cloud of white and gray smoke. She understood the significance of this event. Colonel John Glenn was about to become the first American to orbit the Earth. It had been eagerly anticipated ever since the Soviet Union had beaten the Americans into space. As the rocket cleared the falling gantry, she clenched her eyes tight and whispered a brief prayer for the heroic astronaut.

When she reopened her eyes, she noticed the time on the clock directly above the TV. "Oh, my heavens!" she said excitedly to herself. "Where *has* the time gone this morning?" It was 9:50 a.m., and a caseworker from the welfare department was due to arrive in ten minutes. Angela rushed across the foyer and into the kitchen to clean up the breakfast remains. She collected all the empty baby bottles from the kitchen table and set them in the sink. There was no time to start washing the dishes. They would have to wait until after the caseworker left. She removed the rubber nipples and filled the sink basin with hot, soapy water so that they could soak while she finished cleaning up the kitchen. She slid the two high chairs against the wall and rearranged the remaining chairs neatly around the kitchen table. She was sponging off the table when the doorbell rang.

Angela peaked through the kitchen window curtains before she opened the front door. "Lisa, I'm so glad to see you," she said as she pulled open the heavy door. "Please, come in quickly. It's cold outside." She could see Lisa's breath hanging in the air as she stood on the front step.

Lisa hurried though the door, carrying a large basket overflowing with blankets. She stomped her feet on the door mat to shake the snow off her boots. "Thanks, Angie. I didn't mean to get here so soon, but I needed to get some gas along the way, so I left the office a little early," she said as she gently placed the basket and her large tote bag on the floor.

Angela helped Lisa remove her dark blue wool coat and placed it on a hanger in the foyer coat closet. "Well, I can't wait to see the baby you told me about," she said with a smile. "Let's go in the kitchen so we can talk, and I'll make us some coffee."

Lisa picked up the basket and her tote bag and followed Angela into the kitchen. She set the basket on the table, while Angela topped off the teakettle with hot water and placed it back on the gas stove to boil.

"I'm sorry that I didn't have a chance to clean up before you came," Angela said as she removed two coffee cups and saucers from the sage green beadboard cupboard. "One of the babies wasn't feeling well enough to play this morning, so I had to put her back to bed. Sometimes I just lose track of time."

"Angie!" Lisa replied in a playfully scolding tone. "You're taking care of five children for us. I don't know how you keep from losing track of your sanity, much less the time. You've done so much for the department that I truly feel guilty bringing you another."

"Oh heavens, I don't consider this a job," Angela said with a smile as she approached the table, wiping her hands on the apron she was wearing. "I just want to make sure these children find their way into good homes. Now, let's take a look at this little boy."

Angela couldn't wait to see the baby in the basket. Lisa carefully lifted the corners of the blankets, gradually revealing the face of a newborn baby boy. He was fast asleep on his back with one hand tucked in the folds of a blanket next to his face. He had curly blonde hair and a wide, turned up nose that twitched when the blanket brushed his face.

"Oooh, he's adorable!" Angela gleefully exclaimed when she saw the newborn's face. Lisa had heard her say those words whenever she brought a new baby to her house, but she knew that Angela meant it every time. "When was he born?"

"Last Wednesday afternoon. I believe that was the 14th."

"How sweet, a Valentine's baby. I can tell. He's going to make some lucky family happy."

"Well, that's what we hope. We already have several families looking for a newborn boy, so hopefully you won't have to take care of him for too long. We're just thankful that you're willing to help us out. We've got such a backlog right now that we didn't have anywhere else to turn."

"You know you can always count on me to help," Angela said as she gently tickled the baby's tiny hand with her finger. "I'd like to pick him right up and hold him, but he's sleeping so peacefully right now. Has he been fed?"

"I got to the hospital around 9:00 this morning. The nurse told me he'd just been fed and changed. He fell asleep in the car on the way here. He'll probably sleep well for a couple more hours."

"Does he have a name?" Angela was familiar with the process and knew the answer, but she always asked anyway.

Lisa reached into her tote bag and pulled out a manila file folder as she responded. "No, he doesn't have a name. According to the hospital nurse, the mother didn't even ask to see him when he was born. Sometimes I just don't understand these people." Her tone turned critical. "So many of them don't have husbands or decent homes, yet the good Lord gives them all these beautiful babies. Then they just turn them over to the state like they were someone else's responsibility. It just seems so unfair."

Angela didn't like it whenever Lisa started criticizing the less fortunate, but she understood why she felt that way. Lisa's parents had to work their way up the ladder. They were poor when they married, but her father was a tireless worker. He bought a struggling hardware store in downtown Portsmouth, turned it around, and soon became a well-respected man in the business community. Lisa had worked hard too and became the first member of her family to graduate from college. She had to work her way through school. She felt that, if her family could break the bonds of poverty, then others could do it too. She believed they just lacked the proper motivation. From her perspective, it was a very reasonable expectation. After all, neither she nor her family ever benefitted from any easy breaks.

Angela didn't share her own views openly, and she didn't want to start an awkward and uncomfortable debate. So, she just smiled politely at Lisa as she turned away from the table to check the water on the stove, which was now beginning to boil. She used the distraction of the whistling teapot to change the direction and tone of the conversation. She placed the coffee cups on the saucers, spooned some instant coffee into them, and filled them with boiling water. As she turned and carried the cups to the table, she began the conversation anew. "Well, I don't know about you, but I think a baby that cute ought to have a name. That's the least we can do for him. Now let's see..., what would make a good name for a boy?" Angie pondered wistfully, as she ran her hand along her chin. "What about Michael—no, how about Greg?"

Lisa didn't say anything as she stirred her coffee and reached for the cream and sugar that had been left on the table. She didn't feel comfortable getting too close to the babies she worked with. As Angela began to stir her own cup of coffee, Lisa quietly opened the file and rifled through the papers. She could hear the other children babbling playfully in the living room and the sound of the television in the background. She recognized the sound of Walter Cronkite's voice, but she couldn't hear precisely what he was saying.

"Oh, I almost forgot!" Lisa exclaimed as she suddenly realized what was on the television and seized her own opportunity to change the subject. "Did he make it okay?"

Angela was still trying to think of a name for the baby and was caught off guard by the sudden change in subject. "I'm sorry, what was that you asked?"

"Did Colonel Glenn make it okay? I was listening to the coverage of his launch on the radio as I was driving here. I just wanted to know if his launch was successful."

"Oh, yes, I guess so. His rocket was just lifting off as I came downstairs before you arrived," Angela responded in a matter-of-fact manner. Then something clicked in her mind and her faced beamed. "Lisa, that's it! We'll call him Glenn. It's the perfect name for a baby boy."

"That does sound nice," Lisa said hoping that it would end the quest for a name. She relieved her discomfort with the subject by wrapping her stiff fingers around the warm coffee cup to soothe them from the numbing cold outside. "Here, I'll even put it on his records for you—Baby Boy Glenn. Of course, you know it'll probably change, once he's adopted. The new parents have the right to name him what they want. Now, let's take a minute to go over the file so you can sign the release forms."

Angela nodded and smiled in appreciation. She felt better knowing that the baby had a name while it was staying with her. It just felt more humane even if she knew it was only temporary. After all, every person deserves a name.

Angela never liked the paperwork, but there was always a lot of it. It always made foster parenting seem so complicated and bureaucratic. To her it was all about sharing her love for children. But it was the price she had to pay, since she knew she couldn't have children of her own. So, she obediently sat down next to Lisa and pretended to listen attentively to the standard spiel. She had heard it all many times before. Lisa was not the only caseworker she had worked with over the years.

By the time the paperwork had been completed, they had finished their cups of coffee. Lisa gave Angela her copies of the forms, closed the file and tucked it back into her tote bag. "Well, that about does it, Angie. I know you're busy, and I don't want to keep you too long. I really want to thank you again for helping us out. I don't know what we'd do without you. I feel guilty saddling you with another baby when you are already caring for so many."

Angela always downplayed the compliments. "I'm just doing what I can. It's the children who really need the help. You just find this baby a nice home, and don't worry about me. I'll take good care of him until then."

Angela accompanied Lisa back into the foyer and retrieved her coat from the closet. As Lisa put it on, she peeked into the living room at the three children in the playpen. They were all playing contentedly, babbling away. Lisa said her goodbyes to them and Angela, then walked out the door.

Angela went back into the kitchen and admired the sleeping baby. She carefully slid her arms under the infant and lifted him out of the basket. He stirred only slightly while she cradled him in her arms. She sang a lullaby as she carried him up the stairs and into the nursery, placing him in a bassinet she had prepared for him earlier that morning. As she turned to leave the room, she stopped briefly to glance at the baby girl she had put to sleep before Lisa arrived. She looked closely at the little girl's face then looked curiously back at the baby boy in the adjoining bassinet. Their hair and the features on their faces seemed so strikingly similar. She pondered her observation for a moment then shook it off. *No, they just couldn't be related*, she thought to herself. *They're only ten-and-a-half months apart in age, and the little girl was only placed in temporary foster care.* She left the room and slowly closed the door. *Still*, Angela thought as she walked down the stairs, *they really do look a lot alike.*

## Wednesday, April 25, 1962

Sally had been in the office for less than an hour when the phone rang. "Now what?" she muttered to herself as she reached for the receiver. Work had been hectic for her over the past few months and her frustration dealing with it in an understaffed office was making it hard for her to maintain her normally pleasant demeanor. She took a deep breath to collect her composure before picking up the receiver. "Good morning, Chelsea welfare department, Sally Kesselman speaking."

"Hi Sally, it's Bill," came the hurried reply. "I know you're probably busy, but I've got a little problem here that I need your help with. I want to talk to you about the Baby Boy Glenn adoption. Do you have the file handy?"

Bill was usually chatty when he called. Now he sounded hurried and formal. Sally suspected that something was wrong whenever he got right down to business instead of engaging her in small talk. She cradled the receiver between her head and shoulder, as she rifled through a pile of files on the corner of her desk. She was working on three adoption cases, twenty-five active welfare assistance cases, and a number of new applications that varied almost daily. "Yes, just a second. I have it here."

"Have you met with the adoptive family about it yet?"

"Yes, I met with the Smiths early last week. They've signed all the paperwork, including the release forms, and I was going to start on the family background check later this week. Why do you ask?"

Bill ignored her question. "How well do you know them?"

"Ellen Smith and I grew up together here in Chelsea. We were good friends in high school, and I know her family well. We lost touch for a while after she graduated and moved to Laconia. She got a job there as an operator for the phone company. She said she quit when she married her husband, Robert. I've met him, but I don't really know much about him, except that he was born in Concord and grew up in Laconia. They moved back here in 1960 to buy a farm in North Georgetown. They've been married for about six-and-a-half years, but they haven't been able to have any children. They want to adopt a son and start a family. Is there something specific you want to know?"

"Do you feel comfortable with them?"

"Of course. Ellen and I have been friends since we were kids. We grew up in the same neighborhood. I told them about the baby, and they really want him."

"How soon do you think you can get them over to Portsmouth?"

"Over to Portsmouth?" she repeated in a puzzled tone. "Well, I haven't even started with the references yet. It'll take me at least another..."

Bill cut her off in mid-sentence. "No, no, no; that's not what I'm asking. We're trying to expedite this case. The baby's in a foster home with five other kids, and we need to get the boy out of there soon to take the burden off the foster mother. We can deal with the background check later, if necessary. If you feel comfortable with the parents, I'd like to get them over to Portsmouth to pick up the baby as soon as you can. Do you think they'd be willing to pick him up next week?"

"Well, I don't know..." Sally responded, somewhat perplexed. "I mean, I'm sure they'll be excited. I'll call and ask, but I thought I'd be bringing the baby to them. Can't you just relocate the baby for a few more weeks?"

"No, we thought about that, but we'd really like to process this case quickly, Sally. I'd like you to make arrangements with Lisa Banks over at the Portsmouth office for the Smiths to pick up the baby sometime next week. Lisa's working with the foster mother. Please call me back when you've got it all arranged. I know you've got a lot you're working on, Sally, but I really would appreciate your help with this one."

Sally paused for a second before warily responding. "Sure, Bill...I'll do what I can."

"Thanks Sally. This is really a big help. I'll get everything in order here in Concord. Don't worry about a thing. I'll talk to you later. Bye." Sally heard Bill's phone click before she had a chance to respond.

Sally didn't know what to think, as she hesitantly hung up the phone. Not only was it one of the stranger telephone conversations she'd had with Bill, it was also odd that he was asking her to make such quick arrangements to transfer the child. It really wasn't standard procedure, even in New Hampshire. Adoptive parents did not receive their babies until all the paperwork was finished, and she didn't know of any case where the adoptive parents were asked to travel so far to receive their children.

She stared at the open file for a moment as she fingered the pages with a bewildered look on her face, before closing it and placing it on the top of the stack. She was glad to know that her friend would finally have the baby she wanted. She knew Ellen would be excited. Still, Sally hesitated as she picked up the phone again and started dialing. It all just seemed very unusual. Then again, with all the work that had been given to her, she could at least understand the desperation she sensed from Bill.

***** *****

Ellen Smith had just finished washing the breakfast dishes when Sally called. Robert had gone back out to the barn to turn the cows out and finish the morning chores. She was naturally surprised to get the good news so soon. Sally had led her to believe that it would be at least another month or more before they'd see the baby. Earlier in the week, she had arranged for a local attorney to represent them during the adoption process. She told Sally that they'd be ready to go whenever the arrangements could be made, but that was just two days ago. She was so excited that she cried when she hung up the phone.

For Ellen, this was a dream come true. Finally, they would be starting the family she always wanted. As the youngest of four children, Ellen was the only one who really never left the nest. Having a family of her own would mean, in her mind, that she had finally grown up, even if she still wanted to live near her parents. Her sisters, Karen and Brenda, both had children of their own, and she was feeling more than a little concerned about her inability to have children. This insecurity was aggravated by the circumstances surrounding her brother, Craig, the oldest of her siblings. After years of suspicion, innuendo, and pressure, he had finally admitted privately to the family that he was "involved" in a secret relationship with another man.

The news devastated Ellen and her sisters, each of whom reacted differently to it. Karen immediately developed a vocal hatred of homosexuals and refused to acknowledge that her brother had ever existed. At the time, she and her husband were living in the Lakes Region of central New Hampshire, so most of her close friends knew nothing more about her family than what she told them. In later years, Karen divorced her husband and moved out west to Oregon to "start a new life" and distance herself from her former husband and her brother. Like everyone in the family, Karen feared the reaction of her long-time friends in Chelsea if word of her brother's 'affliction' got out. Chelsea was a small, conservative, and close-knit community, and Karen couldn't handle her fears about the scandal his revelation would cause.

Brenda, who had the most visible insecurities, became increasingly devout in her faith and pretended her brother had died in an automobile accident. She secretly prayed for him to repent, but she knew she could never face him again. Since Craig was living in New York City at the time the revelation occurred, Brenda thought that no one would question her story. She and her family would eventually move away to Ohio, where she would experience less pressure to face reality, and her story would be easier for others and her to accept.

Ellen really didn't know how to feel about it. She was the baby of the family—a full ten years younger than her brother—and she had developed a strong admiration for him as she grew up. She didn't want to pretend he no longer existed and she couldn't simply abandon him, but she experienced the same intense feelings of shame and fear that the rest of her family felt. In fact, she couldn't avoid the nagging fear that some genetic defect had caused her brother's dysfunctional behavior as well as her own inability to have children. She knew none of her friends would accept that kind of behavior—at least, not publicly. It was a haunting fear that intensified her desire to have a "normal family" of her own. Little did she realize her efforts to hide the truth and project a false "image of normalcy" with respect to her family would cause her to continually manipulate reality throughout the rest of her life. Yet she desperately needed that image to soothe her personal anxieties and to protect her from public scrutiny.

The news was especially hard on Ellen's parents, who just couldn't accept the intense reactions that Karen and Brenda had, but who internalized the greatest disappointment and guilt about their son's situation. Over time, the family chose not to discuss the situation privately or openly, preferring to deflect questions about Craig's whereabouts by just saying, "He had moved away to New York and was doing fine, but his job kept him too busy to visit very often." They were a puritanical New England family that never liked to discuss or express personal feelings. Ellen eventually felt that this "story" was best, because most of her friends in Chelsea knew that Craig didn't visit his family anymore, and he had lost touch with his childhood friends in town. There were few job opportunities in Chelsea, so it was not unusual for the children to move away after high school and rarely return. She could never get over her love for her brother and wanted to remain in contact with him, but she never initiated any calls, never went to visit him, and never invited him to visit her. Ellen didn't want to do anything that would remind her parents of the embarrassment and guilt they quietly sheltered. She also wanted desperately to cling to her former image of him. As a result, she always felt trapped in the middle of the issue and was constantly worried—like the rest of her family—that her social circle would someday learn the truth—a truth that no one in her family had the courage to face publicly.

As Ellen struggled to control her tears, a list of things that needed to be done raced through her mind. She needed to call the attorney, prepare the nursery, buy baby clothes and supplies, and call her mother. But first, she raced out the door to the barn to tell Robert. As she opened the heavy barn door, she found him scraping cow manure into the gutters with a hoe. "Bob! Bob!" she yelled excitedly as she ran towards him. When she reached him, she threw her arms around him before he had a chance to rest the hoe against the wall. "Sally just called to tell me the news. We're going to get the baby. We can pick him up next week. Isn't it wonderful?"

Bob felt Ellen press her head against his shoulder, as she began to cry again. His initial reaction was to stiffen against her emotional displays, which always made him feel uncomfortable. Like Ellen, he was stunned by the suddenness of the news. He dropped the hoe where he stood and gently placed his arms around her. "Yes, it's wonderful news," he said in a cautiously pensive tone. He really hadn't taken enough time to fully resolve his feelings about adoption. He wanted a son, and he knew how badly his wife wanted children, but he, too, was privately haunted by his own insecurities.

Robert was an only child. He never met his biological father, Martin Smith. His mother, Donna, told him that Martin abandoned her just before he was born. He grew up with the belief he was a bastard child. His mother said that Martin always liked to party and drank excessively, and she was tired of being embarrassed by his behavior. He would become abusive when he was drunk, and she needed to escape. She also told him that, after the divorce, Martin never wanted to see his son and refused to contribute any child support. Donna never said a kind word about Martin, but it would not be until after both his mother and father died that he would fully understand and accept the truth. Everything she ever told him about Martin was a lie.

Robert was raised by his mother and stepfather, Walter Carr, who Donna married only months after her divorce from Martin. Walter owned a small, hardscrabble farm near Laconia, where the family lived until after Robert married Ellen. Known throughout the community as a rugged, emotionally distant man, Walter refused to adopt Robert because he felt that Martin should be responsible for him. Walter always treated Robert with disdain, as though he was a constant reminder that Donna was once married to another man.

Likewise, Robert never felt close to his stepfather. He always called him "Mr. Carr," never "Walter" or "Dad." When he married Ellen and wanted to take over the family farm, Walter refused to allow it. He told Robert to his face that he didn't have what it took to be a farmer, and he'd rather sell the farm than let Robert "run it into the ground." Several years later, Walter did sell the farm to a local developer, who built a shopping plaza on it. Robert was devastated, but he swore he'd buy his own farm and prove "Mr. Carr" wrong. That's when Robert and Ellen decided to move away and buy an 80-acre dairy farm along the Connecticut River in North Georgetown.

Unfortunately, times were tough for Robert and Ellen during the first few years on their new farm. They hadn't made a measurable profit since they bought the farm in 1960, and they were beginning to incur substantial debt for supplies and replacement equipment. His need to hire part-time help to keep up with the demanding farm work didn't help. Robert always kept the books and managed their finances privately, so Ellen never knew how close they were to bankruptcy. For him, it was a matter of pride. To her, living on the margins was simply becoming an accepted fact of life. Their financial struggles and inability to have children reinforced Robert's emotional insecurities and low self-esteem. Perhaps Walter had been right about him all along. This fear made him hesitant to assume the role of father, especially to someone else's child. But Robert knew how much this adoption meant to Ellen, and he didn't want to fail her, too. So, he swallowed his nagging anxieties, as he was accustomed, and agreed to adopt a child. He just didn't stop to think that it would happen so fast. He needed more time to feel more comfortable with the idea.

After a moment of silence, Ellen looked up at Robert and said through her tears, "You know, I think that things are finally looking up for us, after all."

Robert smiled reassuringly. "I hope so, Ellen. I really hope so."

## Tuesday, May 1, 1962

The late afternoon sun made it hard for Robert to see the road ahead of him. He and Ellen were returning from Portsmouth with their new adoptive son. They had expected to be home by now, but the meeting with the caseworker and foster mother took much longer than they originally planned. Now they were only halfway home, and it was getting close to milking time. Robert wanted to press on, but the setting sun was becoming harder and harder to battle. He needed a break. Fortunately, they had arranged to stop at Uncle Andrew's house on the way home. Uncle Andrew was Robert's favorite relative on his mother's side of the family. Ellen adored him for his gentle good nature and warm sense of humor. They so admired him that they decided to rename their new son after him...David Andrew Smith. Ellen couldn't wait to tell him.

Robert turned to Ellen as they drove up the narrow, dusty driveway. "We can stay until the sun sets, but we need to get back on the road as soon as we can. I've got to milk the cows before it gets too late."

Ellen only smiled. From the moment they started home, she was enthralled by the baby she held in her arms. She fed him a bottle of milk as they were leaving Portsmouth and then played with him until he fell asleep. "That's okay, Bob. He's asleep now anyway," she whispered.

Robert opened the car door for Ellen, and she carefully got out of the car. Before they could get to the front steps, Uncle Andrew and Aunt Sue were standing in the doorway waiting to greet them.

"Come in, come in," Aunt Sue urgently implored, motioning with her arm. "We've been waiting to see the baby."

Robert raised his finger to his lips as she was welcoming them. "Shhh...He's sleeping," he said in a hushed voice. "We can't stay long, but we wanted you to see the baby."

As they entered the house, Robert and Ellen were greeted by the aroma of a fresh cooked meal. Aunt Sue was a marvelous cook and the scent of her meals was always an irresistible invitation to stay. It was not going to be easy to convince her that they needed to leave so soon.

Ellen carefully tilted the baby towards Aunt Sue and Uncle Andrew, as they entered the generously furnished living room. "See, isn't he cute?" she asked as she turned the corners of the blankets away from the baby's face.

"Ohhh, would you look at that?" Aunt Sue softly replied. "He's so adorable, isn't he, Andrew?"

"He's a real lady killer all right, just like his great-uncle. Come on; let's go sit on the couch. You know, we were thinking we were going to have to send the Mounties out after you," Uncle Andrew said, as he led them to the sofa.

"We'd have been here sooner, but the meeting with the caseworker took much longer than we thought it would," Ellen said as she settled down between Aunt Sue and Uncle Andrew. "We didn't even leave Portsmouth until after 3:30."

"So, what's his name?" Aunt Sue interjected.

"Well, the foster mother named him Glenn, after John Glenn. But we thought we'd name him David Andrew," Ellen said with a smile. She turned to Uncle Andrew. "What do you think?"

"Hmmm..." Uncle Andrew pondered as he scratched his chin with his thumb and forefinger, "That's a fine name. But I think it would sound a little more impressive, if you called him Andrew David."

"I like the name David," Ellen replied. "Besides, there's only enough room for one Andrew in this family."

"What about his birth certificate?" Aunt Sue asked. "What will his name be on that?"

"The caseworker said that the city will issue a new birth certificate for him. It won't contain any information about his original name or mother. The new birth certificate will list his name as David Andrew Smith and list us as his parents."

"Did they tell you anything else about him or his family?"

"Well," Ellen responded, "we know he was seven pounds, thirteen ounces, and nineteen inches long at birth. He was born on February 14 at the Portsmouth General Hospital. We met the foster mother, and she told us he eats and sleeps well. He apparently got a case of thrush mouth shortly after she got him, but the pediatrician took care of it right away. Other than that, he's been healthy. They did tell us some information about his former mother. We know she was in her early twenties, widowed, and she had some children by her deceased husband. They told us more, but we're going to forget all that. He's *our* baby now."

Aunt Sue detected the possessiveness in Ellen's statement. She knew that, deep down, Ellen could be very selfish at times. She only hoped that she wouldn't lie to the child about his past. It seemed to her that lies could be more devastating to the child than the truth. Little did she know at the time, Aunt Sue's hopes would not be fulfilled.

# Part II: A New Beginning

After adopting me in 1962, Robert and Ellen adopted a second child, a thirteen-month-old girl, in 1964. They named her Jeanette. Then Ellen gave birth to three natural children, all of whom were girls: Daphne in June of 1965, Leslie in December of 1967, and Anita in August of 1975. Since Anita was born so late, relative to the rest of us (I was thirteen-and-a-half years old at the time), her experiences within the family were quite different. A sixth child, Ellen's only natural son, was stillborn in 1973. We all lived together on the family farm in North Georgetown, until I moved away to college in 1980.

Ellen's parents, who lived in the neighboring city of Chelsea, visited us often and were major influences on our lives. We spent many days at their house where they had lived all their married lives. In the earliest years, we also spent a lot of time with Ellen's sister, Brenda, and her four children. They also lived in Chelsea, where Brenda's husband, Keith, managed a local laundry. We always enjoyed spending time with Brenda's children, even though two of them were considerably older than us. In 1969, Brenda and Keith moved away to Ohio, and we saw them only rarely after that. We never met Ellen's brother, Craig, and we didn't first meet her oldest sister, Karen, until she visited us briefly from Oregon in 1977, just before their father passed away.

Robert's mother visited occasionally for Christmas, and we visited her and her family only infrequently. The most interaction I recall with Robert's relatives was the annual family reunion, which was always a dull and boring affair. Only one of his mother's siblings had children, so there were very few kids our age at the reunions. What few kids we did meet at the reunions always seemed spoiled to us (probably because we were so poor), so we never really liked to play with them. I spent most of my time answering the same general questions asked by a horde of older relatives that I really didn't know well. Eventually, we stopped going to the reunions. Either our parents finally became bored with the affair or enough of the key older relatives passed away that there was no longer anyone left to organize them. We never really knew for certain nor—to be perfectly honest—did any of us really care.

I don't remember when I learned that Jeanette and I were adopted or what it meant to be adopted. In fact, I don't recall any family or even any one-on-one parent/child discussions about it or what it meant. During the early years, it never seemed to matter. We all played together and quibbled as normal children do. Actually, the fact that two of us were adopted didn't become an

---

important distinction between the adoptive and natural children until I was roughly ten years old. Around that time, a series of events occurred that would gradually create a rift within the family. These events and their effects on our relationships would never be openly discussed or resolved, but they would have serious consequences for my self-image and my ability to consider myself a legitimate member of the Smith family.

My childhood is not an easy subject for me to write about. For a number of reasons, I had very low self-esteem throughout most of this period in my life, and I tend to be a very private person. I also harbored a lot of anger and frustration that I turned inward on myself. I was not a happy camper, and I knew it. In fact, I was so embarrassed about my childhood, for multiple reasons, that I tried to hide it all away when I left home for college. My upbringing with the Smiths had taught me that it was a sign of strength and integrity to bear your personal problems privately. Although I was successful in repressing my memories of the events from my consciousness, the anger and resentment I felt about them remained in the back of my mind, manipulating my perceptions of the world around me. It was like a dark, evil puppeteer pulling my strings from behind the curtains. Eventually, I had to understand and face those childhood memories in order to exorcise the demons that haunted me.

When I finally revealed my childhood experiences to my wife, she reacted to them with some measure of skepticism. When I asked her why she felt that way, she said that she could accept the fact that I had many unpleasant experiences as a child, but she couldn't understand why I never mentioned any happy times. She felt, quite reasonably, that my childhood couldn't be filled only with unpleasant experiences.

I spent a lot of time thinking about her point. In fact, I could recall many experiences from my own childhood that most people would consider to be happy times, such as occasional family day trips to the beach, chasing fireflies on a warm summer night, the annual Fourth of July fireworks displays in Chelsea, and trips to the county fair. In later years, I have found it easier to appreciate many of my childhood experiences and the heritage I gained from them. Although I did enjoy these activities and have fond memories of them, the joy I obtained from these experiences never seemed to last very long, and they always seemed to be overshadowed in my mind by the anxieties and fears that I carried. Why? Was I just a naturally unhappy person? I have been much happier as an adult than I was as a child, so I don't believe that I was simply incapable of being happy.

The only explanation I can give is that, as a child, I was never able to feel any lasting sense of satisfaction or fulfillment from the pleasant experiences in my life. During most of my childhood years, I felt so guilty about being part of and dependent upon my adoptive family that I was never able to gain any lasting sense of contentment from even the most pleasant of experiences. I often felt like I was a burden or a long-regretted obligation, rather than a legitimate member of the family. And without that sense of contentment, I had nothing to use as ballast against the rising tide of guilt, fear, and anger that hovered like a dark cloud in the back of my mind and tainted my perceptions of the world and people around me. I don't know if this explanation is easy to understand, but it's the only way I know to explain it. I think it is important, though, to understand why I felt so bad about my childhood experiences.

# The Great Divide

Of the five children in our family, Jeanette, the second adopted child, was the slowest to mature. She always seemed to have a very difficult time comprehending things. Her attention span was very short at times, and she often had problems focusing on tasks that challenged her abilities. She also had a somewhat annoying tendency to behave in a very immature manner or retreat to a child-like state when confronted with a challenging situation. At times, she would babble incoherently then laugh loudly and uncontrollably at her own behavior—regardless of whether it was truly funny or not. When it occurred unexpectedly, she almost seemed like a possessed child. We never knew what caused this behavior, but my other sisters and I were often shocked and frightened by her sudden behavior swings. Jeanette always had a very limited ability to understand the world around her and her place within it. I felt for many years that she may have been mildly retarded, but I guess I'll never know for sure.

Jeanette's developmental handicap became more apparent as she grew older and the gap between her chronological age and her cognitive development grew wider. She apparently had a very difficult time in kindergarten—or at least more so than the rest of us. At the end of the year, her teacher recommended that she repeat kindergarten before beginning first grade. I never knew the specific reasons for it, but I do know that Mom was not about to allow it. When she could not persuade the teacher to let Jeanette advance to first grade, she took her case to the superintendent's office. Eventually, the school relented, and Jeanette moved on to first grade. Although she would have difficulties throughout her school years, she received very little formal counseling, and no attempt was ever again made by the school to hold her back.

Jeanette's difficulties were not limited to school. She also had a bed-wetting problem until she was ten or eleven years old. These incidents were especially frustrating to Mom, who refused to accept that there was anything wrong with Jeanette. While I can't say for certain why Mom never sought any outside help or guidance dealing with Jeanette's problems, I believe she feared anything that threatened the "image of a normal family" she always worked so obsessively to project. Her solution to Jeanette's developmental problems was to punish the undesirable behavior, in the hope that Jeanette would eventually learn to behave properly. When Jeanette wet the bed at night, Mom would force her to scrub the sheets and blanket in the bathtub the next morning. If she wet the bed again the following night, Mom would make her get into the bathtub with the soiled sheets and blanket and scrub them clean in cold water. If it happened yet again, the washing routine would be accompanied by a harsh and often brutal spanking.

I can't say that this approach ever met with much success. The punishments Jeanette received never helped her learn how to act appropriately, and she received no positive reinforcement when she did behave properly. In fact, the only thing she did learn to do in an attempt to avoid punishment was to lie about her accidents. Unfortunately, her inability to think through the potential flaws or contradictions in her lies made it hard for her to be very convincing. She often tried to blame Daphne, Leslie, or me for her mistakes or accidents. This caused the rest of us, including me, to turn on her, even though it was usually obvious that she was lying. In the end, whenever Jeanette's lies failed, she would receive harsh punishment from Mom then face some form of torment or retribution from the sibling she had falsely tried to blame. From her perspective, I'm sure there was no way to win.

Since Dad spent most of his day working in the barn or in the fields, it took quite a while for him to realize what was happening to Jeanette. When he finally did begin to understand how Mom was treating her, he objected. This led to many loud arguments between them. A typical argument would begin with Dad criticizing Mom's treatment of Jeanette. Mom would then blame Dad for not supporting her and for not helping her control Jeanette's behavior. Occasionally, she would try to deflect Dad's concerns by reminding him that he never really wanted to adopt children anyhow, so he had no right to tell her how to raise Jeanette. Invariably, Dad would then accuse Mom of favoring me over Jeanette, because I was her only son. In the end, the arguments always centered on the adoptive children, and they were always fierce and bitter.

As children, we were frightened by these arguments. When we heard Mom and Dad begin to argue, we would hide in a bedroom until we heard a door slam. That usually meant that either Mom had retreated to her bedroom or Dad had left the house. Either way, it was a signal that the fight had ended. I guess Mom and Dad weren't aware that we could hear everything they said during these arguments. Once a fight had ended, nothing was ever said about it, as if it had never happened. Sometimes, Mom and Dad wouldn't even speak to one another for hours after they had argued. We children certainly never asked about them. In fact, we rarely talked about them amongst ourselves, even when we were hiding together.

However, I think that each of us privately realized that our parents were divided over the adopted children. As we grew older and more frustrated over the fighting, Mom and Dad's arguments would begin to trigger subsequent squabbles between the adoptive and natural children after the initial fight ended. Sometimes, we would bicker over unrelated issues, just to vent our frustrations and anger. On other occasions, we would argue over who or what was to blame for our parents' fight. Quite often, our anger and resentment were directed at Jeanette and her actions.

However, I do remember one defining incident that occurred when I was around nine or ten years old. After a particularly long and loud argument between Mom and Dad over the adoptive children, Daphne—who was only six or seven years old at the time—defiantly approached Jeanette and me and said in a sneering tone, "*You're* not part of our family. If you weren't here, *our* mom and dad wouldn't fight so much." I remember feeling angry about her allegation, but I said nothing. After all, how could I argue with her? Everything we heard Mom and Dad say when they fought seemed to prove it. Daphne was just the first of us to acknowledge it out loud. It was the first time that I began to perceive myself as an outsider living within the family. It also marked the beginning of Daphne's intense jealousy and guarded hatred of Jeanette and me.

I certainly can't claim to have been a model child by any measure I know. I would have to say that my biggest and most visible childhood liability was my fiery temper. Even my great-aunt Sue, who I considered to be my staunchest supporter within the family, often said that, as a child, I was usually a good boy, except for my temper. When I lost control, I would usually just yell, say something mean, or slam things. However, I did once put my fist through the cellar door. A few years later, I punched a hole in my bedroom wall. I tried to hide the hole behind a picture, but my mother found it several years later, when she repapered my room. There were times when I could control my temper, but not very often. Only after I had vented my anger, would I begin to feel any regret for my actions.

I was usually punished or chastised for my temper, but I was never able to completely restrain it. In most instances, I wasn't even aware it was controlling me until after I had vented it. But, when Daphne said to me what I knew and feared to be true, my anger instinctively turned inward. I could no longer blame Jeanette, Mom, or Dad. I couldn't even blame Daphne for saying it. All I could do was wish that I didn't exist. For the first time in my life, I felt like a truly evil influence. That's when I knew in my own mind that I *was* different because I was adopted, and I would struggle with that awareness throughout the rest of my childhood.

Daphne's assertion never seemed to affect Jeanette the way it affected me. I don't think that Jeanette was ever able to comprehend it the way that I did, and she was used to being blamed for things like that, anyway. I was always a deeply reflective person, even as a child, and Daphne's words struck a chord deep within my psyche. The more I remembered what Daphne had said, the angrier I became with myself. I also remember feeling scared. What if the fights got worse? What if Mom and Dad decided it would be better to get rid of Jeanette and me? What if they would punish us for causing their disputes? These unanswered questions only increased my fears during subsequent arguments. I couldn't bear the thought of being in the same room as Daphne and Leslie during another fight. I struggled with my feelings for weeks, maybe a month or two, after it occurred, before I had to say or do something about it. As usual, though, what I did say about it was not the best choice of words.

Sometime after the incident with Daphne, we went to my grandparent's house in Chelsea for a family cookout. I don't remember if it was a special occasion, only that it was a hot summer day. Mom took all of us kids to the house early to help prepare the meal. Dad remained at home to finish his morning chores before joining us closer to lunchtime. Grandfather was in the back yard, setting up the grill. The four of us children were playing in the front yard, as Mom and Grandmother began setting up the tables under a large maple tree near the front porch. I don't remember what we were playing, but a squabble soon erupted between Daphne and me. To break us up, Mom directed me to get the lawn chairs and set them up near the table. Whatever Daphne and I had quibbled about must have aggravated my feelings of guilt about being part of the family. Mom made it worse by making me feel like the one who had to be separated. So, when Mom and I were conveniently alone near the table, I just blurted out the simple question that plagued my mind, "Why did you adopt me, anyway?"

As far as I was concerned, it was time for me to know the answer to that question. I was quite tired of thinking about it. My mother, of course, was stunned. Not only was it one of those issues that was not openly discussed, it also came up without warning or preparation. Her face went blank for few seconds, as she struggled to find a way to evade my question. I must have interpreted her silence as a hint that I would not like her answer. So, I proceeded to fill the gap with my own feelings on the subject. Although I can't remember my exact words, I doubt that they were very sensitive of her feelings. When I was finished, Mom just dropped what she had in her hands, turned around, and ran crying into the house. Years later, Great-Aunt Sue told me that, according to my mother, I had said that I wanted to find a picture of my real mother and carry it in my wallet.

I sincerely doubt that was everything I said, but it was clearly representative of my feelings at that moment in time.

It certainly didn't take long for me to realize that I had made a mistake. Shortly after Mom disappeared into the house, my grandmother barreled through the front door with an expression of sheer rage on her face. Nothing I would ever say or do again would cause such a vengeful look. The blind fury in her eyes caused me to freeze, as she thundered down the front porch steps. By now, the events had caught the attention of my sisters. Grandmother marched up to me and grabbed my upper arm with a vice-like grip. Her voice trembled with rage as she screamed at the top of her lungs.

"Just who do you think you are?" she yelled, yanking on my arm as if she could shake an answer out of me. "Why do you have to be so hateful to your mother? Do you have any idea what she's done for you? If it wasn't for her, you would have grown up on the streets or in an orphanage!"

I remember feeling her spit hit my face as she berated me for what I had said. As she paused for a second to catch her breath, she pulled me over to one of the lawn chairs I had just set up and slammed me into it so hard that I thought it would break. She let go of my arm and then shook her finger at my face.

"You just sit right here and think about what you said. I have *never* in my life seen such an ungrateful child. Don't you move from this chair until you're ready to apologize to her. I don't know what's gotten into you, but don't you *ever* say anything like that to your mother again. Do you hear me?"

I didn't answer. I just sat there, mesmerized by the rage in her voice. Satisfied that she had spoken her peace, she caught her breath again, turned away from me, and marched back into the house, slamming the door behind her. I looked back at my sisters, who were equally shocked by the scene that had just unfolded. They were all staring back at me, their cheeks tracked by tears. On their faces, I saw only scowls. It was the old familiar, "What on earth have you done now?" look. I felt like a spectacle. It was as though a giant spotlight had been turned onto me, and there was nowhere to hide from it. I wanted to yell at someone, but there was no one to yell at except myself. Then, as I became aware of what I had done, I could feel guilt taking hold of me. Once again, I was a source of division within the family, and that feeling would nag at my conscience every time I reacted to the way I was treated. It was only then that I, too, felt tears begin to trickle down my cheeks.

Eventually, my guilt got the better of me. Perhaps I was an ungrateful child. After sitting in the chair for what seemed like an hour, I sheepishly got up and shuffled up the stairs of the house. As I entered the front door, I could hear Grandmother in the living room softly consoling Mom, as she continued to sob. Their voices fell silent when I emerged in the living room doorway. I stood there for a second, as if lost for words, and then meekly proclaimed that I was sorry and that I didn't mean what I had said. I don't remember what my mother said or did, but I do remember seeing my grandmother beam a smile back at me, as if nothing had ever happened. From that point on, I never trusted the sincerity of her smile again.

These events caused everything to change. Although Mom continued to punish Jeanette harshly for her mistakes, we rarely overheard any future arguments between Mom and Dad. By the time Anita was born in 1975, any disagreements they might have had were virtually invisible to us. Although we did see occasional periods when they refused to speak to one another, it was unusual for any of us to hear the disagreements that triggered them. The subject of my adoption was also never mentioned again.

Over time, Daphne became increasingly resentful and jealous of my place in *her* family. She treated me as if I had illegitimately and deliberately stolen her role as the eldest child and first in line to take care of her mother. She always compared herself to me and couldn't stand to view herself as second best. She, too, had a sharp tongue and was not afraid to use it. As she got older, she blamed me for everything that happened to her that she didn't like. In 1983, three years after I left home for college, Daphne decided to attend the same school. Although I wasn't even around when she made her decision and was never involved in her deliberations, she always said that it was my fault that she chose to go to the same college. I stopped speaking to her in 1995, because she blamed me when Mom was diagnosed with breast cancer. She claimed that the cancer was caused by my efforts to persuade Mom to visit my family in Georgia, after we moved away from New England in 1991. Her remaining list of accusations rarely made any better sense.

As for myself, I could never look at my adoptive family the same way again. I had already learned to feel guilty about my uncontrollable temper. Now I felt guilty for anything I did that created any further division between family members. For a time, I quietly believed that I was possessed by an evil alter ego that took control of me whenever I let my guard down. But once I felt like an outsider living within the Smith family, my guilt rose to a new level. I wanted to run away many times, but I was too afraid of the outside world to act on my impulses. I had little self-confidence and knew nothing of life outside the interminably sheltered sphere of the farm community in North Georgetown. How could I survive? Where would I go? How could I get there? There were no obvious answers to these basic questions.

Instead, I basically resigned myself to life in the Smith family. I felt guilty whenever they did special things for me, but I could never discuss my feelings with them or anyone else. I forced myself to do what they expected of me, whether I wanted to or not. I even tried to impress them when I could, in the hope that they would not be disappointed with me. But worst of all, I learned to hate myself for not wanting to be a part of the family. Every time I argued with my father or I despised Daphne for the way she treated me, I would hate myself more afterward. I was gradually digging my own grave, and I didn't even realize it. It just seemed to be my lot in life.

## *The Prodigal Son*

The fondest memories I have of my adoptive father date back to when I was about four or five years old. Life was hard for him in the early years, but his determination always remained strong. I always admired him for his inner strength and resolve, and I still do so, even today. I respected and deeply internalized the traditional values he lived by, even as we didn't always see things the same way. As he grew older and failed to achieve his own personal goals, he began to lose his motivation, and his outlook became increasingly negative. Eventually, Dad and I began to disagree on many issues, and our relationship deteriorated.

Dad was convinced, and always said, that there was no future in farming, and that we all needed to get a college education and find a good job in the outside world. He seemed genuinely convinced that I didn't have what it took to be a good or successful farmer, which I later learned had been his father's assessment of him. Even today, I can't be certain if his casual indictment of my farming abilities was his own genuine assessment, part of his persistent efforts to discourage me from farming, or just his subconscious way of deflecting the criticism he received as a child by passing it along to me. Whatever his true intentions were, it tarnished my respect for him, and became another reason for me to bury my childhood experiences when I finally left home. The last thing I needed on my resume was any prior experience as a poor, incompetent backwoods hick. It would be many years before I could discover and acknowledge any practical value in my traditional rural upbringing.

Despite Dad's persistent efforts to discourage me from farming, I was genuinely eager to farm as a young child. So much so, that I eagerly assumed my first regular farming chores when I was about six years old. I can remember following him around the barn as a young child, like a loyal puppy, while he milked the cows and did his chores. I know that I often wanted to help, and I would try to lift the heavy buckets of milk after he filled them. To me, I was testing and building my muscles. I also liked to ride with him on the tractor and often dreamed of driving it myself.

Even as a young child, I had a somewhat lean, but rugged build, so I was physically capable of handling a number of simple jobs. Since I liked to ride in the grain cart when Dad fed the cows, I quickly learned the amount of grain each cow received before milking. So, he eventually allowed me to scoop out the grain for each cow at feeding time. He also let me prepare the powdered milk formula and feed the calves. I would do other odd jobs, such as breaking apart hay bales and distributing them to the cows, scraping manure into the gutters after the cows were turned out, stacking chopped firewood, and carrying partially filled milk pails to the milk room, so Dad could pour their contents into the bulk tank. They seem like little, meaningless tasks now, but to a six-year-old child, they felt like big responsibilities. Eventually in later years, I was paid the extravagant sum of 50 cents per day for my work. My work responsibilities increased gradually over time, but always seemed limited to the more mundane and routine jobs that my father was more than willing to pass along.

There was always plenty of work to do on a small family farm. Before I was old enough to work, Dad hired a part-time man to help him with the heavier chores during the summer months. I don't remember his name—only that he was a tall and lean man with skin that always felt like finely tanned and buffed leather. Around the time I began working on the farm, a new helper arrived on the scene. He was my first cousin, Carl (Aunt Brenda's younger son). Carl was built for farming. He was a rugged, roly-poly, red-haired, freckle-faced kid, about three or four years older than me. He was also fascinated with farming. He loved to work with his hands, and he loved to be around the cows. He seemed to be a natural for the job. He also admired my father.

Carl was eager to work on our farm during the summer, and Dad was more than willing to oblige. Since he was a few years older than me, Carl was given the more "glamorous" and responsible jobs of driving the tractor and helping Dad with odd repair jobs. Carl wasn't a scholar by any means, but he was trustworthy, motivated, and endowed with a compensating supply of common sense. He quickly earned my father's respect, and they developed a strong bond that was apparent to anyone who saw them together.

When Carl first began working on the farm in 1968, I admired him, too. He was friendly and fun loving, which were two qualities I wanted, but never believed I possessed. However, by the end of the second summer, my admiration began turning to envy. Whenever I followed Dad and Carl around, I felt like a fifth wheel—and a flat one at that. In many instances, the only time I was noticed was when I asked to help or got in the way. Dad's love and respect for Carl became more apparent the longer they worked together. I remember sitting quietly through many supper conversations, as Dad regaled the family with stories about what Carl did and how well he did it. I must admit, Carl expressed a deep and sincere admiration of my father, and Dad was only returning it the only way he knew how. However, expressions of love were not offered generously in our family, and it was much harder for me to earn the kind of respect that Carl freely received. In the end, I felt that Carl was the son my father always wanted, but never got. Although my jealousy of Carl grew throughout the summer of 1969, I never let it show. I just buried it deep inside and laughed respectfully with everyone else at the stories Dad was so fond of telling.

I felt somewhat relieved when it was announced that Carl's family was moving to Ohio at the end of that summer. I believe that Carl did come back for part of the summer in 1970 to work on the farm, but he didn't stay for long, and he never spent any significant time on the farm after that. Still, the memories of Carl remained strong in our family, and a picture of him was always displayed prominently on the desk in our living room. It was a constant reminder to me of how I envied him.

Several events occurred shortly after Carl left New Hampshire that served to reinforce my feelings about him and his relationship with my father. First of all, it was not long after Carl moved away that I first became aware of the arguments that Mom and Dad were having over Jeanette and me. Those arguments taught me that Dad was not entirely enthusiastic about adopting me. That understanding made it hard to believe that Dad's casually negligent treatment of me whenever Carl was around could be unintentional. However, at that time, I blamed Carl for it, not my father. I responded to it by working harder to earn my father's respect. I thought that was what he expected of me.

The second event occurred several years later in 1973. During that summer, Mom was expecting her third child. It was clear that Mom and Dad were hoping it would be a boy. My reaction to their enthusiasm and anticipation was fear. If they did have a son, how would they treat me? I never spoke about my fears, but I guess my trepidations about it were obvious. Several family members went out of their way to tell me how wonderful it would be for me to have a little brother. Perhaps their assurances were intended to avert any additional thoughts I might harbor about wanting to find a picture of my birth mother.

Then, for some odd reason, the family's preparations for the impending baby abruptly stopped and concern mounted. Within a month of the expected birth, my mother no longer felt the baby's movements. Soon thereafter, she went to the hospital and stayed there for several days. When she finally returned, we were told that the baby had died. While the news of the baby's death was a shock to everyone, the most disturbing aspect of it to me was that the baby was indeed a boy, and they had decided to name him Carl. For a long time after that, I felt guilty because my parents lost the son they really wanted—their *own* son—and they were stuck with me instead. My mother never got over the loss, which I always felt was aggravated by the fact that his namesake had moved away. In fact, her intense reaction to the loss also made me wonder if I ever would have been adopted into the family, had Carl been born first. After all, they had stopped adopting children once they began having children of their own.

The third and final event happened shortly after the baby's death. By that point in time, I had begun to lose interest in farming, and my father and I were beginning to argue frequently. Although I wanted to please him and make him proud of me, everything I tried to do seemed to fail. I gradually became disinterested in farming, because I was always assigned the most menial tasks, and my efforts to do more than I was asked to do were often met with criticism. Whenever he criticized me, my thoughts would turn to my cousin Carl, and I would feel like a failure. Besides, Dad had told me many times that he wasn't going to let me take over the farm, because I wasn't cut out to be a farmer. However, an opportunity arose during that period that would give me one last chance to prove him wrong and earn his respect.

Our family's financial situation was not good in the early 1970s. The gas crisis of 1973-74 caused inflation and a downturn in the local economy that nearly pushed my father into bankruptcy. Dad was beginning to feel that the only way to sustain the farm was to get a second (part-time) job. He heard about an opening at Agway (a northeastern farming supply store chain) for a sales representative, and one of his friends urged him to consider it. He knew most of the farmers in our area on both sides of the river and would be a good marketing asset to them. At least the hours would be flexible, so he could continue working on the farm. To improve his chances of getting the job, he was advised to attend a two-day Agway conference in Springfield, Massachusetts. Springfield was at least an hour-and-a-half drive away from North Georgetown, so he couldn't commute from home. If he wanted to attend the conference, he would have to spend the night in Springfield. However, before he could attend, he needed to find someone willing to milk the cows and take care of the farm for two days. I was determined to do it!

When Dad announced that he had decided to attend the conference, I immediately offered to do the chores for him. By then I was at around twelve years old, and I knew the entire milking routine. It was the first opportunity I had found to show Dad what I could do on my own. Of course, he didn't immediately accept my offer. First, he called every friend he knew in Georgetown to see if he could find someone else to fill his shoes. I was more hopeful than insulted by his efforts to find someone else to help, because I really wanted this opportunity. By the time he decided to attend the conference, none of his friends had enough advance notice to shift their own work schedules. It was not long before he came back to me and reluctantly told me that I could do it.

Once the reigns of authority were placed in my hands, I never let go. I worked like a man possessed. I followed every procedure to the letter. I even made sure I cleaned and scrubbed every square inch of the milking machines and other equipment after each milking, including the insides of every hose, which my father usually only rinsed to save time. I cleaned the barn from one end to the other, picking up tools that had been left out. I cleaned all of the residue hay out of the waterbowls. I cleaned out the gutters. Fortunately, nothing went wrong. By the time he returned from the conference, I was confident that he would be proud of and pleasantly surprised by the work I had done. Finally, I would receive some credit from him for a job well done.

When Dad returned late in the afternoon, he quickly changed his clothes and headed for the barn. I followed him confidently, asking him about the conference all the way. After opening the door, he stood in the doorway and surveyed the barn. The fruits of my labor were obvious. A fresh coat of sawdust was spread evenly behind the stanchions. The gutters were clean. All of the equipment was neatly put away. All of the loose hay that was usually scattered in the walkway between the stanchions had been swept neatly into the mangers. I waited eagerly for his first statement, but he said nothing. He just turned and walked into the milk room.

"How did you rinse out the machines?" he interrogated, as he carefully inventoried and inspected the milking machine components. It was as if he didn't trust what he saw—as though it was just window-dressing, and he was searching to find something I hadn't done properly. I told him that I didn't just rinse them out with a bucket of water and iodine (as was his expedient practice); I took them apart and cleaned them with the brushes.

"How many scoops of grain did you feed Lucy?" Lucy was our leading milk producer at that time and was fed more grain than the other cows. I knew that she received three scoops of grain before each milking.

The list of questions went on and on. He led me all around the barn, grilling me about every detail he could think of. Never once during the questioning did he say "thank you" or "good job." All I got was the Spanish Inquisition. Yet, I immediately and correctly answered every question he asked. And with each correct answer, I detected his frustration level increasing. When he was finished, he dismissed me with a cursory "Looks okay, then," as he turned his back to me and began his preparations for the evening milking. I was furious with him. All of the anger I had felt towards Carl, I now directed at him. I wanted to explode, and I think he knew it. But I bit my lip, walked away silently, and vented my frustration in the confines of my own bedroom. That's when I punched a hole in my bedroom wall. We didn't speak to one another for at least two days.

That final event effectively destroyed my relationship with my adoptive father forever. From that point on, our disagreements became more frequent and more intense. It didn't help that Dad and I had different ways of thinking. To my father and all of his farming friends, life always seemed easy to understand, if you had a good measure of "common sense." It never mattered how little knowledge or practical understanding we had about how the outside world really worked. Everything was either right or wrong–good or bad. I tended to be a deliberative thinker. Where Dad saw only black and white, I saw shades of gray. The simple answers that Dad offered for every question I asked never seemed to completely satisfy me, when I thought about them in greater detail. Since no one else in our social circle thought the way I did, I eventually came to the conclusion that I was so stupid that I couldn't even recognize the simple sense in my father's reasoning. I thought too much only because I was incapable of understanding. At least, that's what I led myself to believe. Whenever Dad and I discussed complex issues, I would ask many probing questions in an effort to understand his position. In most instances, my questions were received as challenges to his way of thinking, and he would quickly become frustrated. His frustration would only make me feel stupid. Then, our discussion would quickly degrade into an arguement. This pattern grew worse and reinforced itself as our relationship deteriorated.

By the time Dad's life ended in April 1984, we could barely have a discussion about the weather without ending it with an argument. It was many years later before I learned the real reason why he seemed so offended by my efforts to impress him with my ability to farm. In 2000, my great-aunt Sue told me some of the unspoken details about Dad's relationship with his stepfather. Only then did I realize that his own self-esteem had been shattered by the awful and demeaning things that his stepfather had told him when he was aspiring to be a farmer. I now believe that every effort I had made to make him proud of my accomplishments and capabilities only made him feel more and more inadequate or incompetent. He probably thought I was trying to outdo him. Neither of us ever talked about the incident, so we never knew how each of us felt about it nor why we reacted to it as we did. That shortsightedness was a trademark of my adoptive family, as well as its eventual undoing.

## *School of Hard Knocks*

During my early years, we had very few opportunities to play with other children in the community. The closest homes in our neighborhood with children our age were nearly a mile away, and there were always plenty of farm chores to occupy our spare time. I normally played by myself or with my sisters whenever I had no chores to do. My lack of social interaction with children outside our family didn't become an issue until I began school. Although I don't remember my first day of kindergarten, I do recall being very shy and withdrawn when surrounded by other children. I also remember being afraid to start first grade, because I knew I would be in a different school surrounded by children I didn't know well, even though they lived throughout our community. I think that all five of us experienced some problems adapting to the public school environment, after spending so many years in a sheltered family setting. Yet each of us tended to adapt in different ways.

Despite my fears and insecurities about the social environment in first grade, I did quite well. Through first, second, and third grades, I attended a small, two-room schoolhouse in North Georgetown village, less than a mile from home. All of the children that attended our village school, fewer than 40 in all three grades, were from our small community on the northern end of Georgetown. Since the families of the village were somewhat familiar to us, it was relatively easy to be accepted by the other children and to make friends. I made several good friends among the children of our village, including Ricky DeMark. Ricky and I became such good friends, in fact, that we had to be separated in first grade, because we talked too much during class.

My social environment did not change again, until I entered fourth grade. Due to classroom limitations at the North Georgetown School, all of the children in our community were bused to the central primary and elementary schools in Georgetown village for grades four through eight. These schools were roughly seven miles from North Georgetown and included older and unfamiliar children from all corners of town.

To make matters worse, this transition occurred at a very awkward point in my childhood. By the time I began third grade, I had developed vision problems. I couldn't read the chalkboard or watch TV without squinting. My eyesight was tested, and I was diagnosed to be nearsighted. From then on, I wore glasses, which greatly changed my appearance at a point in time where children become more sensitive about it. In addition, the transition to the central schools occurred at roughly the same point in time that my relationship with my father and the rest of my adoptive family began to change. The changing social environment only complicated the emotional difficulties I faced during that period of my childhood. To put it mildly, I did not adjust well.

During the time I attended the village school in North Georgetown, the children either walked to school or rode a small yellow school van that collected the children living in the outlying rural areas surrounding the village. Although I lived less than a mile from the school, Mom refused to allow me to walk to school, as I often wanted to do. She was always afraid that someone was going to kidnap me on the way to or from school, even though such occurrences were very unlikely in such a rural environment in the late 1960s. I never did understand her reasons, until after my final search for my biological family. In any event, my sisters and I all rode the little school van during the time we attended the village school.

When we started attending the primary and elementary schools, we began to ride a larger standard school bus. This bus not only picked up all the younger school students in North Georgetown, it also took the high school students in our community to a transfer site at the elementary school, where they boarded a second bus to the regional high school. To us younger kids, the high school students were "cool," and everyone wanted to be accepted by them. I was dealing with a lot of difficult emotional issues at that time, and I acted very withdrawn and awkward around the new and older students. It did not take long for the older adolescent kids on the bus to pick me out as an easy target for teenage abuse. The first thing about me that they attacked was my appearance, especially the horn-rimmed glasses that I wore. They also noticed that I frequently smelled of the family farm, which provided them with additional ammunition. Everyone who grows up on a dairy farm knows that each farm has a distinctive odor that permeates everything and is difficult to detect by the people who live there, but is immediately apparent to everyone else. It's not unlike the scent of cigarette smoke that can be detected in clothing by any nonsmoker. I spent so much time in the barn during my early years that my clothes, shoes, and jackets often carried the odor of our farm with me.

The initial criticisms I received from the kids on the school bus made me very conscious and insecure about my appearance. I began to study my reflection in the mirror from time to time. I had always known that I didn't look remotely like anyone else in my adoptive family. In fact, most adoptees I have talked to seem to become aware, at some point in their childhoods, that they look quite different from their adoptive families. People don't stop to realize how alienating that realization can be. If you think about it, relatives and friends often comment on how much a baby or child looks like its siblings, parents, or other relatives. That rarely happens with adoptees, and no one ever thought that way about me. I carefully studied every individual aspect of my reflection, and I found no similarities at all to anyone I knew in my adoptive family. To me, it was as if my reflection had no depth. When most people look at their reflections in the mirror, they can see their mother's eyes, their father's nose, or some other physical trait that links them to a family and gives them a sense of belonging or connection. My reflection began and ended with me and me alone. It made me feel different and peculiar. That feeling seemed to legitimize the scathing attacks I suffered and led me to accept the thought that I was ugly. Rather than fight back, I accepted their judgments of my appearance and tried to make myself as invisible as I could. Although I knew that my glasses were part of the problem, I was afraid to change to a different style. I thought the change would draw more attention to me, and I certainly didn't want to make myself any more visible to them than I already was.

When I did try talking to Mom about the abuse I received on the bus, she would try to console me with some old cliché. She never wanted to discuss it and never expressed any sincere concerns about it. Her suggestion was to "ignore them" or "don't pay any attention to it." That might be fine advice for an adult who has already developed some measure of self-esteem and can look at comments like that from a broader perspective and life experience. However, for a child who was just beginning to perceive his self-worth from the reactions and impressions of older and presumably wiser kids, it was useless advice. How could I simply ignore the only feedback about myself that I was getting? I just decided to quietly accept the abuse, and I rarely talked about it again. In the end, it just became one more reason to hate myself.

As I became a target for continued abuse and taunting by the older kids, I began to lose the allegiance of my friends from the village school. When faced with the choice of defending a social outcast (who would not even defend himself) or being accepted by the "in-crowd," they quite logically chose the latter. Of course, it did not take long for the treatment I received on the bus to pervade the school environment. By the time I began fifth grade at the elementary school, I was an awkward, reclusive pariah, who cowered on the fringes of the school society. Suddenly, I was standing outside looking in at both my social circle and my adoptive family. The only potential source of friends open to me was the pool of other social outcasts like me. I was determined not to be an outcast among the outcasts.

Making friends was a frightening challenge for me in elementary school. I felt ugly, stupid, and inherently unlikable, so I wasn't going to win them over with a smile. However, I did manage to contrive a way to build friendships with the other social outcasts. I decided that, if I could not be liked for who I was, I would simply become a different person. The first step was to carefully observe the behavior of the person I wanted to make my friend. I studied his mannerisms, attitudes, interests, and other behavior patterns, in an attempt to understand his personality. I then altered my own behavior and interests to replicate or reflect those of the person I wanted to befriend. This was not an easy task, and it meant that I usually had to focus on only one friend at a time. I found it too difficult to pattern myself after two different people at the same time, as there was often a wide range of personality traits among the outcasts.

Using this approach, I managed to maintain a loose association of rag-tag friends throughout elementary school. However, my interests tended to swing wildly to accommodate my best friends, from auto racing, to science fiction, to baseball. After a while, I had no idea what I really liked—nor did it matter much to me. Of all the friends I had in elementary school, the one I spent the most time with was Craig Dobbins. Those who knew him well called him "Dubber." To this day, I still don't know what that meant. Craig was a short, odd, and awkward character, obsessed with UFOs and science fiction. The strange nature of his interests and his obsession with them placed him on the outer fringes of the outer fringes. To me, that made him an excellent candidate for a friend, since there would be little competition for his friendship. However, my friendship with him also reinforced my own outsider status within the school environment.

Dubber and I spent a lot of time together during and after school between sixth and eighth grade. He was the first friend I was allowed to spend nights and weekends with largely because he lived only two doors away from the elementary school. My parents would agree to let me stay, because I didn't need a ride from my parents to get there from school, and Craig's mother would usually agree to bring me home. Although Dubber's interests and character set him apart from everyone else, he had a surprisingly cheerful and outgoing disposition. These personality traits made it possible for him to find additional friends among the social outcasts, but he always spent most of his time with me. Still, the lighthearted attitude he managed to project, despite his social status, earned him a measure of respect from some of the kids who were part of the "in-crowd." He never appeared to be as insecure about it as I did. Although I, too, admired this trait, it was the one aspect of his personality that I was never able to emulate. I simply did not possess the level of self-confidence that he seemed to have.

At the end of eighth grade, Craig informed me that he would soon be moving away to Massachusetts. Apparently, his parents were divorcing, and Dubber's mother was taking him and his sister home with her. The loss of our friendship was painful to me. I had few other friends at the time, and I really didn't want to face high school on my own. But, on the last day of school, Craig shared something with me that only made me feel worse. He showed me some of the comments that our classmates had written in his yearbook. The one that caught my eye was written by my old village school friend, Ricky DeMark. As a consolation to Dubber, he had written that he thought Craig was an okay guy, except that he hung around too much with me. Suddenly, I realized that even my former best friends from the village school were convinced that Craig's outsider status had more to do with his friendship with me than anything about his odd beliefs and fantasies. As far as I was concerned, that said it all.

## *The First Search*

My adoptive family was not very communicative. The majority of our group discussions occurred around the supper table. Even then, our conversations were not very substantive or meaningful. We would talk about almost anything trivial, but never individual family members, our feelings, or our relationships. I remember one supper conversation when I was in seventh grade that focused on U.S. geography. I don't know how the subject came up, but my father had acquired a good basic understanding of geography from his schooling, and he seemed intent on testing our skills in that area. Dad rarely had any interest in helping us with homework, unless we had to build something. Perhaps he felt a little inadequate on the subjects we normally needed help with, so he wanted to see what we knew about a subject of which he did possess some knowledge.

I believe the discussion began with a quiz about state capitals. I knew most of the major ones, but I probably missed a few of the smaller, more obscure cities, like Carson City, Pierre, or Bismarck. They only existed in another world far away from our farm. Satisfied that our education or knowledge in this area was somewhat lacking, he proceeded to test us on major cities. Our performance in that area was much less impressive. At that time, I couldn't even tell you whether San Antonio or San Diego was in California, and I was easily confused about large cities that could be found in multiple states, like Springfield or Columbus. Geography clearly was not my forte. By that point in time, I was convinced that Dad had little confidence in my abilities. I already felt stupid when measured by his standards, and his persistent challenges on the subject of geography that evening only made me feel more inadequate. I didn't like feeling so stupid all of the time, so I decided I needed to learn more about geography. After all, it was a very specific subject, so it couldn't be all that hard to learn.

I found an old Rand McNally travel atlas in the living room closet that was about 10 years old, and during the next few weeks I studied it thoroughly. The atlas had short descriptions on each state and basic information on the major cities. I hadn't realized how immense the U.S. really was or how many cities there were. At first, I was a little overwhelmed, but as I started studying it, I actually found the information easy to digest and engaging to read. It quickly taught me that there was a whole world of exotic and intriguing places out there beyond the confines of my own little community. I so hated my life in North Georgetown at that time that my mind became easily captivated by the thought of running away to these distant places and beginning a new and exciting life. I often daydreamed of what my life might be like in the various cities I discovered in the pages of that beloved and colorful atlas. I knew I didn't have the means, the courage, or the street-sense I needed to follow through on my desire to run away or even to survive on my own. So, the atlas became the only escape I had during that period in my childhood. At least I could read about the cities, look at the pictures, and travel there in my mind. With my dreams to inspire me on, it did not take long for me to develop a broad knowledge of U.S. and Canadian geography from that atlas. I learned the names of cities, the counties and states in which they were located, their 1960 populations, and a little about their histories.

Of course, I could not let my newfound knowledge just languish in the dark recesses of my own mind. I had to show Dad what I had learned. After a month or so of quiet study, I casually raised the topic of geography at the supper table. This time, though, the shoe was on the other foot, and he had no idea of what he was facing. Not only could I answer every question that Dad threw at me, I was quickly able to put him in the interrogation chair. I think it took everyone by surprise, especially my father. Suddenly, I could name and talk about more cities and towns in California or Texas than he knew in New Hampshire. This time, I was not trying to make him proud of me, I was getting even. It was a subtle way of venting my frustrations and embarrassment. I no longer even desired his pride or confidence. I just wanted to feel the satisfaction of beating him on the battlefield of his own choosing. On that one evening in the fall of 1975, I did it for the first time in my life, and it was right in front of the entire family.

Having digested the fraying and worn atlas, I desired new sources of information about the places I had discovered. I soon found a 1968 Information Please almanac and realized that it had a lot of additional information about U.S. cities, even if it was a little outdated. I began to devour that as well. Then, I discovered that the city descriptions in the almanac included mailing addresses for the local chambers of commerce. For weeks, I saved all the money I earned from my meager allowance to buy a $15.00, circa-1940, Remington typewriter. I used it to write formal letters to the chambers of commerce and collect packages of new information on the cities that were of greatest interest to my fantasies. Now I possessed a wealth of detailed and truly boring information about scores of cities to complement my expanding knowledge of American geography.

To my surprise, I had acquired too much detailed information on the subject to be of interest to anyone other than myself. My prized sword soon lost its luster, and my knowledge of cities and geography became just another measure of my quirkiness. However, my private fantasies of life outside North Georgetown drove me on obsessively. I eventually discovered that my little AM clock radio could receive stations from distant cities at night when the two local stations went off the air. These stations came in even clearer during the long, cold winter nights. I soon realized that I could receive stations from Baltimore, Cleveland, Fort Wayne, Chicago, Detroit, Charlotte, Atlanta, Cincinnati, St. Louis, and even Dallas and Denver. I found so many stations, that I eventually had to compile a written catalogue just to remember where to find them on the dial. My passion to learn more about these places just built on itself. The more I learned about a new city, the easier it was to dream about escaping my tortured existence and living there. At least I could pretend in my mind that I was a different person living somewhere else. The more I dreamed about escaping, the more I wanted to learn about the distant cities. I never realized at the time that this passion was actually the initial catalyst for my future career, as well as my first attempt to find my biological mother.

Eventually I became fixated on St. Louis. Don't ask me why. It was just an interesting city to me, with a colorful past. It was the primary starting point and outfitting center for nineteenth century Americans traveling to or exploring the western frontier. To me, it was a city of hope and an appropriate place to begin a new life. I became fascinated with every aspect of the city, including the St. Louis Cardinals (baseball and football), the St. Louis Blues hockey team, even the majesty of the Gateway Arch. I listened avidly to baseball games on KMOX radio out of St. Louis. I loved to hear Jack Buck's voice and his dramatic and colorful description of the games. I still claim to be the only person in New Hampshire who heard Lou Brock break Ty Cobb's stolen base record live on the radio. They were playing in San Diego at the time, so the closest station broadcasting the game was KMOX out of St. Louis. I doubt anyone else in the state even knew that station existed, much less listened to it regularly. To this day, I remember and repeat their daily late-night advisory, "It's 10:00 St. Louis; do you know where your children are?" I didn't understand it at the time, but I guess they had a city-wide curfew. My obsession with St. Louis became so great that I set the alarm clock in my bedroom to central time, and I bought a one-year mail subscription to the St. Louis Post Dispatch. St. Louis was the primary escape I used to avoid facing my shattered life in North Georgetown.

Then, during the early stages of my dreams of escaping, something truly incredible happened. Unbeknownst to him, Dad's biological father died sometime in 1975 or 1976, and shortly thereafter, a couple of strangers came to our house. They were his biological father's sister, Sarah, and her husband, Ernest James. It was the first time in his life that he met a biological relative on his father's side of the family. Sarah knew how much her brother had always wanted to meet his son and be a part of his life. Apparently, Dad's biological father, Martin, had followed him throughout his life from a safe distance, afraid to reveal himself. As Sarah revealed the story of Dad's past, a hidden truth was revealed. His mother had lied to him all his life about his real father.

It was actually Dad's mother who had left his father and sought divorce, not the other way around, as Dad had been led to believe. She also left him *after* Dad was born—not before. She was not a person who liked to celebrate life, and she hated Martin's passion for dancing and parties. Apparently, the separation and divorce deeply hurt Martin. He never remarried and never had any other children. He tried to visit his son many times when he was a child. However, every time he tried to visit, his ex-wife had an excuse. His son would always be sleeping, away visiting a relative, or too sick to receive visitors. When Donna married Walter Carr, Martin began to feel unwelcome, but he continued to persist. His attempts to send child support were spurned by Donna. She wanted nothing to do with him or his money. Yet, Martin's love for his son could not be denied. He took every chance he could get to spy on him throughout his childhood, just to make sure he was doing okay. Martin had even driven by the farm in North Georgetown wanting to stop and meet his son. But by then he knew that Donna had poisoned his son's mind, and he couldn't face the rejection he might receive from Dad. Sarah had tried for years to encourage her brother to stop and introduce himself, but he couldn't muster the courage to do it. When Martin finally died, Sarah felt compelled to meet Dad and tell him the truth. It was the least she could do to honor her brother's memory. Before they left, Sarah presented Dad with some of Martin's personal effects that he had always wanted his son to have. Dad treasured them always, and kept them in the top drawer of his dresser. It was all he would ever have by which to know or remember his real father.

Dad never expressed his emotional reactions to this visit, but I know that it did affect him. First of all, he learned that his mother, the only true family he ever knew, had lied to him. I don't believe that Dad ever revealed to his mother what Sarah told him, but I can't say for sure. She was ill at the time, recovering from a stroke that eventually caused her death a short time later in 1977. Second, Dad learned about his father's true love for him only after Martin had died. After being raised by a stepfather who treated him with contempt, I believe that Dad must've wished that he could've had a chance to meet his real father. Soon after Sarah's visit, we made many trips to her house near Concord and came to know her well.

As it progressed over the subsequent years, Dad's successful reunion with his biological family affected me as well. First of all, it proved that it was possible for a person to be successfully reunited with biological family members that were never known. Second, it proved that those unknown family members could still feel love for a long-lost child. Third, it suggested that those unknown family members could be searching for their long-lost child. These were timely revelations for me. I had been dreaming of running away for a few years, and the thought that my biological family could be out there searching for me provided a new focus and impetus for my fantasies. I began to feel that there might be a way to escape and set things right, if I could only find my own biological mother. Perhaps I had a whole family somewhere out there. Perhaps they might accept me as one of their own. I began to focus my geography research on my birthplace, Portsmouth, NH. My first search was just beginning.

My research skills were now well honed, and I put them to good productive use. I learned a lot about Portsmouth during my early years in high school. I even wrote a school paper on Strawberry Banke, a living history museum that contains many of the original homes built in and around the city. I studied maps and learned the street patterns. During study halls, I went to the school library and used reference books to learn even more about the city. I even found an AM radio station from nearby Rochester that I listened to whenever I could receive it. It was not a powerful station, so I could receive it only when the weather conditions were right.

During one of our rare summer day trips to the beach in York, ME in 1977, I managed to convince my parents to drive through Portsmouth. They had always avoided the city before, so I had never been there before in my living memory. I remember how desperately I studied the landscape in the faint hopes that I would see someone that might resemble me in some way. I also remember how nervous my mother acted as we drove through the city, and how she cast aspersions on virtually every aspect of my birthplace. "What a dirty place...Look at all the traffic...They really need to fix these roads." In reality, I could have easily made the same comments of her hometown, Chelsea, which had been in economic decline for many years. When we finally drove across the Piscataqua River Bridge into Kittery, ME, Mom clenched the door handle and hissed in fear all the way across, because the length and height of the bridge scared her so. It didn't seem that frightening to anyone else in the car.

While I was successful in learning a great deal about Portsmouth, I couldn't figure out how I was actually going to find my biological mother. None of the information I learned contained any clues, and I didn't know how to find out who she was. My adoptive mother always told me she knew nothing about my original parents, and she had once said that all my birth records were destroyed when the Portsmouth Hospital burned. Both of these stories would later turn out to be lies. Still, I needed to find some way to make a connection, or my search would end in vain.

At some point in late 1977, I learned about a mother who had found her long lost son, when he responded to a classified ad she had placed in the local newspaper. I don't remember how I learned about it or where it happened, but it eventually gave me the thought that my own mother might be doing the same thing to find me. So, I went to the high school library and found a reference book on newspapers across the country. I looked up the Portsmouth Herald and found their mailing address. As I had done with the St. Louis Post Dispatch, I ordered a one-year mail subscription to the paper. By now, my parents had become accustomed to my quirky behavior and apparently never suspected a thing when I started receiving the Portsmouth Herald in the mail. I certainly never revealed why I had subscribed, because I feared that they would force me to cancel it. I read the paper thoroughly every day, hoping to find some article or ad from my mother. I always anticipated the holiday issues, under the assumption that she would be thinking of me at those times. I was especially eager to receive the February 14, 1978 issue. I thought for sure I was going to find something in those pages. I must've read that issue twenty times, before conceding that there was nothing in it. I managed to hold onto my hopes until Mother's Day came and went, and I still found no ad or article. My hopes soon faded, and I reluctantly allowed the newspaper subscription to lapse.

I tried to think of some other way to find my biological mother, but it was no use. I simply did not have the knowledge or the access to the basic information that I needed. By the summer of 1978, I had resigned myself to the idea that I wasn't going to find her. It seemed that I was destined to be a part of the Smith family forever. It was not a comforting thought, and it offered me no solace.

## *Seventeen*

After completing eighth grade at Georgetown Elementary School, I advanced on to Bald Mountain High School. Bald Mountain was a regional school serving Georgetown and five other neighboring rural communities. It was the ultimate adolescent melting pot. It brought students from six different towns together during the most sensitive adolescent years. The social competition in the school was fierce, but how you felt about it depended, in large part, on your status within it. Each town's students had built its own defined social hierarchy in the lower grades. Now the "in-crowd" from each community was forced to compete with one another for social influence and dominance within the larger school environment. The ultimate prize was to become the one in-crowd that all the other in-crowds from the remaining communities admired and followed. The tougher kids who couldn't fit into a specific in-crowd formed their own rogue band of bullies.

The battles between each leadership group for social supremacy were rarely fought directly between the groups, although some fistfights among rival leaders did occur. Instead, they were waged against the disorganized band of social outcasts, whose ranks had swelled. Actually, I often wondered why so few social leaders fought each other when the competition between them was so intense. However, later in life, I came to realize that when children have little hope or are insecure about their social status, they will often belittle or bully those they perceive to be beneath them in order to feel superior or to demonstrate their superiority. I wish I could have known that as a child. Perhaps I would not have internalized the abuse I faced so intensely.

Like an Olympic competition, each in-crowd's status within the school hierarchy was judged and revered by the boldness of their acts and the level of cruelty they could exact against the hapless social outcasts. Taunting and bullying became commonplace, as each in-crowd group drew firm social parameters for appearance and behavior around their chosen leaders. Drugs, cigarettes, drinking, and teenage sex were the principal rites of passage into adulthood. There were even a number of suicides by students who couldn't handle the stress or face the abuse. In one locally high-profile case, two students from one family committed suicide on consecutive Christmas Eves. It was, in effect, adolescence run amok. Some of the characters in the school would have found themselves quite at home in the pages of _Lord of the Flies_. If not for the regimented administrative structure of the school, there would have been no control whatsoever. To make matters worse, I began to suffer from a bad case of acne. Obviously, I was not going to have a fun time at Bald Mountain High School.

When I first started high school, I was bewildered by the complexity of the social environment. I had just lost my best friend, and I was thrust into a giant institutional building with a sea of strange faces. Of course, my first instinct when confronted by this bewildering environment was to withdraw even deeper within myself. Now more than ever before, I wanted to be invisible, but my gradually deteriorating physical appearance made it increasingly difficult for me to avoid the spotlight. I quickly learned that being an outcast in high school was even harder than being one in elementary school. Not only did I have to face abuse from the older kids, but I also faced the insulting realization that I was not respected by the younger kids. Respect is an important thing for an adolescent. If you have it, you feel in control of your life, and you receive a "get out of adolescence free" card. If you don't, you feel totally worthless, and it becomes a struggle to outgrow your adolescent failures. I felt totally alone, worthless, stupid, and ugly. I was batting for the cycle.

The taunting and abuse I faced at Bald Mountain took many forms. In the early days, most of it was simple verbal abuse, tripping, incidental bumps and nudges, and knocking books out of my hands. My appearance and demeanor had immediately identified me as "outcast material." Now, I was being carefully stalked and deliberately tested to see how much abuse I would take. I did not disappoint them. It was about the only test in high school that I passed with flying colors.

Once I had passed outcast boot camp, I quickly rose up the ranks. I soon became a star attraction for abuse. Kids tried to goad me into fights. The insults became increasingly vile and demeaning. Even the girls tried to tease me, just to see if I would respond. I can honestly say that I never saw the interior of a bathroom at Bald Mountain. I was too afraid to use them. I feared being trapped and attacked by the worst bullies, who spent as much time in the bathrooms as they could to buy and smoke pot. I also didn't want to see what was written on the walls about me. I actually used the bathroom at home every morning, just before I left for school, and I held it in until I returned home in the afternoon. I was always the first one in the bathroom after getting off the bus. It may have been difficult to do, but at least I never gave them an opportunity to dunk my head in a toilet. Still, despite all of the abuse, I rarely stood up for myself. As children, we were always taught never to fight. However, it was only a matter of time before my explosive temper would get the best of me. It finally happened towards the end of my sophomore year.

***** *****

During my first two years of high school, I was required to take physical education classes. Although my work on the farm made me physically strong, I was no athlete. I was inept and uncoordinated. I was also too intimidated by the jocks to participate in school sports or enjoy gym class. I usually did only what was asked of me and kept to myself. What I hated the most, though, was "hitting the showers" at the end of gym. I usually lagged behind everyone else and took my sweet time, so I wouldn't have to shower and change with the jocks. I was following this pattern one morning in the spring of 1978, when one of the jocks decided it was time for an in-crowd plebe to face his initiation test. The plebe's name was Derek Sanders. Derek was relatively short and skinny, but popular with some of the girls. On that day, I was to be his hazing target.

By the time I dragged into the locker room, the showers were full. I waited patiently on a bench with my belongings. Some of the jocks had already finished their showers, and they were dressing near the lockers. Derek Sanders and his idols were among them. After a few more minutes, the showers began to empty, and I decided it was time to make my move. I picked up my books and clothes and started to carry them to a now empty bench next to the showers. Derek, who had finished changing his clothes at the time, reached out behind me as I passed and knocked my books out of my arms and onto the damp floor. When I turned around, I saw him standing there, laughing at me and brashly spouting taunts and insults. He approached me at the urging of the other jocks, who seemed quite pleased with the developments and asked me what I was going to do about it.

I don't know why, but something inside me snapped. Perhaps I had already been taunted earlier that day. All I remember is being consumed with rage. I suddenly yelled at the top of my lungs and attacked him. My aggression clearly took him and everyone else by surprise. I think he expected me to be an easy target. As I made my move, he ducked and tried to escape. I chased him across the locker room and into a corner, where I finally caught up to him. I grabbed the back of his shirt collar with my left hand, pulled him towards me, and wrapped my right arm tight around his neck. I then grabbed my right hand with my left hand and began to strangle him with all my strength. Derek was helpless. He flailed his arms wildly at me in an attempt to brush me away and force me to let go, but it was no use. He was in no position to land a solid blow. I just kept tightening my grip, as he gasped desperately for air.

The rest of boys in the locker room were so stunned by my uncharacteristic reaction that they just stood where they were, yelling at me, "Let him go!" After a few seconds, the coach emerged from his office to see what was happening. He raced towards me, grabbed my arms, and tried to break my grip. To my own surprise, not even he could break the chokehold I had on Derek. The coach yelled at me to stop, but I didn't listen. Then, as suddenly as I had exploded, I threw my arms open and let Derek fall to the floor. His face was flushed, and he was choking and gasping for air. I had nearly strangled him. The coach immediately bent down to help Derek, and I backed away, glaring wildly at the other boys who had now crowded around us. No one said a thing.

After Derek stood up, brushed himself off, and said that he was all right, the coach came back to me, grabbed me by the shoulder, and led me to the Principal's Office. I was still wearing my gym clothes, and I was drenched in sweat. He sternly instructed me to sit in the principal's meeting room, while he spoke with the principal. Suddenly, the knowledge of what I had done struck me, and I began to panic. I felt certain I would be suspended, and my parents would be called. I sat in that room for at least twenty minutes, until the principal came in and asked me what happened. I explained the story as I experienced it. We talked briefly about my feelings and why I did it. He seemed to show some measure of concern. After our conversation, he rose from his chair and told me to wait in the room until he returned.

I sat there obediently by myself in my shorts and tee shirt for at least two hours. It seemed like an eternity. I couldn't see into the rest of the office from the meeting room, so I didn't know what punishment I was going to face. I thought I was waiting for my mother to arrive and take me home, but nothing happened. Towards the end of the school day, the principal came into the room and told me to go back to the gym, change, get my things, and go to my final class of the day. To my surprise, I never heard anything about the incident again. My parents said nothing about it when I got home, so I never mentioned it.

I felt a little relieved the next day, but I kept my guard up. I really didn't know what to expect, but I was prepared for some form of intimidation or retaliation. I had briefly stepped out of my place in the social order, and I knew that would not be tolerated for long. Then, one morning later that week, Derek and his friends cornered me at the lockers in a dead-end corridor. Once again, his friends prodded Derek to challenge me and exact revenge. But, before he could do anything, I threw a quick sucker punch with my right arm and hit him squarely on the cheek. Derek stumbled clumsily back into the lockers, but remained on his feet. He rubbed the side of his face with his hand and checked for blood. I had not broken the skin, but I knew it hurt. It hurt my knuckles, but I didn't let it show. In the confusion that followed, I turned and walked away. To my surprise, none of his friends tried to stop me. That was the last time Derek Sanders ever faced me. I'm sure the incidents with me also ended his chances of joining the in-crowd. He would have to resolve himself to remain an outsider. That's how the social order at Bald Mountain High School worked.

Although I had won my first physical confrontation, the Derek Sanders incident did little to elevate my social standing. After all, I had only beaten a plebe, not a fully accepted member of the in-crowd. If I had wanted to earn respect from the in-crowd, I would have to challenge and defeat one of the bigger bullies, and I didn't have the self-confidence I needed to do something that daring. For a time, though, my victory reduced the intensity of the abuse I received, but not for long. I know that I faced many other embarrassing and insulting incidents of abuse during my junior and senior years. Fortunately, I can't remember many of them. My confrontation with Derek may not have made me feel any better about myself, but in hindsight, it probably made me a less inviting target. It also may have made the in-crowd leaders a little leerier about personally testing my physical abilities. At least, for the remainder of my sophomore year, I had earned some relief from the harassment. It was a trophy that I could silently accept.

When I began my junior year, things went back to normal. One could not expect a single victory to build a lasting impression. In the wild, a single kill sustains a lion for only a couple of weeks. Persistence and consistency were the keys to maintaining your social status at Bald Mountain. There was always another hungry challenger waiting quietly in the wings for an opportunity to move up the ladder. The competition to remain on top was always rejuvenated with each incoming class of freshmen and the loss of each departing senior class. It did not take long before I was reminded of my position in the social order.

I took my junior year in stride, largely because my failed search for my birth mother had virtually destroyed my hopes of escaping. However, I made some effort to rejuvenate my fantasies of escaping to another place. I enrolled in a geography class during my junior year, in the hope that I might learn new information or stumble across some new way to approach my search for my birth mother, but it didn't work. By the end of my junior year, I faced a real emotional crisis. I was an ugly outcast in school with very few friends. I felt alienated from my adoptive family and guilty about wanting to escape it. My father and I argued often. My dreams of escaping had failed, and I was unable to find my biological family. I had no future aspirations, and I was afraid of entering the real world unprepared. My failure as a person seemed complete, and my world began to spiral in on me. Yet, despite my growing sense of despair, I had yet to face one last incident that confirmed my greatest emotional insecurities and triggered what would become the darkest and most self-destructive episode in my life. It would occur in 1979, when I was seventeen years old.

***** *****

Although I can't remember everything that happened during my junior year, I do clearly remember how I felt. My intense fears of retribution and abuse after the Derek Sanders incident heightened my suspicions of everyone. Every time that I saw a group of kids looking in my direction, I thought they were talking about me. I would even shudder whenever I heard laughter behind my back. The nagging thought that I might once again have to prove my ability to fight worried me. Like a roach when exposed by a light, I would scamper away as discretely as I could. I shied away from anyone who looked trendy or popular, just because I didn't want to see his or her reaction to me. I was becoming a paranoid recluse. Like my passion to learn about cities, it became self-reinforcing. The more I feared abuse, the more abuse I thought I saw. The more abuse I thought I saw, the more it fed my fears. The intensity of my fears and growing paranoia reinforced my emotional anxieties.

Throughout my junior year, my growing anxieties caused me to become increasingly withdrawn. When at school, I avoided crowds and group activities. I spent a lot of time in the library, where I found undisturbed privacy and solitude. It was the only place in the school where student behavior was strictly controlled. It also allowed me access to reference materials for my research. I kept my circle of friends to a minimum. The few friends I did have were outcasts like me, so I felt that they could be trusted. My reclusive behavior even followed me home after school. I began spending more time in my bedroom with the door shut. I would place a piece of folded paper under the door to hold it closed without having to shut it tight. I felt that made my desire for privacy less obvious, although I don't really know why. I also found places outside the house where I could seek refuge from my family. I often walked down the bluffs to the shores of the Connecticut River, where I could think in privacy. I took long walks in the woods— even at night. I even created small hiding chambers in the hay bales stacked in the loft above the barn. As my fantasies of running away and creating a new life in a distant city seemed more and more futile, I used these escapes to take their place. It was not a healthy trend. The unfocused and undirected time I spent alone made it easier to dwell on my problems and more difficult to feel that I was making progress towards a solution. I soon began to experience a deep and overwhelming depression and listlessness.

Depression really began to take control of me during the 1979 summer vacation between my junior and senior years. I was stuck at home almost all of the time. My adoptive father had been diagnosed with terminal emphysema in 1978, and he was gradually forced to give up farming. When he could no longer smoke his Camel unfiltered cigarettes, he began drinking his way through the traditional evening milking hours. His lungs were deteriorating, his energy levels dropped, and he was soon placed on 24-hour oxygen support. To support his medical bills, he sold the cows and farm equipment then began selling pieces of the farm estate. By the summer of 1979, there was little farm work left for me to do (not that I was really interested anymore). So, I tried to find odd jobs in the surrounding area. The local economy was not healthy at the time, due to a recent plant closure in the machine tool industry, and I was only able to find a few short term or temporary part-time jobs. For the first time in my brief life, I had a lot of spare time with which to dwell on my problems, and I was certainly skilled at that.

As the long, hot summer days wore on, I became increasingly listless and reclusive. I remember lying in bed for hours after waking up on many mornings, feeling that there was little reason to get up. I would just lie there, stare at the walls and let the patterns in the wallpaper empty my mind. After a while, I began to feel disconnected and removed from the world and the events that occurred around me as though I was watching a television program. I rarely spoke, unless requested. I had little motivation, energy, or enthusiasm to do anything. Simple chores, such as mowing the lawn, became overwhelming tasks that I tried to avoid. If I did have to work, I did as little as I could. When I was asked to do something I hadn't planned to do, I would become agitated and uncooperative as though I was being asked to amputate my own arm. Many times, I had no appetite, even for things that I truly liked. I was just plain miserable all of the time, and I really didn't care if anyone knew it or not. I hated myself and my life with a passion I'd never felt before. I even began to experience brief blackout spells during this period. They never lasted for more than a couple of minutes, and I never revealed them to anyone at the time. Eventually, I began to consider suicide as a way to free myself from my misery. Years later, when I finally asked my adoptive mother why no one in the family ever noticed my wild mood swings during this period, she said, "Everyone just thought you wanted to be by yourself, so we left you alone." I found that to be a convenient excuse for a family that would rather eat fresh cow manure than deal with its emotional problems.

I don't know how, but I managed to survive the summer. Once again, I faced the usual anxieties about the impending school year, but I knew it was my last, and I'd be a senior. I knew that my class status would help insulate me from the incoming freshmen. The only people I had to worry about were the other seniors. That thought made it a little easier to face the start of another school year. Yet, when the fall semester began, my defense mechanisms kicked into gear, and I began to closely monitor the behavior of everyone around me. It did not take long to find what I was looking for.

During my senior year, I took a political science class. The teacher, Tim Harvey, was well liked by the students, which meant his course was easy. Consequently, several in-crowd jocks of the senior class took the course. Since the class was large, extra seating was required to accommodate the students. The center of the classroom contained rows of arm-table chairs. To provide the extra seating that was needed, a series of long folding tables were arranged in a C-shape around the arm-table chairs. The in-crowd jocks always sat at the folding tables along the sides and back of the classroom. Several of the more popular girls in the class would join the jocks at the folding tables. One of these girls was

Amanda Decker. Amanda was a pretty girl with bright blue eyes and long, wavy blonde hair. She always dressed neatly in stylish clothes. She was also known in the school for her artistic talents. Amanda loved the attention she got from the jocks in the class and always chose to sit with them. I could never sit with the in-crowd or jocks, so I sat at one of the arm-table chairs in the center of the room.

I always felt exposed in that class, because of the seating arrangement. I was surrounded on three sides by the students I feared the most. The size of the room and the large number of students in the class made it hard for Mr. Harvey to make sure everyone was paying attention, so the students sitting at the back tables had ample opportunity to whisper and pass messages back and forth. It was a liberty they exercised regularly. After all, it was an easy course, so they didn't need to pay attention all the time to earn a passing grade. Besides, most of the students who sat around the tables were seniors, and they were on top of the world. I always watched them diligently out of the corners of my eyes. I had received so much abuse from the in-crowd that I was sure they were whispering about me. Whenever they snickered, my heart would begin to race, and I would feel a chill run down my spine.

One day during the first few weeks of the semester, I heard some muffled snickers coming from the table to my right. My attention was drawn to a couple of the senior jocks sitting on either side of Amanda. I could tell that Amanda was busy writing something on a piece of paper. The two boys were looking intermittently at Amanda's paper and me, trying desperately to contain their laughter. Every muscle in my body froze under the intensity of their penetrating stare. My senses were heightened. I could feel my fear and anger building, as I monitored the scene. I just *knew* they were laughing at me.

After several minutes, Amanda stopped writing. I watched her inconspicuously fold the paper in half, when Mr. Harvey wasn't looking, and pass it to the boy sitting to her left. The paper was passed along, one by one, to each student along the back table. Each time it was unfolded, I heard another muffled snicker. One student sitting behind me was so amused by it that he almost laughed out loud. He tried to cover it with a faked cough. Mr. Harvey heard it, though, and he asked the student what he thought was so funny. The entire class turned around and the student just sat there with a smug smile on his face and shook his head. Eventually, the piece of paper made its way back to Amanda, and she carefully tucked it in her notebook. I had to know what was on that paper.

As luck would have it, Amanda and I were in the same class following political science. When the class ended, I watched her carefully for a chance to peek at the notebook that contained the mysterious piece of paper. She went straight to our next class, and I discretely followed her all the way. I spent the entire class trying to think of some way I could see what was in that notebook. I decided that I would accidentally bump into her hard enough to make her drop her books, then I would help her pick them up. If I did it right, the paper might fall out, and I could see what it said.

I waited eagerly for the class to end. I sat two rows behind Amanda in that class, so I watched her like a hawk. Just before the end of the class, the teacher began to pass out the tests we had taken the day before. As Amanda opened her notebook to put the test away, I saw her remove the folded piece of paper. To my surprise, she crumpled it up, got up from her desk, and threw it away in the wastebasket. I pretended not to notice her, as she returned to her desk. What luck! All I had to do now was lag behind after the class ended and retrieve Amanda's paper from the wastebasket.

When the bell rang, I began to shuffle papers in my own notebook, as the classroom emptied. I saw another student approach the teacher to ask a question about the test. I seized my opportunity. While they were talking, I got up and started to leave the classroom. As I approached the wastebasket near the door, I accidentally dropped one of my own books. When I bent down to pick it up, I looked into the wastebasket. There were several wads of paper in the can. I grabbed the two on the top and stuffed them in my pocket. One of them had to be the paper that Amanda had thrown away. Once and for all, I would finally know the truth!

I stopped at my locker between classes and, screened from view by my open locker door, I removed the two pieces of paper from my right pocket and carefully unraveled them. I felt my heart sink, as I immediately recognized the one that Amanda had thrown away. On it was a sketch of a monkey dangling by one arm from a tree limb. It was scratching its head with the other hand—no, not its head, *my* head. She had drawn my head on the body of a monkey. My heart began to race, as I realized the significance of my discovery. In my mind, it confirmed that every suspicious stare I had noticed, every snicker I had heard behind my back, and every whisper I had ever detected was directed squarely at me. All my paranoid fears had instantly become reality. There was no hiding from it now. No remote chance that my fears were misplaced. I was truly the awful person I had always suspected I was, and everyone else knew it! That sketch was the final straw that broke my self-tortured spirit.

Although I threw the sketch away the first chance I had, the image of it remained rooted in my mind. I can still see it as clearly today as I did the day I found it. When I returned home that evening, I shut myself in my room, sat down at my desk, buried my face in my hands, and cried. As far as I was concerned, my failure was complete, and that sketch was the epitaph for my gravestone. The weight of my high school experiences, my adoptive family, and my own self-hatred was too much to bear. I was an evil person that made everyone else's life unpleasant. There was no longer any benefit to my existence—not even to myself. That mid-September night in 1979, I began to plot my suicide. I was certain that by killing myself, I would make everyone's life better–my classmates' and my family's.

During the summer months, my father kept a .22 caliber rifle in the barn. He used it to shoot the rats that lived in the tall grass behind the barn. He would pick them off one by one from the barn window. He was a good marksman. When I was still in elementary school, he taught me how to load and shoot the gun. Although we had stopped farming earlier in the year, I knew the gun had been left in a storage room in the barn. I also knew that he kept the bullets in the top drawer of his dresser, along with his biological father's personal effects. I decided that shooting myself was the best way to commit suicide. It was quick, and if I did it right, I believed it would be painless.

The thoughts of my pain and desire to commit suicide haunted me for the rest of the week. I could focus on nothing else. There were times when the feelings of despair were so strong that I just wanted to scream or explode. When I was alone at night in my room, it was hard to sit still. I remember pacing back and forth thinking about it. So many thoughts were rushing through my head at the same time that I couldn't stand it anymore. When Saturday morning came, I just had to write it all down. I began writing my suicide note. The note wasn't directed at anyone specifically; it was just a rambling jumble of thoughts and feelings. I spilled my anguish onto the paper. I worked on it one piece at a time that day, hiding it under the blotter on my desk. When it was finished, it was about three or four pages long. I didn't sleep well at all that night.

The next morning, I found the opportunity I needed. Mom went to the store to do some shopping, and she took the girls with her. I stayed at home with Dad. When he went into the bathroom, I quietly snuck into the bedroom, stole a bullet from the carton in his dresser, and dropped it into my shirt pocket. I went back into my own room, took the note out from under the blotter, and placed it on the center of my desk. I then closed the door to my bedroom, as I normally did when I was hiding from the rest of the world, and snuck out of the house before Dad came out of the bathroom.  With bullet in hand, I went straight to the barn and removed the gun from the storage room.

Normally, Dad would leave the gun in the barn only during the summer months.  In the fall, he would clean it and store it in the house for the winter.  However, his lack of motivation must have caused him to forget about it over the past year.  The sides of the gun were splattered with specks of dirt, white wash, and dried cow manure, and the gun was covered with cobwebs.  The base of the barrel was even showing signs of rust.  I used my heavy flannel shirttails to rub as much of the debris off the gun as I could while keeping a wary eye on the front door of the house through the barn window.  As I pulled on the trigger guard and loaded the bullet in the side chamber, I noticed that my hands were damp with sweat.  In fact, the small bullet almost slipped through my greasy fingers.  Then, I positioned myself and prepared for the final step.

The base of the barn walls was lined with large square timbers, which formed a low sill.  When I was younger, Dad and I would sit along that sill and talk while we waited for each cow to be milked.  I sat down on that sill one final time and placed the butt of the gun firmly on the concrete floor between my feet.  I then tipped my head forward, resting it on the end of the barrel and placed both of my thumbs gently on the trigger.  The cold steel barrel of the gun felt like a spear pressing against my forehead.  My thoughts raced with fears of every kind and fleeting images of haunting incidents from my past.  It felt like the disks of a slot machine after the arm has been pulled.  When the wheels in my mind stopped turning, all I could see was the image of Amanda's sketch.  The game was over.  With sweat beading on my forehead and tears pooling in my eyes, I closed them tight and pushed my thumbs against the trigger.

I think I remember hearing a sharp click, but nothing else.  Did I die before I heard the blast?  No, I could still hear the sound of flies buzzing around my head.  Suddenly, I realized I was still alive.  My heart began to pound and my body began to tremble, as I opened my eyes.  I gasped for breath as I threw my head up and pushed the barrel of the gun away.  I flinched when I heard the gun slap against the concrete floor.  Beads of sweat were running down my face and back.  Nothing had happened, and I was completely stunned.  I don't know why the gun never fired.  Maybe I hadn't cleaned it well enough.  Maybe some of the key parts in the gun had corroded or rusted from age and exposure.  Maybe the bullet was defective.  I had no idea, and it didn't matter.  All I knew was that I was sitting there, racked with fear, my eyes glued to the gun lying lifeless on the cold concrete floor.

For the first few seconds, I felt nothing but fear. I couldn't even think. I felt my arms and legs tremble, but I couldn't move them. All I could do was breathe. Then, my mind snapped back to life, and I realized I was becoming aware of my surroundings. I felt scared and emotionally spent. I was panting. I stood up and secretly peeked out the barn window towards the house. My father hadn't left the house. I didn't want anyone to see what I had tried to do. I felt a sudden concern for the person who had pulled the trigger, as if he was a different person. I quickly picked up the gun, removed the bullet, and threw it out the open window, then returned the gun to the storage room. Walking was difficult. I kept losing my balance, as I stumbled along. I would not hold another gun in my hands for more than 30 years.

I walked out behind the barn to collect my thoughts and feelings in privacy. Suddenly, I discovered I was shedding tears, even though I didn't realize I was crying. I couldn't understand why I was still alive. I became angry at the gun. After a while, I came to conclude that I had failed again. I couldn't even kill myself. Yet, there seemed to be a part of me that wanted to survive. I had thrown the bullet away, and I wasn't trying to think of an alternate way to do the job. I didn't feel truly relieved to be alive, but I also didn't feel as burdened by my anxieties as I had when I was preparing to die. It was as though my mind had been divided into two parts. One part retained the anxiety, anger, and self-hatred I had cultivated over the years. Over time, I repressed that part of my mind deeper and deeper into my psyche. The other part gradually became intensely analytical. It was as though the logical part of me wanted to survive despite the need of the emotional part to die. For a long time after my suicide attempt, the emotional part of me would reveal itself only to vent anger or fear. I couldn't even cry again for years. The analytical part of my mind gradually took control of my everyday life. It was all that kept me alive.

After a while, I went back into the house. My father was sitting at the kitchen table, reading the Sunday paper. I said nothing as I walked by him and went to my room. For a while, I just looked at the suicide note I had left on the desk. Part of me wanted to throw it away, another part didn't. I eventually decided to fold it in half and tuck it carefully in the pages of a hardcover book on my bookshelves. It remained there long after I left home. About six years later, after Dad had died, my adoptive mother sold the farm and moved away. Before she left, she had a yard sale to get rid of the things she didn't want to take with her when she moved. Included in her yard sale were many of the things I had left behind, including the book in which I had placed my suicide note. If she found it, she never mentioned it. Perhaps it was one of the books she that couldn't sell and later threw away.  Maybe someone out there still has it on his or her bookshelf.  I may never know for sure, as I can't remember which book contained it.

Somehow, I managed to finish my senior year and graduate.  I dreaded the political science class, but I survived it.  For some reason, I didn't fear the muffled snickers and stares of my classmates so much, because I already knew how they really felt about me.  There was really nothing more I could do about it.  Whenever I was teased or abused, I just turned and walked away from the situation.  I just kept my focus on the end of the school year.  In November, I was accepted at the University of Hartford, and I would finally be leaving home for a big city.  At least I knew that part of my dream would come true.  Now all I wanted to do was start a new life.  I was going to a place where no one knew me.  I could leave my past behind in the dark recesses of my mind.  I could throw away the person I was as a child and become someone else.  At least, that's what I thought—and hoped.

# *Part III: One Flew Out of the Cuckoo's Nest*

As with most personal decisions I made during my adolescent years, fear was the primary influence that drove me on to college. My father never encouraged me to farm because he saw no future in it, and he had no intention of turning the farm operation over to me. I knew nothing of the business community because I had virtually no interaction with it. I was afraid of entering the local work force with my classmates and of being stuck at home. I was petrified by the thought of facing the life I was destined to lead in North Georgetown. In short, the only chance I had for a different future and a new life was to attend college. At least I was finally getting away from home and my tortured existence there.

Unfortunately, my mediocre academic performance in high school did not make it easy for me to get into college. My Scholastic Aptitude Test scores were marginal at best, and my high school grades averaged in the low Bs to the high Cs. I might have been capable of doing better, but I never really applied myself. After all, there was little incentive or reward for academic achievement in my community and even less if you were a social outcast. The primary industries in the Chelsea/Georgetown area were the dwindling farm operations and a number of machine tool, textile, and forest products manufacturing plants. All of these industries were declining when I was growing up, and the kids my age all knew it. I would estimate that roughly one-third of my high school graduating class went directly into the armed services, which was the primary means of escaping the area for those who were not college-bound. The majority of the remaining students found traditional jobs in the local economy; most followed in their parents' footsteps. Only a small minority of the students from my graduating class went on to college. I became one of those fortunate few. When I returned briefly to the area nineteen years after graduating, many of those who stayed behind were still living in the area working in the same job tracks that they had entered after high school. That's why there was so little incentive to do well in school. Most of the kids my age knew there was little opportunity to succeed in the local economy, so they chose instead to enjoy themselves during their "carefree" high school years.

When the University of Hartford first accepted me, the administration wanted me to enroll in their College of Basic Studies, which was a two-year remedial high school program for marginal college students. I managed to evade that sentence only by taking a college-level night school course at a local state college during the second half of my senior year in high school. The B+ grade I received in that class was apparently enough to convince them that I was ready to take college level classes. My father strongly encouraged me to enroll as a computer science major. He was convinced, rightly so, that people in that field would make a lot of money in the future. Since he agreed to help finance my education, I followed his advice. It helped alleviate the guilt I felt about accepting his help. In reality, the majority of my undergraduate college expenses were covered by my student loans and the local scholarships I received. Actually, the money he contributed, which I always presumed had come from his pocket, was money from his mother's inheritance, and her will specifically directed that it be used to help pay for his children's college educations. Of course, that little detail was never revealed to me, until many years later.

The knowledge that I would be leaving home for a new life in Hartford, Connecticut was the only thing that kept me going through the final semester of my senior year at Bald Mountain. I was determined to leave my failed childhood behind and start a new life in the big city. The analytical side of my mind focused on that goal, and I began to think of ways to recreate myself. I decided to hide the truth about my embarrassing and shameful past. My childhood on the farm was over, and I was determined to leave it behind like a snake shedding its skin. I planned to watch the new people closely and learn to emulate their behavior using the skills I had honed in elementary school. This strategy had been fairly successful with the other outcast students, so I naturally thought I could make it work for me at college. I decided to buy new clothes and dress differently. I even changed the style of my glasses and let my hair grow longer. The thoroughness and highly detailed nature of my plans convinced me that they would work. As my high school graduation approached, the anticipation I felt about finally leaving home helped me overcome my depression. I had a sense of hope for my future, and I was determined to make the best of it. My past life was ending, and I was ready to wipe the slate clean and begin anew. However, I was not really as healthy and confident as I thought I was and needed to be.

As I began my college career, my life did begin to improve. However, I soon learned that I couldn't completely hide from my past. As with my adoptive parents, the insecurities I harbored deep inside continued to affect my attitudes and behavior thereby making my adjustment difficult. I didn't understand anything about the outside world and felt awkward within it. My new life had begun, but it didn't quite follow the course I had initially planned. I found many new obstacles to overcome on the long, unpredictable path to recovery. My rebirth would take many years and much more work than I had anticipated. At least I had found the determination and intestinal fortitude I needed to persevere the long road to recovery.

# Rebirth

When I began college at the University of Hartford in September 1980, I had been away from home on my own for an extended period of time only twice before in my life. In June 1975, Aunt Brenda and Uncle Keith took me to visit them in Ohio for about a month, and I spent a week in April 1978 with one of my father's aunts in Covington, Kentucky. She had promised to drive me to St. Louis to see a Cardinals baseball game, if I came to visit her for a week. Those two trips represented the sum total of my experience living away from home and outside rural New Hampshire and Vermont, and both times I stayed with relatives I knew.

The experience of being truly alone in a strange and very different place for the first time in my life was far more overwhelming than I had expected. At first, I didn't understand why I felt so uneasy about it. After all, I was out of the house and away from North Georgetown. I was living in an exciting, vibrant, big city, just as I had dreamed for the last four years of my life at home. I was enrolled in a small, private college that had no significant athletic program and no on-campus fraternities or sororities. This meant that I would not have to face a bunch of jocks or party animals. Logically, it was the ideal environment for me to begin the new life I had carefully planned for myself.

Yet, I felt afraid and intimidated by all the new faces and the fast pace of city life. I was never comfortable around strangers, and now they surrounded me. Every person I saw or met was a stranger. I was afraid to say much to any of the people I met until I had to a chance to understand them and their personalities—presumably so that I could imitate them. I really didn't know how to act around them which also made me afraid that I might somehow accidentally reveal my hidden personality flaws. My distinctive rural New Hampshire accent and manner of speaking also made me stand out. I certainly didn't want to be perceived as a hick fresh off the farm.

I was especially overwhelmed by the speed at which everything and everyone around me moved. Even the people I met seemed to talk fast, as though they never had enough time to say everything they had to say. There was so much activity occurring around me constantly that I couldn't comprehend it all at once. I found it hard to sleep at nights with all the urban noise outside. How I longed to hear nothing but the breeze whispering through the trees, the haunting twilight call of a whippoorwill echoing in the distance, or the sound of crickets chirping again. All the familiar and comforting night sounds were suddenly replaced by the sounds of car horns and traffic on the streets, car engines revving, muted conversations and occasional arguments, intermittent sirens that gradually waxed and waned along the surrounding highways, slamming doors, and neighbors watching television or listening to loud music late at night. It was a constant, restless cacophony of overlapping artificial noises that I was not accustomed to hearing throughout the daytime, much less during the night. I hadn't learned how to filter out all the irrelevant background noise and activity that can make city life stressful. Adjusting to city life was not as simple or easy as I had hoped. Wanting to live in a different environment does not alleviate the sense of alienation, nor does it make the adjustment any easier. I knew there was no going back, and I didn't want to admit it, but I was beginning to feel afraid that I would fail to make the transition. The sense of yet another impending personal failure only served to amplify my fears and frustrations.

The stress became so intense for me at times that I suffered an increase in the frequency of the blackout spells that I first began to experience in 1979. Eventually, they became so frequent that I went to the college physician to learn the cause. He sent me to the Hartford Hospital for an electroencephalogram to determine if I was suffering petite mal seizures that might be a symptom of epilepsy. The doctor asked me, as all have done, for my family history, but as an adoptee, I had none to provide. Fortunately, the tests were negative, and the doctors just attributed the problem to severe stress. Although the frequency of the blackouts declined over time, I still experience them on rare occasions even today.

Although I felt uneasy in my new environment, the guys who lived on my dormitory floor were warm and engaging. One of my two freshman roommates, Greg Dayton, became my best friend. I still think of him today as the brother I never had. We remained roommates for three-and-a-half of our four years at the University of Hartford, and we maintained our friendship for many years after that even though the distance between us and the evolving demands of our lives eventually pulled us apart. I still remember the names of the other guys who shared our dormitory suite during my first two years just like it was yesterday: Calvin Palmer (my other freshman roommate), Joe Torrance, Chris Bachelor, Mark Weiss, Larry Stanton, Dana Setzer, and John Ely. I was pleasantly surprised by their persistent efforts to make me feel a part of their social community, even though I acted so withdrawn and hesitant. Never had anyone worked so hard to know me as the guys who lived on the first floor rear of Reeve Hall. For the first time in my life, I was encouraged to become part of a loose in-crowd, and I didn't want my hidden "true" personality (whatever that was) to destroy it.

I tried to limit my interactions to one or two of them at a time, so I could successfully alter my personality and interests to reflect theirs, but it became impossible. I was constantly placed in group situations where I had to relate to multiple people simultaneously. Of course, it frustrated my efforts to mold myself after them. I just couldn't become so many different people at the same time. I didn't realize it at the time, but they could sense I had problems relating to people, and they were deliberately forcing me to interact with several of them at once to help me realize and face the problem. Instead, I became even more scared and withdrawn. At my worst, I would spend long evening hours sitting by myself in our dormitory floor lounge with the lights out, so I wouldn't be seen by passers-by. Sometimes, I would go for long, brooding walks around the campus by myself. I didn't want to be alone so much of the time, but I couldn't handle the pressures I faced adjusting to my new environment. Things clearly weren't working according to plan.

Many times, during my first semester, I felt I wasn't going to make it. I could handle most of the classes (although my test scores weren't as good as they could have been), but I really didn't like my major. I just hadn't anticipated how hard it would be for me to adapt to this new environment. I had convinced myself before leaving home that my extensive knowledge of cities and my deliberate scheme to make people like me would work. That was my first mistake. These early lessons convinced me that all good theories are good in theory, but not necessary in reality. All theories regarding how large, complex systems work are always built, to some degree, on a set of predetermined assumptions. Unfortunately, reality does not have to obey assumptions. I was beginning to learn that the theory I used to decide how I should interact with my friends was based on some faulty and unrealistic assumptions. However, I lacked the knowledge and experience I needed to determine which assumptions were wrong or how to correct them. The more I struggled with the problem, the more I could feel myself becoming depressed again, but I didn't want to admit it. I was beginning to fear that my new friends would soon realize that I was a social failure, and I'd quickly become an outcast again.

To escape, I reluctantly went home every two or three weekends during my first semester. I didn't like going home to stay with my adoptive family, but it was easier to face being a failure at home than it was at college. After all, I didn't have to feel like I was disappointing anyone at home. I just limited my interactions with my family and used the familiarity and serenity of my old home environment to relieve the stress and think of new ways to adjust. I decided I needed to make some major changes or my long anticipated new life was doomed to fail, too.

The first change I made was to seek advice from the people I trusted. After all, I clearly didn't have the answers I needed, and I wasn't going to get them from my adoptive family. My roommate, Greg, was someone I believed I could trust. From the first time we met, he struck me as a quiet and reserved person like myself. He was sincere, friendly, and receptive, but not overly outgoing. It also appeared that he, too, was trying to find his own way in our new environment. During the first few days of school, we did almost everything together, largely because we were both a little nervous about the strange surroundings and all the other students we were both meeting for the first time. He also was a psychology major, so I thought he might be a source of good advice. Since we were roommates, we had plenty of time for private discussions.

I also had many conversations with the resident assistant in our dorm. I don't remember her name, but she was very friendly and willing to talk about anything. She had encouraged me to talk to her on several occasions, once she noticed that I wasn't adjusting well. I guess it was more obvious to others than I thought—perhaps because I was so reluctant to admit it to myself. I began to reveal selective bits and pieces about my past and my anxieties to both of them. They soon suggested that I seek free counseling through the university's on-campus health services program. The thought made me uncomfortable at first, but by the middle of the semester, I decided to follow their advice. I began formal counseling and continued it for nearly two years.

I also decided that I did not want to pursue a major in computer science. I wasn't doing well in the advanced mathematics classes I was required to take. My interest in computers had emerged in high school as a result of my brief friendship with a social outcast who was a first generation computer geek. He had built his own simple computer and was fascinated with high technology electronics. I really wasn't that interested in the subject, but I had no other idea of what I really wanted to do after I graduated from college. If I had an interest, it was to understand the dynamics of social interaction and human behavior in the hope that I might learn why I had failed to relate well to people as a child. I decided I couldn't fix myself until I understood why I couldn't socialize well with other people. The only answers I could give myself were the standard conclusions I had drawn from my childhood—I was ugly, awkward, and unsociable. However, that information lacked the detailed reasons for those characteristics and what made them so apparent to the people I tried to befriend. That was something I would need to understand, if I was ever going to be successful in changing those perceptions.

At one point early in my first semester, Greg introduced me to his college adviser, Dr. Ofslager. He taught archaeology and Native American anthropology classes in the sociology department. Dr. Ofslager was a kindly old professor with a genuine interest in the people he met. He always encouraged his students to follow whatever interest they might express, regardless of how strange it might sound to someone else. I was drawn to that quality like a magnet. Through my many conversations with him, I decided to pursue a major in sociology at the start of my second semester. It seemed to be a good way to understand the intricacies of human social behavior, and that was something I had a vested personal interest in understanding. I also asked Dr. Ofslager to become my student advisor, and he consented.

The worst part of this decision was breaking the news to my father. I did it over the Thanksgiving holiday. I approached him one evening when he was sitting alone at the kitchen table drinking a bottle of Manischewitz wine (as had become his nighttime custom). As I anticipated, he hit the ceiling. After calmly and delicately explaining my desire to change majors, he pounded the table with his fist. "What the hell do you think you're going to do with a sociology degree?" he bellowed at me. Before I could even try to answer, he began his next response. "After everything we've done for you over the years, that's the *best* you can do? I *never* should've agreed to spend one dime on your education." I had let him down again. I was destined to be a failure in his eyes. So, what else was new?

To be perfectly honest, I couldn't have answered his question even if he had given me the chance. I really had no idea of what I was going to do with a degree in sociology or even what a sociologist did for a living. I couldn't have told anyone what I really wanted to do with my life. I didn't even know who I really was. I just knew I didn't want to be a computer programmer. It seemed technically difficult, boring, and lonely to me—not something I really needed. I decided that when I did discover what I eventually wanted to do with my life, it would stem most naturally from something that was of interest to me, and that I had a natural ability to understand. In all reality, I don't think I could have explained that to him in a way that he would accept. Instead, my response to Dad's criticism was to spend progressively less time at home. That decision drove me to make better use of my support resources at the University of Hartford. It also forced me to face my fears of social situations. It was difficult at first, but in retrospect, I had made the right choice. The formal counseling that I received helped me immeasurably.

When I first began my counseling sessions, I was very hesitant to discuss my former life in North Georgetown. Personal problems were not openly discussed, and my problems were especially embarrassing to me. I just wanted an expert on human behavior to tell me the secret of making friends. I was convinced that there must be a simple formula to life that I just didn't understand. The only problem I had was the counselor. He didn't seem to have any answers for me or else he was hiding them. All he wanted to do was ask questions and listen to me. What was the value to that? If I had the answers I sought, why would I need him? It seemed like a game we were playing to see who would give in first. I really didn't see much benefit in talking about my problems because I had already spent what I thought was more than enough time thinking about them. I simply needed better direction. I needed to know how to reconstruct myself so that I could fit into the social environment. Why couldn't he just tell me that so I could get out of his hair—that is, what little of it he had left? I attended many frustrating sessions before I surrendered and hesitantly started discussing my embarrassing past.

When I finally did begin to discuss my past life, I was very careful about what I said. I didn't reveal anything about my suicide attempt because I was afraid I'd end up in a psychiatric ward. I was also afraid it would somehow end up on the front pages of the Chelsea newspaper. That revelation wouldn't make my relationship with my adoptive family any better. I talked a little about my relationship with my family, but I didn't mention that I was an adoptee. I still felt very guilty about being a source of division between my parents, and I didn't want to be indicted for it. I focused instead on my failed relationship with my father. I also talked openly about the abuse I faced in high school, including Amanda's sketch and my fight with Derek. Those issues seemed to be the best symptoms of my social failures and the primary sources of my immediate anxieties and fears. Maybe if I revealed those tidbits to satisfy his incessant curiosity, he would finally give me the advice I was seeking.

After a few difficult sessions, I began to feel a little more comfortable talking about my negative self-image. I remember that it eventually became a relief to express it, even though I feared that it would change the way others perceived me. I even talked to Greg and our resident assistant about it and found that my concerns were totally unfounded. Their attitudes towards me did not change, as I had initially feared. That alone made it easier for me to trust the efforts that my new dormitory friends were making to involve me in their social activities. Fortunately, they didn't let me down. As I began to trust them, they rewarded me generously. They exposed me to their interests. Mark Weiss introduced me to his favorite group, Genesis, and I quickly developed an interest in their music. They encouraged me to join them when they played games. Dana Setzer and I played many Othello tournaments. I think I lost every single game we played, but I never had more fun in my life. I was also invited to enjoy their regular nickel-ante poker games. I was beginning to actually enjoy life. Without even realizing it, I was also becoming more comfortable with myself as an individual thanks to the encouragement they offered freely.

Through our association with our third freshman roommate, Calvin Palmer, Greg and I eventually became honorary members of the "Techies," a band of engineering and technical college students at the university. Calvin was a Ward Technical College student and one of the leaders of the rag-tag group. They included Greg "the captain" Norre, Mark Streitfeld, Craig Zoal, and Dan Shoop, to name a few. They were often rambunctious, inquisitive, and eccentric pranksters, but they rarely did any harm. They had a customary dining table that they frequented in a corner of the university commons, and Greg and I would usually join them during meals. By the middle of my sophomore year, I was no longer trying to pattern myself after someone else. I was finally beginning to discover and develop a personality of my own, but it was still too early for me to know if it was truly mine.

## The Yellow Brick Road

As I began to develop my own personality and interests, other aspects of my life began to take shape, including my career interests. Although my father was not going to let me take over the family farm, he always pushed me to decide what I wanted to do with my life, as though I could be expected to know. Unfortunately, I didn't have a lot of experience to draw upon in making that decision. By the time I finished high school, farming was the only line of work about which I had any practical knowledge. I had little exposure to any other careers until my father's health gradually deteriorated in 1979. After that, I began to work a number of part-time and temporary jobs to earn spending money for college. Between 1977 and 1987, I worked as the janitor of the village school in North Georgetown, an inventory specialist for a firm that conducted grocery and department store inventories, a self-employed house painter, a short order cook, a surveyor's assistant, an electrician's assistant, a carpenter's assistant, a research assistant, a computer assembly line worker, and a shipper at a large computer company warehouse, among others. None of these jobs were very inspiring or profitable, and they offered little opportunity for advancement. However, that knowledge helped me focus on my college education as the primary tool to discover the career path that I truly wanted to follow.

After I changed my major from computer science to sociology, I took a wide range of courses to expose myself to a variety of different career opportunities. In fact, I almost transferred from the University of Hartford to the University of Southern Maine between my freshman and sophomore years to pursue a geography major. It was becoming difficult to afford my education in Hartford. I also felt that my father would be less disappointed with me if I studied geography because it was a more concrete and practical field than sociology. Also, the guilt I felt about accepting my father's financial help for my college education encouraged me to consider attending a school I could afford on my own resources. However, I changed my mind at the end of the summer and decided to return to the University of Hartford anyway. I could not bring myself to leave behind my new friends and the counseling support I was receiving. I just didn't feel emotionally secure enough to start over again in another strange, new environment. To me, the University of Hartford had become my first and only true home.

During my junior year, I took a course in urban sociology. This class exposed me to the works of Herbert Gans, Kevin Lynch, and Donald Appleyard, all of whom had contributed to the field of urban and city planning. Their writings and perspectives on urban development and cognitive mapping fascinated me. Their works also appealed to my childhood interest in cities, so I approached my advisor for additional information on the field of planning. He introduced me to Dr. David Hoover, a city planner, who taught a graduate-level introductory course in planning at the university. Dr. Hoover helped me secure an internship at the Hartford Planning Department (the oldest in the nation), and I eventually took his graduate planning course. Even though I was still an undergraduate student at the time, I did quite well in the class.

Dr. Hoover also encouraged me to attend graduate school and continue my studies in planning. I followed his advice and applied to five colleges that he highly recommended. Based on my references, practical internship experience in Hartford, and exposure to introductory graduate-level planning and statistics classes, I was accepted at all five schools. Dr. Hoover encouraged me to attend the University of California at Berkeley because he felt I needed to experience life outside New England. I knew he was right, so I accepted the offer from Berkeley and moved to California in August 1984.

Graduate school was much more challenging than I had anticipated. Everything was more expensive than I had planned. Not only were the classes demanding, I also found myself all alone again in an even more alien environment. At first, I missed all my friends at Hartford and the security of an environment I had finally grown to know intimately. I also had difficulties finding affordable housing in Berkeley, and I eventually rented a bedroom in an old, two-story bungalow in an area of the city colloquially known as "the Flats." Although my living conditions were marginal at best, the most depressing aspect of my life in Berkeley was my lack of connection to the student community on campus. I had finally reached a point in my growth and development where I actually wanted to be around other people my own age, but I still lacked the confidence I needed to meet strangers in an open, unstructured social environment. In the final month of my first semester, I went to the university housing office, and they helped me secure off-campus student housing at Mills College in neighboring Oakland. Although Mills College was a small, private women's school, the college had two vacant dormitories that they leased exclusively to the University of California for graduate student housing. In exchange, Berkeley allowed Mills College students to attend some specialized classes at the University of California that Mills College did not offer.

The rather aloof Mills College students generally did not mingle with the Berkeley students, but I did discover a small, but engaging community of Berkeley students living on the Mills campus. Unfortunately, I did not have enough time to build friendships within that community before my first semester ended. I had expended most of my financial resources, and the university informed me that they would not renew my out-of-state tuition waiver for the spring semester. Overall, I was disappointed with my life at Berkeley, and I had grown uncertain about my determination to pursue a career in planning. My grades were good, but my attitude was deteriorating. I was spending too much time thinking about the friends and good times I left behind in Hartford. So, in December 1984, I withdrew from Berkeley and returned to Hartford.

Although I returned to New England, I spent little time at home with my family. I spent most of my time in Hartford, staying with my remaining underclassmen friends at the university. I tried to get a job in the Hartford area through the university's career development office, but my sociology degree was not in great demand in the local job market. My adoptive father would have glibly said, "I guess you should have listened to me." I tried to recapture my former social life on campus, but it wasn't the same. Most of my best friends had graduated and moved away. I felt increasingly out of place in the college community and by mid-February 1985, I was again losing my direction in life as well.

I spent a lot of time with my former advisors, Dr. Ofslager and Dr. Hoover. They both encouraged me to return to Berkeley and continue my career in planning. For the first time since I met him, Dr. Ofslager was actually encouraging me to pursue a career path I felt I no longer wanted rather than just supporting what I wanted to do that day. He finally saw something in me that made him realize that planning was more than just a passing fancy to me. I had a passion for it, and he didn't want to see me throw it all away just because I had to work a little harder for it than I had anticipated.

I had many lengthy heart-to-heart discussions with Dr. Ofslager. Through them all, he remained persistent in his assertion that I continue my work in planning. No matter what defense or rationale I used, I couldn't convince him otherwise. Although my adoptive father had told me what I should do in the past, the advice I received from Dr. Ofslager was different. He truly cared about me and understood me in a way my adoptive father never did, and it showed. I trusted his advice because I knew that he was genuinely concerned about my well-being, and he understood my potential even though I didn't. He was truly the father figure I never had. Over time, he convinced me that I needed to leave the security of my past life at Hartford behind and return to Berkeley with a new determination. My future path was now clear. I had confirmed my direction in life, and it did indeed emerge from my original interests, just as I had hoped it would when I decided to change my undergraduate major to sociology. Unfortunately, my adoptive father never lived long enough to see it.

By early March, I returned to my old home in North Georgetown and made preparations for my return to Berkeley. I got a full-time temporary job as a shipper/receiver at a computer company warehouse near Concord to earn the extra money I needed to pay for my tuition and expenses for the 1985-86 school year. I worked at the warehouse for seven months, eagerly accepting any overtime, weekend, and third shift work I could get just to earn extra money. Commuting from home allowed me to manage my expenses and save most of my earnings, and the long hours that I worked helped minimize my interactions with my adoptive family. Even though my adoptive father had died in the previous year, I was never able to feel completely comfortable living with my adoptive mother and sisters. I applied for readmission, obtained an additional guaranteed student loan, and returned to Berkeley in early September 1985.

The experience I had returning to Berkeley also gave me a new sense of confidence. First of all, I was returning to a school and setting that I recognized rather than a strange, new environment. Things that first seemed alien to me when I began my studies at Berkeley now seemed familiar the second time around. I was also able to return to the Berkeley student housing at Mills College, which made it easier for me to interact with students my own age. All in all, I began to feel more in command of my life and more familiar with my surroundings. I soon became part of the Berkeley social circle at Mills College, just as I had done at the University of Hartford. Aside from the 1985 Christmas break and a 1986 summer internship at a regional planning agency in Portland, Maine, I remained in California until I completed my graduate work in December 1986.

To help manage my education costs and reduce my dependency on the out-of-state tuition waiver, I applied for residency status once I had lived in California for six months. At that time, I felt it would be best for me to stay in California and begin a new life far away from the memories of the past. As part of the process of establishing residency, I applied for a California driver's license. I went to the department of motor vehicles office in Oakland, filled out the application, and took the written test. However, before I could receive my new license, I was asked to provide a copy of my birth certificate to verify my date of birth.

That request caught me by surprise. I had never been asked to provide a copy of my birth certificate before. In fact, my mother told me many times during my childhood that my birth certificate—along with all of my birth records—was destroyed when the hospital in which I was born burned to the ground. At that time, I didn't realize that birth certificates were actually issued by the city or town of birth not the hospital, and that the story was a lie. In fact, I didn't learn that my mother actually *did* have my amended birth certificate until I told her that I was required to provide a copy of it for my first professional job. Although I was angered when I learned about the deception, I said nothing about it. All I knew when I was trying to get my California driver's license was that I didn't have a birth certificate nor did I know of any way to obtain one. I explained that I was an adoptee and my birth certificate and records were destroyed by fire when I was a child. After a lengthy debate, I was given a piece of paper and asked to make a signed, written statement attesting that I was born on February 14, 1962 and that my birth certificate and records were destroyed by fire. They accepted the statement, and I was issued my license. Once I had my new license, I was able to apply for residency, which eliminated my out-of-state tuition costs for my final year at Berkeley and made it easier for me to afford the rest of my graduate school expenses.

As my graduation approached, I realized that I needed to begin looking for a planning job. I applied for jobs in California, but there were few opportunities and many qualified applicants looking for work. In the face of such fierce competition, I was not successful. I hoped that my internship in Portland, Maine would lead to a job opportunity there, but no entry-level jobs were available. It soon became apparent to me that my job search would take some time, and I reluctantly made preparations to return to New Hampshire. During 1986, my adoptive mother sold the farm in North Georgetown and moved to a small, lakeside resort town in central New Hampshire. I decided to use her new home as a base for my job search, and I began sending my resume to regional planning agencies across northern New England. When I finally completed my degree requirements, I was proud of my achievement. I wanted to attend the graduation ceremony, but my mother refused to make the trip out to California. So, I decided to just skip the ceremonies and return to New Hampshire. Without a job and a decent income, I had nowhere else to go.

During the first few months of 1987, I searched long and hard for a planning job. I interviewed for openings across New England. Although a number of job opportunities were available, I was competing against applicants who had far more experience in the field than I did. By the middle of February, I was becoming concerned that I would have to take a job outside my profession just to make ends meet. I just couldn't bear the thought of becoming dependent upon my adoptive family again. Before giving up, I made one last attempt to get some practical work experience. I went to the Lakes Region Planning Commission (LRPC), the local regional planning agency serving the town in which my mother now lived, and asked the executive director, Kim Koulet, for an internship. I told him I would work for free, if he would give me a work reference and a chance to gain some practical experience. Kim said that he couldn't let me work for free, but he did offer me a full-time paid internship until I could find a permanent job.

I enjoyed my work at the LRPC and the people I worked with. I dedicated myself to the job in the hope that it might eventually turn into a permanent position. I found it easy to work with the small towns that the agency served, and for the first time in my life, I actually began to feel that I was gaining some measure of self-respect in my native state. It was an exciting experience for me to feel that way, since virtually all of my anxieties were tied to my experiences growing up in rural New Hampshire. I began to realize that I had become an entirely new and better person, and I could conquer my old fears and insecurities by conquering my new job. I soon felt a deep sense of dedication to the LRPC, my co-workers, and the communities it served which only heightened my desire to work there. I was now eager to make my own mark on life.

Despite my affections for the agency, I realized that I needed a permanent job to get the health insurance coverage I needed and an income that would allow me to support myself. While I occasionally pestered Kim to give me a permanent job, I continued to interview for jobs across New England. Eventually, in late March, I was offered a salaried position at a regional planning agency in Worcester, Massachusetts. I felt I had no choice but to accept it, even though I preferred to work at the LRPC. The job I accepted in Worcester had two negative aspects for me. First of all, it was a transportation planning position, and I didn't want to be channeled exclusively into one area of the field. I wanted to experience a little bit of every aspect of planning which was my primary reason for seeking work at a regional agency. The other negative aspect of the job was that it was funded by a specific grant from the state, and my continued survival at the agency was not guaranteed unless the state decided to fund future phases of the grant-funded project.

From time to time, I kept in contact with Kim at the LRPC and even agreed to do some consulting work for him while I was working in Worcester. I wanted to keep the communication channels open in the event that a new job opportunity would develop at the LRPC. To my surprise, the opportunity I was seeking became available in July 1987, and Kim invited me to return. I eagerly accepted, and within a month, I was back at the agency I had come to love—this time as a salaried employee. Unfortunately, I had to accept a significantly lower starting salary, but the job seemed more secure, and it offered me the variety of work I desired. I decided I could continue living at my mother's house until I could find an affordable place of my own. This time I felt a little better about it, because I could afford to pay my mother a monthly rent. It wasn't much considering the high cost of living in the Lakes Region of New Hampshire, but it certainly eased my guilt and gave me a greater sense of independence than I had ever felt living with my adoptive family. Fortunately, I would not have to stay there for long. My professional career was off to a flying start, and the feeling of confidence it gave me would soon propel my life to the next level in my personal growth.

# *Learning to Love*

Like many adoptees, I have always had a problem with feelings of love and affection. It's hard to deal with the knowledge that you were once abandoned by your mother or parent, especially when you are not allowed to know the reason why you were relinquished, as though it were some deep, dark secret that would cause shame or ridicule. Many adoptive parents are advised to tell their adoptive child that he or she was "the chosen one" to help ease the feelings of abandonment and rejection that the child might feel when he or she learns what it means to be adopted. In reality though, an adoptive child is rarely, if ever, *chosen* by his or her adoptive parents. It is a nice sentiment, though, and I suppose it does work for some adoptees that are placed in truly loving families. However, the frequent arguments my adoptive parents had when I was a child made it quite easy for me to know that I wasn't "chosen." As a result, I had to deal with two rejections—one by my biological mother and the second by my adoptive family, within which I usually felt like an outsider or a regretted burden. To top it all off, the difficulties I encountered adjusting to the social environment in the public school system only made it harder for me to feel worthy of any love or affection.

As an adolescent, I actually feared any feelings of affection and attraction that I felt for girls in my school. I certainly didn't believe that any girls could be attracted to me, and I didn't want to be embarrassed or ridiculed for having expressed any feelings of affection for girls that I knew in my own mind to be "out of reach" or "above my station." Oh, I wouldn't be truthful if I didn't admit that I had crushes on several girls at Bald Mountain High School. Those unfulfilled affections merely became another frustration for me as well as another reason to despise myself. Now that I look back on it all with a deeper level of understanding, it's easy for me to realize why I had so few romantic relationships. While I felt a strong *need* to love and to be loved, I came to the conclusion at an early age that a romantic relationship was unattainable for me. Therefore, I never sought one.

Although I never did have a "romantic" relationship with any of the girls I met in high school, I did have a brief encounter with one girl during the last month of my senior year. Her name was Denise Smithers. She had red hair, a face full of freckles, and a soft, almost inaudible, voice. Although I wouldn't describe her as obese, she was quite stocky for her height. I can't be certain what grade she was in, but I think she was a year behind me. Like me, she was from a poor family and one of the social outcasts in the school. I didn't really know her at all. Although I wasn't aware of her feelings, she tried on several occasions to place herself in situations where I might notice her. I really wasn't very observant or cooperative. She finally found an opportunity to talk to me during a weekend school sponsored field trip that we both took to Boston. I went on the trip to get away from North Georgetown and to see the big city, although I have never been enamored with Boston. She sat next to me on the bus during the two-and-a-half-hour ride to Boston, and engaged me in a long, running conversation. I had no other friends with me, so I timidly responded to her initial questions and soon found myself engaged in a pleasant, if meaningless and non-threatening, conversation. I ended up accompanying her and her two friends during our excursions in Boston, and she rode with me again on the return trip.

On the way home, Denise asked me if I could drive her home, which was only a couple of miles from the high school. I innocently agreed. When we arrived at her house, she invited me in to meet her parents who she said would want to thank me for bringing her home. The brief introduction turned into an hour-long conversation. Eventually, I realized that it was getting late, and I needed to go home. Denise walked with me to the car. After opening the door, I turned to thank her for a nice time. However, before I could realize what was happening, she reached up, placed her hands on my shoulders, pulled herself up onto her toes, and kissed me on the lips. I don't remember what I said, but I'm sure I handled the situation quite awkwardly and probably made Denise feel as embarrassed about it as I did. I just got into the car as quickly and politely as I could and drove away. I was too stunned to feel comfortable about the encounter, and I really didn't feel any attraction to her, so I tried to let it go. Denise and I had a few awkward conversations during my final weeks of high school, but I never spent any time alone with her again. However, I did refer to Denise as my "girlfriend" during my first semester at the University of Hartford, as part of my effort to leave my past behind and build a new image for myself. I even called her from school a few times that semester to help validate my image with the guys on my floor and to talk with someone more familiar. After a few telephone conversations, she soon lost whatever misguided interest she had in me, and my first "relationship" with a girl ended as abruptly as it began.

The counseling I received during my first two years at Hartford helped me realize some of the mistakes I made in high school. Over time, I began to acknowledge that I did have an interest in women, even if I was too shy and afraid to do anything about it. It took a long time for me to believe that I could have any kind of a relationship with women so—at the advice of my counselor—I began with friendships. My developing relationships with the guys on my floor and the

Techies helped expose me to several women who were otherwise unattached. Every time I had interactions with these women, I discussed them in my counseling sessions. However, none of them turned into opportunities for meaningful relationships.

One of the college women I met at Hartford through my own initiative was Geri Collette. She had placed a notice in the student union building seeking a Thanksgiving ride to northern Vermont during my sophomore year. I called her since I was heading in that direction, and I felt I could use the company. She lived in Newport, Vermont, near the Canadian border, which was about two hours north of my destination. So, I offered to take her as far as Chelsea where she could arrange to be picked up by her mother. Geri was a very attractive, petite, and outgoing young lady, and I was eager to build a friendship with her. Although our relationship never became more than a good friendship, I did meet many other eligible women through her. Geri knew that I was not an outgoing person, so during the first half of my senior year, she set me up with one of her friends, Shirley Kowalski. Her efforts led to the first serious relationship of my life.

Geri introduced me to Shirley at a dorm party I attended early in the semester. Geri met her in one of her classes at the beginning of the year. Shirley was a transfer student from a small college in New Jersey, and she was only just beginning to feel comfortable with the social environment at Hartford. Geri introduced her to everyone else at the party and then brought her to me. When introducing me to Shirley, Geri told her how helpful I had been to her by assisting her with her studies and driving her home at holidays. She told me about some of Shirley's interests that reminded her of me. Like me, Shirley was from a small family farm in the west-central part of the state, so we had somewhat common backgrounds. Before either Shirley or I realized it, Geri had engaged us in a comfortable conversation and quietly slipped away.

Shirley was shy and innocent. She had long, wavy brown hair and bright green eyes. Her shyness and reserved demeanor immediately put me at ease. As we talked, I learned that we had many mutual interests including our tastes in music, our struggles adjusting from life in rural areas to life in the big city, and our shared sense of humor. It was not long before we were talking by ourselves in a corner of the room for the rest of the evening. After a couple of hours, we left the party early, and we walked back to her dorm, arm in arm.

When we arrived at her room, the hallway was dark and her roommate was gone. We had spent just enough time together and had talked enough to realize that we had an immediate mutual attraction for one another. Shirley unlocked the door to her room and hesitated in the doorway. It was another awkward situation for me. It was that uncomfortable point at the end of a first date that you realize it's time to leave, but you aren't sure how to properly conclude it. She was too shy to make the first move, and I was too scared. Although I had seen this situation many times before on TV, I never expected to face it myself. Somehow, after a few moments of silence, I gathered my courage (or what little of it I had), placed my hands around her waist, looked squarely into her eyes, told her that I really enjoyed being with her, and kissed her gently on the lips. Afterwards, she looked up at me, gave me a demure smile, and told me she would like to see me again. I nodded reassuringly, as we said our goodbyes.

That scene certainly didn't seem to go as smoothly as it sounds when I write about it today, but it didn't matter to me at the time. I felt like I was on top of the world. I probably didn't stop smiling privately about it for a week. Perhaps the most embarrassing aspect of it all was the realization that I had forgotten to ask for her telephone number. However, Geri stopped by my room the next day to ask me how things went with Shirley, and I was able to get the telephone number from her.

Shirley and I dated many times in the coming months. We often studied together, and I helped her with some of her class assignments. On nights that we had no specific plans or homework, we would often lie together on the bed and listen to music. It did not take long for us to become a topic of discussion among our friends. Although our affections for each other grew, we never made love. She had strong religious convictions about sex and marriage, and I lacked the bravado to press the issue. I was just so overjoyed by the thought that she wanted to be with me that I never felt unfulfilled by our limited romantic encounters. Just having someone to hold close and kiss was comforting and satisfying enough to me. I had never felt that close to another person before in my life.

Shirley was the first girl that I ever introduced to my adoptive family. When I told them I was bringing her home with me for the weekend early in my final semester at Hartford, they were stunned. I don't think I brought her with me as much to gain their approval of her as I did to validate my own feelings that I had conquered my past insecurities and to demonstrate that I had become a person who was truly worthy of someone's affections. Throughout my childhood with them, I had never been able to feel worthy of any love or basic consideration. That was a primary source of my eternal frustration and negative self-image. My relationship with Shirley made me feel on top of my world for the first time in my life, and I truly wanted to revel in it.

Our relationship remained strong throughout the remainder of my senior year. However, just before my graduation, she told me that she wasn't going to return to Hartford the following year. The cost of tuition was more than her family could afford, and she had no scholarships or income to make up the difference. I went to visit her at her home in Belle Meade, New Jersey during the summer of 1984, so that we could spend some time together before I left for California. We had a good time, but it wasn't the same. Both of us privately knew our lives were going in different directions, and our relationship would be the ultimate victim. It was the last time I ever saw her. We tried to keep in touch by phone and letters while I was attending school at Berkeley, but it didn't last. My first and only true romantic relationship had ended. The loss of our relationship was but one of the disappointments I experienced during my first semester at Berkeley, and it contributed to my decision to drop out at the end of the semester.

I still think of Shirley from time to time, although not because I can't accept the end of our relationship. She was the first woman in my life to make me feel desired in any way, shape, or form, and I'd just like to know that she is happy and doing well. I will always remember her fondly for the way she made me feel about myself at a time when I needed it most. I guess it's hard to forget your first love. But, then again, I'm not sure why I'd want to do that.

I had no meaningful relationships with the women I met while I was at Berkeley—only a few brief encounters. My classes were far too demanding, and I had to work on the side occasionally just to make ends meet. What little spare time I had I spent with the other Berkeley students living at Mills College. We had a good circle of friends, and we'd often play football, go bowling, or play a few rounds of miniature golf on the weekends. By the time I finished my graduate work at Berkeley, I had readjusted to a life without romance and became focused instead on my career goals and ambitions. At that point in time, I felt that I needed a purpose in life more than I needed a girlfriend. That may be the real reason why my next relationship caught me completely off guard.

When I returned to the Lakes Region Planning Commission in July 1987, I was determined to make my mark in the planning field. I attended as many night meetings in the local communities we served as I could fit into my schedule—sometimes as many as four per week. I even went to the office on weekends to work on my projects. I had two personal incentives to work hard. First of all, I had to live with my adoptive mother because I couldn't afford to rent an apartment on my starting salary. The cost of living in the Lakes Region was outrageous at that time, and I also had to make significant monthly payments on three college loans. The extra hours I spent at work made it easier to accept living with my adoptive family. At least I didn't have to spend all of my spare time at home, and I was living life on my own terms. That gave me some small, reassuring sense of control and independence.

Second, I thought that I would feel better about myself and become more self-confident, if I could be successful in my career. For the first year or so, it worked. I found great personal reward in my work, and I made many friends among the local officials I served. However, planning is not always the most professionally rewarding line of work. It's often difficult for a community to reach a political consensus on what it needs or wants to achieve today, much less ten or more years into the future. Although I was committed to my work, many of the plans and studies I wrote ended up on the shelf shortly after they were completed. While the citizens I worked with appreciated the work I did for them, the lack of implementation after the project was done occasionally made my efforts seem futile. I wanted to write plans that would be useful, not just printed reports collecting dust that no one would read. Most planners I have met throughout my career experience those feelings in their early years and learn to accept it—as I eventually did. You may be able to lead a horse to water, but you can't make it drink. But, at that point in my personal and professional development, it was a great disappointment, and it made my work seem less fulfilling at times.

Fortunately, my co-workers in the office were all more experienced than I was and were able to help me put it all into perspective. Tom Martin, the agency's senior planner, always had an amusing anecdote to draw upon when the work became frustrating. Collin Morris, the agency's semi-retired transportation planner, had some counseling experience through his church and was often able to provide moral support. Jim Klinger, our draftsman, seemed to have more life experience than a man twice his age. I always enjoyed his carefree nature and gentle good humor. When my work became frustrating, I often turned to them for support and guidance. Eventually, we began to do activities together outside the office, and I gradually began to divert my energy into outdoor recreational activities with my co-workers. It was during this transitional period that she arrived.

Her name was Karen Hollings. She was relatively short, but she had a naturally pretty face adorned with black curly hair and a reassuringly pleasant smile. She began working at the commission in May 1988 as an entry-level planner. Her specific planning specialty was historic preservation, but she started out working with me on a number of community plans that our agency was under contract to prepare. Like me, she had only recently received her graduate degree, so she needed some help getting acclimated to the agency and the region. I was asked to help her "learn the ropes."

Karen was a quick study and soon learned how our agency operated. Eventually, she began to talk about herself and her reasons for accepting the job. Karen was in the process of divorcing her husband to whom she had been married for less than a year. The break-up did not go smoothly, so she decided she needed to get as far away from him as she could. They were living in Spokane, Washington at the time, and Karen wanted to return closer to her mother's home in a suburb of Springfield, Massachusetts. The divorce proceedings were a terrible strain on Karen's attitude and outlook, so I decided to introduce her to the various forms of entertainment available in the region. I thought the activity would provide a pleasant distraction from her problems. It also gave me a good opportunity to have some fun outside of work.

It all began innocently enough. I took her to a large arcade complex in Laconia, and we went to a number of the popular tourist traps in the area. On a couple of occasions, we joined some of our co-workers in their off-hours activities. As time progressed, we started going out to restaurants and movies together. I found her to be quite fun to be around, when her mind was not focused on her divorce or past relationship with her husband. In fact, I think we each became the distraction that the other person needed. I helped her take her mind off her stressful divorce, while she gave me a pleasurable new distraction from the emerging frustrations of my work and my adoptive family. Before I even realized it, we were spending a lot of time together. I never really stopped to consider my feelings for her until an incident occurred that changed our relationship.

The summer of 1988 was a scorcher in New Hampshire. From mid-July to mid-August, the daily high temperatures exceeded 80 degrees for a record number of consecutive days with extremely high humidity levels. Karen was renting an apartment in an old converted mill building in downtown Franklin, New Hampshire at the time. As a historic preservationist, she loved living in the mammoth historic brick mill. Her apartment had 15-20-foot-high ceilings with ornate windows that extended almost from floor to ceiling. Unfortunately, the heavy brick walls absorbed the daytime heat, and with the addition of the relentless sunlight through the large windows and poor air circulation, her apartment felt like an oven during those hot summer days. The high humidity levels prevented any significant cooling during the nights. Although Karen was suffering with the heat, she didn't want to move out of the building she loved.

One morning in early August, as I was getting ready for work, the phone rang. I heard a distinctly female voice on the other end of the line, but I couldn't understand a word she was saying. The woman's voice was so slurred and strained that it was incoherent. It sounded to me as though she was drunk. At first, I thought it was just a crank call, and I became annoyed. However, the woman's voice became almost panicky, and I became concerned. Then I realized that she was calling me by name, and I felt my heart sink as I finally understood who it was. It was Karen, and she was pleading for help. It sounded like she was trying to say that she couldn't get up. I was living about twenty minutes away from her apartment, so I didn't know what to do. I told her I would call an ambulance, but she kept objecting. I couldn't get her to hang up the phone, so I ran to the neighbor's house, gave them her address, and asked them to call an ambulance. When I returned to the phone, the line was dead.

I got dressed as quickly as I could, called the office to tell them what had happened and to let them know I'd be late, and I rushed to the hospital. When I arrived, Karen was still in the emergency room, but the doctor met me at the door. He explained that Karen was a diabetic, and she was suffering from severe insulin shock. The intense heat of her apartment had caused her blood sugar levels to drop more than she had anticipated, and she didn't adjust her normal insulin shot accordingly. When she awoke the next morning, she had a reaction to the insulin shot she had taken before going to bed. The ambulance had arrived in time, and she was going to be okay. However, I just couldn't forget the fact that I had almost hung up on her when she had called me for help.

Suddenly, my mind was focused on my feelings for Karen. Every moment I spent with her now seemed more precious and important to me. For the first time since my relationship with Shirley, I was falling in love. I was so inexperienced with those feelings that I failed to consciously recognize them. To my shock, it appeared that Karen was experiencing the same feelings for me. We began to spend more and more time together, as our relationship became increasingly romantic. Then, one Friday evening in early September, I stopped by her apartment with some of my favorite albums. We listened to music together, as I had done four years earlier with Shirley. The conversation gradually grew more intimate, and she eventually invited me to spend the night with her.

Our relationship quickly flourished, and I began spending each weekend with Karen. Within a month, we had found a townhome unit in Franklin that we could lease on a rent-to-own basis, and we decided to live together. By the end of October, I had moved out of my adoptive family's home for the final time. My relationship with Karen became the center of my universe, and I began to trust her in ways that I had never trusted anyone else before.

As the settlement of Karen's nine-month divorce proceeding approached, we began to discuss marriage. One of Karen's biggest concerns was her inability to have children. The physical stress of pregnancy and childbirth is dangerous for diabetics. Although Karen truly wanted to have children, she feared that the risk to her health would be too great. She was also concerned that her decision not to have children would affect my feelings towards her. Any expression of disappointment on my part would only make it harder for her to accept her reluctant decision.

It was then that I revealed to her that I had been adopted, and that I would be just as happy adopting a child with her as having one of my own. I think she was as surprised by that revelation as I was to learn that she was a diabetic. She soon began to ask me questions about my adoption and how I felt about it. Apparently, she wanted to know how an adopted child would feel, since (in her own mind) it was the only way she would ever have a child. For me, though, it was a sensitive topic, and discussing it in depth quickly revived memories and feelings that I really didn't want to face or share. If not for my unconditional trust in her feelings for me, I would have done everything in my power to evade the topic. But for the first time in my life, I began to discuss some of my feelings about it with another person.

I was careful not to reveal all my feelings about my adoption, especially the story about Daphne's confrontation with me over the arguments between my adoptive parents and the reaction I received from my mother and grandmother when I first said I wanted to find my biological mother. Those memories were too painful, and I was still too embarrassed to face them. Over time, I did talk about my long-standing desire to know who my biological family was and my feelings about my adoptive parents' general attitudes towards them. From what little I was ever told, I had been led to believe that my biological mother was probably a dockside hooker who catered to the naval personnel stationed at the Portsmouth Naval Shipyard. Yet, despite my adoptive family's concerted efforts to tarnish the image of my biological family and birthplace, I was always resolute in my desire to know about my dark and hidden past. I expressed all these feelings to Karen, but I never realized at the time how much of an impact they had on her or me.

Although in the beginning, Karen and I had a wonderful, romantic relationship, it did not last long. I guess Karen's affection for me was driven as much by her fears and anxieties over her divorce as it was by any genuine affection for me. Her feelings towards me began to change as the divorce drew to a close, and she was confronted with the prospect of having to face our earlier discussions of marriage. By February 1989, she was beginning to secretly reconsider her future plans, and I was not a part of them. I didn't even begin to learn about her changing feelings until one afternoon in March when I picked up the mail and found that it contained a couple of college catalogs addressed to her. When I asked her about it, she said that she was seriously thinking of going back to college to earn a graduate degree in historic preservation. Since the college she wanted to attend was in Indiana and she hadn't discussed her plans with me, the ramifications for our relationship were abundantly clear. I tried to convince her and myself that our relationship could survive, but it was futile. Once again, one of my fleeting romantic relationships was coming to an end as suddenly as it had begun.

I was crushed. The realization that our whirlwind fairy-tale relationship was ending hit me like a ton of bricks. Suddenly, I felt more alone in my life than ever before. I had trusted her like no other person I had known. I had even accepted the idea that I would soon have my own rewarding life apart from my adoptive family. Of course, I didn't blame her for our break-up. It was always much too easy to blame myself. All of Karen's questions about my adoption had reawakened many of the most unpleasant memories from my childhood, as well as my desire to know my biological family. I just couldn't face the idea of being abandoned again by the one I had finally come to love. Once again, my roller coaster life was heading into a tailspin, and I just knew I couldn't go back to my adoptive family again. Soon my enthusiasm for my work at the LRPC began to wane. Everything about the office and my co-workers reminded me of my relationship with Karen. I desperately needed a change of environments. So, I quietly began searching for a new job.

Early in June 1989, I was offered a position at a smaller regional planning commission in Middlebury, Vermont. Professionally, I was drawn to Vermont because the state appeared far more progressive than New Hampshire when it came to community planning issues. I decided I needed to rededicate myself back to my work, and a move to Vermont seemed the best way to do it. I accepted the offer and left Karen and the LRPC behind at the end of the month. I only saw her twice after that, and we soon lost contact with one another. Once again, I would have to pick up the pieces and rebuild my wounded self-esteem.

# Made in Vermont

When I first arrived in the small, quaint community of Middlebury, Vermont, I was a beaten and frustrated person. I was completely alone in unfamiliar surroundings and seriously depressed. I was also nearly broke. It seemed to me as though my life was constantly teasing me–building me up to new heights only to let me down again later. Once again, I turned to support from my remaining college friends and my former co-workers at the LRPC, but none of them lived close by. I was still alone most of the time. I began to build a new friendship with one of my co-workers at the office in Vermont, but he was in the process of marrying his long-time girlfriend, and I just felt like an additional burden at the time.

Middlebury was an "established" community with very few young, single people to meet. Those that did live in the community were largely invisible and disconnected. Many were young college students and they socialized exclusively within the campus. Most of the special events that occurred in the area were geared towards families. If you weren't a part of the Middlebury College student community, you had no comfortable way to meet other single people. I spent most of my evenings watching TV, renting movies, and going for long walks–all by myself. My reclusive life began to remind me of my early months at the University of Hartford. The lack of any nightlife or opportunities to meet other people made it impossible for me to forget my relationship with Karen. I could feel my frustrations deepen, and on the advice of a friend, I soon decided to seek counseling again.

This time, my counseling experience was different. My relationship with Karen had forced my feelings about my adoption to the surface. For the first time, I began to discuss them in my counseling sessions along with all my other "ghosts" from the past. Suddenly, no topic was off the table. I talked about my high school experiences, my failed relationship with my adoptive father, and my feelings about losing Karen. After a few months of intensive counseling, I began to realize just how many conflicting intertwined feelings I had locked away deep inside that I now had to face and resolve. I remained in counseling for nearly two years. While it didn't resolve all of my buried feelings, it opened my eyes and enabled me to take charge of my life. Step by step, I began to reconstruct my life and recover my hope for a brighter future.

The first step I took on my road to recovery was to become more active in the community outside of the office. I discovered that the local public access cable TV station in town, Middlebury Community Television, offered a training program for aspiring local program producers. I took the three-week course and began to videotape community events. I also helped maintain the station's scrolling video bulletin board that filled the broadcasting time between regular programs. I even tried to produce a program highlighting local volunteer and community organizations called Middlebury Area Focus, but I couldn't find a reliable on-air narrator. I certainly didn't want to appear on camera. I did manage to produce the longest program broadcasted on the station at that point in time. It was a performance by the Vermont Symphony Orchestra of The Creation, by Franz Josef Haydn, in celebration of the Middlebury Congregational Church's 200th anniversary. It was about two-and-a-half hours long, and I spent nearly two months editing it for broadcast. I became such a regular fixture at the station that I was eventually invited to serve on the station's board of directors. I thought my involvement in the community station would expose me to other single people, but many of the station's volunteer producers worked independently outside the community. So, I didn't meet as many people as I had hoped I would.

I also tried meeting single women through several dating services that operated out of nearby Burlington and Rutland. These services helped me get a number of dates, but none of them ever resulted in a serious relationship. Actually, I felt quite uncomfortable with the dates I had through the dating services. I wasn't the kind of person who could feel comfortable going on a blind date with someone I knew nothing about. I gradually learned that most people who use a dating service are actively looking for a romantic relationship regardless of what they may say at the outset of a first date. Quite often, they are looking for someone who satisfies their predetermined criteria for a potential lover, and if the date doesn't satisfy those criteria, one or the other person will walk away and arrange a date with another person. It seemed like a "hunt and peck" approach to finding a meaningful relationship that wasn't very reliable. I was not a very self-assured person at that time, so I always acted nervous and awkward on first dates, especially when I felt I was being judged by my appearance and actions. Therefore, I really didn't leave a good first impression with most of the dates I had. I just wasn't comfortable in situations like that, and none of the few women I met made me feel truly at ease.

I discussed many of my dating service failures during my twice-weekly counseling sessions. Over time, I grew to realize that blind dates were not a good way for me to develop successful relationships with women. My low self-esteem and discomfort with my appearance made me too nervous around prospective dates to act naturally and leave a good first impression. I certainly wasn't any woman's idea of a fashion plate. I needed to meet women in a less threatening environment, where I could get to know them and establish a rapport before feeling the pressure of being judged. That's exactly the way that my only prior successful relationships had emerged. In both cases, I was not expecting to establish a relationship; it just happened. I needed a way to learn more about the women I was meeting before dating them seriously in order to feel more comfortable and relaxed around them. When I knew nothing about them, I felt too conscientious and nervous to engage in easygoing conversation. However, I had no way to meet women in a more casual setting. Single women weren't simply hanging around on the streets of Middlebury, Vermont just waiting for some man to come along and strike up a casual relationship.

For my first full year in Middlebury, I remained alone visiting my old friends whenever I had an opportunity to do so. On occasion, one of my friends would visit me in Middlebury, and I would plan an agenda of activities to do during the visit. I had made plans for just such a visit during my summer vacation in July of 1990. My good friend and former LRPC co-worker, Jim Klinger, had agreed to visit me during my vacation. He had always wanted to travel the length of Lake Champlain in his boat, and I offered to help him plan the trip and go with him. I bought a map of the lake and marked the locations of the various campgrounds and boat refueling stations along the shore. The lake is over 100 miles long, so it would take a few days for us to complete the round trip on his small boat. I also bought some basic supplies that we would need on our trip. We planned to meet in Burlington, where he could fuel and launch his boat. I was excited about the adventure and had looked forward to the vacation for months. However, something came up at the last minute, and Jim had to cancel the trip just days before my vacation. I didn't have enough advance warning to make alternative vacation plans, so I faced an entire week alone in my Middlebury apartment.

Fortunately, I had spent a lot of time thinking of ways to meet other single people, and my vacation alone gave me an ideal opportunity to put my plan into action. I decided to organize an activity and social group for singles in the area that I named the Middlebury Area Singles club. I learned from my association with Middlebury Community Television that the town library (where the station's studio was located) had a community meeting room in the basement that was available for free use by any community organization. I reserved the room for a meeting date in early August and posted ads for an organizational meeting of the group throughout the town in places that I knew would be frequented by single people—the library, town hall, post office, supermarkets, video stores, and laundromats. I also posted the ad on Middlebury Community Television's bulletin board.

My plan was to organize a group that brought single people together for group social activities rather than just one-on-one dates. I wrote down a lengthy list of activities that the group could plan to do together in the area such as bowling, hiking, bicycling, horseback riding, pot luck dinner socials, and trips to the upcoming county fairs. Each activity would be planned and coordinated by a volunteer member of the group who was interested in that activity. During each monthly meeting, the activity coordinators would provide sign-up sheets for any member who was interested in participating in their activities. The coordinator would call all of the participating members and arrange a meeting time and location for the activity, once he or she knew how many people wanted to attend. The group would collect dues from all members, which would be used to subsidize the cost of participating in the more expensive activities or for scheduling future group trips to New York City, Boston, or Montreal. Members would eventually find other singles who shared their interests by becoming involved in the group's activities. Over time, it would be an easy way to meet people and become familiar with them *before* having to face the pressures of dating. It seemed the only way for me to meet other singles without a dating service.

My concept became a huge success. Nearly twenty singles attended the organizational meeting. While the composition of the group changed greatly during the first few meetings, the number of members remained strong— between twenty and thirty. I was elected to serve as the group's first president. Barbara Hitchcock, who worked as an assistant branch manager for one of the local banks, was elected to serve as the group's treasurer. The group scheduled many different activities during the fall of 1990, and Barbara and I worked closely together to plan activities and to keep the infant organization financially viable. Eventually, we realized that we were attending many of the same activities. Soon thereafter, we began dating outside the group. For only the third time in my life, I was involved in an intense romantic relationship.

Barbara and I spent a lot of time together during the summer and fall of 1990. She was eight years my senior, but we shared a maturity and attitude towards life that more than erased the age difference. Like Shirley and Karen, Barbara was attractive, and we shared many interests. However, Barb was more naturally outgoing and engaging than other women from my past with whom I had built relationships. In this respect, she was more like Geri Collette. As far as I was concerned, Barbara had a magnetic personality, and I was drawn to her. We seemed to have very compatible personalities and enjoyed spending time together. Ironically, we learned that we had missed several opportunities to meet earlier. I did all my banking at her bank. She also had been a member of the choir that performed in The Creation, which I had filmed for Middlebury Community Television. I had even planned to interview some of the local choir members as part of the program, but I ran out of time and videotape by the end of the performance.

Our relationship evolved quickly and by early November, we were engaged. On May 11, 1991, we were married at the Middlebury Congregational Church. It was a truly memorable day for both of us, but it also held a deeper meaning for me. Once again, I had overcome one of my basic childhood anxieties and achieved something in life that I had always felt to be unattainable. I had finally found someone who could truly love me for who I was—faults and all. I later learned that my former girlfriend Karen Hollings was married on the same day. Seven years later, I would learn through another ironic twist of fate that our wedding day held even more significance for me.

While I had rediscovered my ability to enjoy life, certain aspects of my life were changing at a frantic pace, and they challenged my ability to feel in control of them. Less than two months before our wedding day, Barb learned that she was pregnant with our son. It was shocking news to both of us. Due to previous surgeries, Barb's doctor had told her it was unlikely that she would ever bear children. As a result, she believed that she couldn't become pregnant.

The news was especially frightening to me because I didn't feel confident about my ability to be a father. I was still working to overcome my lingering childhood insecurities, and I didn't want to make the same mistakes that my adoptive father had made. Numerous studies had shown that children with alcoholic parents were at great risk to become alcoholic parents themselves. The same pattern had been documented for children of abusive parents. I felt certain that my poor upbringing and inability to establish a bond with the only father I had known would make me a poor parent as well.

I was also concerned about my medical history. As an adoptee I had no knowledge of my biological family's medical history. Therefore, I had no way to know what potential genetic diseases or birth defects I might pass on to my children. I already knew I had an irregular heartbeat, and I had experienced brief blackout episodes for years that no one had been able to diagnose. This nagging fear plagued me for years after the birth of our child. I just wasn't certain that I *should* be a father. Yet, I couldn't abandon my responsibilities to my future child, as my adoptive parents had led me to believe that my biological family did.

Another force of change in my life was the economic recession of the late 1980s and early 1990s. This recession hit New England especially hard. At first, I thought it might actually help us improve our standard of living. Land values in Vermont and New Hampshire had appreciated beyond our reach during the 1980s, and my salary was not keeping pace. The recession created a vacuum in the real estate market, which helped lower the cost of land and housing. So, I initially thought that Barb and I would soon be able to buy our own home. However, the recession also had grave consequences for our jobs. I worked for a very small regional planning office that survived largely on funding from the state. The recession caused a decline in state revenues, which fueled debates over funding cuts for regional planning commissions. Suddenly, my job was no longer secure.

Barb's job at the bank became equally unstable. When the bank's revenue streams began to decline, Barb's job title was changed from assistant branch manager to mortgage loan officer. Their resources could no longer support both a branch manager and an assistant branch manager at that office. Her job and salary now depended upon her ability to secure mortgages, which weren't in great demand during the recession. Most of the mortgage applications she received were to refinance existing mortgages. My concerns about our lack of job security were compounded by the impending birth of our child and the lack of alternative job opportunities for me in Vermont. We eventually decided that we needed to move away to a part of the country that was less costly for starting families and that was better insulated from the effects of the recession. Once again, I was looking for a new job.

Of course, I was very selective in the potential job locations I considered. I used my basic knowledge of local economies to evaluate the areas in which prospective planning job opportunities became available. If we were going to make a major move, I wanted to be certain that it would benefit us and help us remain more financially stable than we were in Vermont. Georgia was high on my list because I knew that Atlanta would host the 1996 Summer Olympics. I felt that the investments that would be made in the city over the next few years would help insulate it from the economic recession and recover more quickly when it ended. I also knew that Atlanta was growing rapidly and that its economic influence would eventually spread to neighboring areas of the state. Finally, the housing market in Georgia was very affordable. Eventually, Georgia's growth potential would drive real estate prices up hopefully carrying us with them.

I applied for several jobs in Atlanta and the surrounding cities in north and central Georgia. Eventually, I landed a position as a senior planner at the Middle Georgia Regional Development Center in Macon. The job offered me a raise, a promotion, and a lower cost of living, so I accepted it. In early July 1991, we began preparing for our move to the deep south. It was both a sad and joyful time for us. While we both regretted leaving New England behind, we knew that the move would give us a chance for a better future. I felt that I owed my unborn son that much.

During the first two weeks of July, we visited our families and friends one last time. Our last visit with my adoptive family was a comfortable affair for me, if for no other reason than the realization that I would never have to be dependent upon them again. I felt more in control of my life than I ever did before. However, my adoptive mother treated me as though I was abandoning my obligation to take care of her. I never asked for nor desired that responsibility, yet it had always been a source of contention and jealousy for Daphne. Perhaps the most revealing aspect of my adoptive mother's bruised feelings were her final parting words to me. By her own admission, she told me, "If you're going to go down there to live, that's your choice, but don't expect to see a lot of me." She knew she couldn't stop us from making the move, but she wasn't going to do anything to condone it. She never went back on her words.

# Part IV: My Final Epiphany

The move to Macon, Georgia was a very positive first step in our new life together. On the strength of my new salary and with my share of an inheritance bequeathed to my adoptive family from the estate of Dad's long-lost biological aunt, Barb and I were able to buy our first home. It was a small, three-bedroom ranch, but it was considerably better and bigger than the mobile home we owned in Vermont. The lower cost of living in the southeast also made it possible for us to live more comfortably than we had in New England. While the separation from our families was initially hard on Barb, I found it to be a relief. I no longer felt subjected to quarrels and ridicule from Daphne, and the guilt I harbored by virtue of being an illegitimate and divisive part of my adoptive family gradually faded with time. In fact, my tongue actually had time to recover from all the times I had bitten it in the past. I now felt free to create my own life and future, just as I had done at the University of Hartford. Barb and I were beginning to build a family and a life of our own.

However, the anticipated birth of my son in December 1991 made the mysteries about my biological roots even more important to me. What genetic health problems might he inherit from me and my unknown family? What would he look like? Would he even look enough like me for him to know in his own mind that I was his father? I didn't want him to experience the same feelings and insecurities of looking different from his parents that I did. I knew how these nagging questions made me feel as a child, and I wanted to know that they would not plague him as well. To a large degree, my ability to feel confident and comfortable about my role as his father depended on the answers to these lingering questions.

Although I tried to search for my biological family only once during my childhood, I never abandoned my private desire to know my lost family. Actually, I had entertained the idea of searching again soon after I began college at the University of Hartford. I was alone one night in my dormitory room watching an episode of "Unsolved Mysteries" when they presented a story about an adoptee who found her biological family. It was only the second time in my life that I had heard about a successful search. Over time, I saw several adoptee search and reunion stories on that show. I eventually contemplated calling them to request their assistance, but I never did. I decided that they wouldn't be interested in my story. Now that I think back upon it, I'm not sure if I actually believed that or it was a convenient excuse to avoid my fears of a second rejection by my biological family. I hadn't recovered enough of my self-esteem at that point to feel worthy of acceptance by the family that had placed me for adoption.

I actually considered searching again several years later, while I was attending graduate school in Berkeley. During my first semester, I was one of several fellow students who volunteered to donate blood at a local Red Cross blood drive. The recent AIDS crisis had spawned fears about contaminated blood supplies, and the Red Cross was helping replenish local supplies with fresh blood. However, to ensure the quality of the new supplies, each potential donor was asked a number of background medical questions prior to actual donation. As an adoptee, I had no background medical information, so I politely told them I could not answer many of their questions. Rather than turn me away, they asked me if I would allow one of the nurses to give me a brief check-up before I donated blood. However, during the check-up, the nurse discovered that I was experiencing an irregular heartbeat. Although I knew from past experience that it would come and go with time, they decided to turn me away and refuse my donation. Soon afterwards, I began to wonder if my irregular heartbeat might be a warning sign of a potential genetic heart problem. In fact, soon after Michael was born, his pediatrician determined that he had a venous murmur, which is a possible sign of an irregular heartbeat. There was no history of heart problems in Barb's family, so I always wondered if it was a warning sign of a potential genetic heart condition in my biological family. I realized that I would never know without searching for my biological family, but my time at Berkeley was so consumed by my studies that I didn't have the ability to follow through on my desire to find the answers.

Although I thought about searching on many occasions, I always had a reason or excuse to avoid it. The fact of the matter was that I was not fully confident in my ability to succeed, and I was always afraid of being rejected by my biological family. I guess I also didn't want to be perceived by others as being ungrateful to my adoptive family simply because I wanted to find and know my biological family. In all honesty, it seemed that searching offered a greater potential risk of failure than success, and I didn't want to risk damaging my emerging (but nonetheless shaky) self-esteem. However, as the distance and separation from my adoptive family grew, I gradually found the personal space and isolation I needed to rebuild my self-confidence and eventually embark on the search that would change my life again.

# *Fall from Grace*

A friend once told me that the three most stressful events in your life are moving away from home, marriage, and having a baby. Barb and I experienced all three of these life-altering events in one seven-month period in 1991. We were married on May 11; on July 15, we moved away from our childhood homes to a part of the country we had never even visited; and our first and only child was born on December 3. In addition, we bought our first home, and I assumed my first supervisory role in my new job. My predecessor had abandoned many of his projects when he resigned, and I quickly learned that the projects I inherited were several months behind schedule. We also had great difficulties selling our mobile home in Vermont. The real estate market was soft, the monthly lot rent more than doubled during the prior year, and our realtor was not working very aggressively to market it. After many months of negotiating with our Vermont bank, the mobile home was sold in January 1992 for a loss, and we had to pay off the outstanding balance. Around the same time, we also faced a number of costly medical bills for Michael's birth. We managed to keep our heads above water, but our finances became severely strained in the initial year of our move to Georgia.

To put it mildly our first six months in Macon were extremely stressful on both of us. Fortunately, Barb's family was very supportive. Barb's parents drove down to visit us at Thanksgiving and stayed for the remaining two weeks during Michael's birth and Barb's recovery. My adoptive family was considerably less supportive. To help ease my adoptive mother's anxieties about our move and my own feelings of guilt about leaving her behind, I made every effort to call her each weekend, despite our strained finances. She very rarely returned the favor.

As Michael's birth approached, I encouraged my mother to visit us for the big event. Our finances were stretched so thin that I couldn't say how long it would be before we could travel back to New England. Although she had the time (she didn't work) and the money (from the inheritance and from the sale of the family farm) she needed to make the trip, she flatly refused. Instead, she offered a series of excuses for not making the trip. At first, she was afraid to fly. When I suggested she could drive (as Barb's parents had planned to do) or take the train, she said she was afraid to travel alone. When I suggested that Anita (who was still living at home) could accompany her, she said she had no one to take care of her dog and cats while she was gone. Every time I offered a solution to her never-ending litany of problems, she would create a new excuse, which was often weaker than the previous one. At one point, she actually said that she couldn't leave her house because her new furnace repairman had told her the furnace was not originally wired properly and might explode at any time. What kind of excuse was that to stay in the house until it could be fixed? She eventually grew tired of the banter and reminded me of her final parting words when we moved. That's when I realized that her real intent was to make me feel guilty about leaving her behind and abandoning my responsibility to be there for her.

That attitude bothered me. With everything else I had to face, the last thing I needed was to be treated by my adoptive mother as though I had abandoned my obligation to her. It was true that she had given me more support than anyone else within my immediate family, but her support was rarely given unconditionally. I was always aware of the expectations that she had of me, and if she didn't make them clear enough herself, her mother would. She also had a way of blaming herself when things didn't go her way to make me and others feel sympathy for her. For instance, Mom very rarely (if ever) apologized for the mistakes she made. Instead, she expressed her remorse in a self-deprecating manner that was subtly designed to court sympathy and pity for her. Her admissions of guilt were expressed through statements like, "I guess I just wasn't a very good mother," and "I just couldn't give them what they needed." On occasion, she would take responsibility for a problem that she caused, but not her actions. Daphne often employed the same technique.

Mom's method of soliciting pity was always very effective with me and only served to reinforce the guilt I felt about being a source of division within my adoptive family. However, I had obligations to my own family and job now, and I wasn't going to allow my adoptive family to manipulate my life that way anymore. Privately, I rejected her selfish attitude, but I still didn't have the courage to confront her about it—at least not at that point in time. I didn't want to give Barb and her family the false impression that I was a cold and inconsiderate son. They still had no idea what my childhood had been like, and I was sure that they wouldn't understand my hostile reaction.

When I could no longer rationalize with my mother on the subject of visiting us, I found a different way to motivate her. In the fall of 1991, Daphne announced that she was going to be married the following May (almost one year to the date after Barb and I were married). Although I wasn't sure that I would have the vacation time or the money we needed to make the trip, Mom insisted that we attend. I eventually agreed to make the trip, but I told Mom that we wouldn't stay with her during our visit if she wasn't willing to make an effort to see Michael when he was born. I guess it was a somewhat selfish thing to do, but I really wanted my son to have the respect from my adoptive family that I never received. When she finally decided that I wasn't bluffing, she arranged to visit us roughly three weeks after Michael was born. It was the first and last trip she ever made to visit us in the south.

Although Barb and I were only able to travel back to New England twice (in 1992 and 1995), Barb's parents visited us in Georgia several times. My mother made annual vacation trips to Prince Edward Island during the summers (a 700-mile trip by road and ferry), but she continued to find excuses for not visiting us. As time passed, I gradually began to shift my focus away from my adoptive family and towards my wife, son, and planning career. My adoptive family didn't communicate well when we all lived together, and that certainly wasn't going to improve as distance and time were added to the mix. From time to time, I encouraged my adoptive mother to visit, but I called less frequently, and I avoided pushing the subject. There really wasn't anything to be gained by it except my own disappointment and frustration.

As we gained control of our finances, our family life improved. We started taking occasional weekend day trips around the state to see as many sights as we could—especially in the North Georgia mountains. It was reassuring to drive the winding mountain roads to experience a landscape that we both appreciated and increasing missed. We also became involved in our neighborhood association and made many friends. Through it all, our son was the center of our universe. Barb and I both did everything we could to make sure he would have the childhood we never had. We took him to places that would be both entertaining and educational for him; we played with him every chance we could get; and we even took turns rocking him to sleep. Rather than place him in a day care center, we hired home-based day care providers to keep him during the day. That way he would not have to grow up in an institutional environment, but he would still have other children to play with while we were at work.

By all accounts, Michael was a happy and well-behaved child. You could even detect it in his smile and his laughter, which were always full and unrestrained. In fact, Michael's obvious contentment as a child gradually made me realize that I was becoming a far better father than I ever thought I'd be. That knowledge contributed to my growing self-confidence, even though he didn't resemble me as much as I had hoped he would. He had the same hair and eye color that I had, but so did Barb. Overall, I had to agree that he resembled Barb and her family much more than he did me, although I wouldn't admit it publicly.

I always wanted to find a more substantial physical resemblance between Michael and me, if for no other reason than to know that some meaningful part of me would be passed on to future generations. Throughout my childhood, I felt different and disconnected from the people around me largely because no one I knew looked even remotely like me. In the back of my mind, I had hoped that Michael would bear a strong resemblance to me, which would reassure me that I was part of something greater than just myself and that my son would always carry with him some small part of me after I was gone. If Michael didn't resemble me in some recognizable way, I wondered if his children or grandchildren would ever be able to sense their connection to me. I didn't want my existence to be "erased" from the faces of my future generations. It felt like an insulting end for a person who had no known beginning. For the most part, I kept my feelings in that respect to myself. As long as no one else was making an issue of the differences in our appearance, I didn't let it bother me.

Fortunately, my career was also progressing well. By the time I had acquired six years of experience in regional planning I had accomplished a lot. I had been involved in a wide range of projects within the field spanning most of the major topics, from comprehensive planning and zoning to housing studies, transportation studies, economic development analyses, and environmental plans. As I discovered early in my career, most of the plans and reports I prepared were only marginally implemented at best. Yet, my involvement in a broad range of planning projects had taught me a great deal about the workings of local government, and I yearned for closer work with the cities and towns I served. I felt that my work would be more effective and rewarding at the local level. My work at the regional level was becoming too repetitive, boring, and unfulfilling.

To satisfy my growing desire to work more closely with towns and cities and to increase my job security and prospects, two of my colleagues and I formed our own private consulting firm in 1993 called Innovative Planning Concepts. We managed to secure a few small contracts from cities and counties outside the Middle Georgia region, but the work was exhausting. The personnel policies at my agency prohibited me from working within the boundaries of my agency's region, so we had to travel great distances to find outside work. My night meeting schedule became crowded with meetings for my daytime job and my consulting business. The strain on my personal time was more than I could manage, so I decided that I needed to make a change. Since the consulting business was not substantial or consistent enough to support any of us full time, I began looking for a new city or town planning job.

By the end of 1994, I was offered a promising job as the planning director for LaGrange, Georgia. I was excited about the opportunity because I would be the city's first full-time planner, and I would be able to build a new planning program for the city. Although LaGrange was small with a population of only 27,000, it owned and operated a wide range of public facilities and services, including water, sewer, gas, electric, and fiber optic cable systems. As a planner, I knew that the city's ownership of these facilities gave it considerable leverage in directing and managing its growth and development. It sounded like a great opportunity to become an effective planner. So, in the winter of 1995, we prepared for our move to LaGrange.

Unfortunately, my new job did not work out as well as I had hoped. I learned only after I accepted the job that I had walked into a volatile political and economic climate. When I interviewed for the job, I was told that the city was creating its own planning department because the former countywide planning agency had taken a political stance the city opposed, and the city didn't want to depend upon the regional planning agency that served the area. My history of work in regional planning agencies apparently did not make me their first choice for the job. LaGrange is a very independent-minded city and had been for many years. What I didn't realize, though, was that a political power struggle was occurring within city hall, and the director of the community development department did not support the idea of creating a new department—especially one that had potentially overlapping responsibilities with his own department. He eventually saw my presence as a potential threat to his position within the city's administrative structure. When I started work, several of my new co-workers warned me that he would feel threatened by my college education, since he was one of the few department heads in the city who possessed only a high school diploma.

Although I began working under the supervision of the assistant city manager, my work program was shifted into the community development department only one month later, after the assistant city manager resigned. I later learned that the community development director had successfully convinced the city council to downgrade my position from department head to supervisor between the time that I accepted the planning director's job and my first day of work. No one at the city even bothered to tell me that it had happened. This change in status made it possible for him to take control of my work program and fold it into his department, where he would have greater control over my work responsibilities.

As if to compound my misfortune, the city also experienced an unanticipated financial crisis soon after I arrived. In late January 1995, one of the city's largest manufacturing plants exploded and burned to the ground. This particular plant was a major consumer of the city's natural gas, power, water, and sewer services. Although the company eventually decided to rebuild the plant at its former location, the sudden decline in utility service demand reduced the city's operating revenues by more than $1,000,000. This revenue shortfall caused the city to look for ways to trim its expense budget, and it did not take the community development director long to advocate eliminating the new planning department altogether. Since he had no cause to fire me, he offered me an alternative job as a senior development specialist to work on the city's developing dark fiber optic network. Of course, I had no experience in that line of work, and I didn't possess the self-confidence I felt was necessary to effectively and aggressively market the system. By the end of the year, it was clear to me that my planning future with the city was not secure, and I felt compelled again to search for new job opportunities. Fortunately, with some support and guidance from my planning colleagues in the area, I soon found a new job as planning director for the East Alabama Regional Planning and Development Commission in nearby Anniston, Alabama. I decided it was better to return to regional planning than to risk my entire career waging a struggle for a dead-end job in LaGrange. After all, I had no political connections or standing in the community, and the community development director had worked there for years.

As my experiences in LaGrange suggest, 1995, was not a good year for my career or me. I spent most of the year contending with my heavy work load and fears about losing my job or being forced to accept a major career change, neither of which I desired. By the end of the year, I was beginning another job search. Ironically, it was during this point in time that my relationship with my adoptive family finally reached the breaking point. Of course, I didn't expect a lot of emotional support from my adoptive family. They had taught me many years ago that I shouldn't depend on them for moral support. Fortunately, I had learned how to stand on my own two feet in that respect. However, I was eventually placed in the position of having to give them my support during that period of time.

Sometime in 1994, my adoptive mother learned that she had breast cancer. I didn't learn about it until after she had received the test results later that year confirming that it was malignant and that she needed to undergo a mastectomy. When I asked her why she didn't tell me earlier, she said she simply didn't want to make me worry about it. However, the tone of her voice made it clear that her concern for me was really intended to serve as a subtle reminder that I wasn't there for her when she needed it. It really wasn't necessary as I was naturally concerned for her well-being anyway.

Although I didn't like some of the things she did as my mother, I didn't want to abandon her. I just wanted her and the rest of my adoptive family to give me the freedom and the support I needed to become my own person without constantly having to feel so obligated to them. I didn't ask to be adopted by them, but I always struggled with the unspoken expectation that I somehow had a greater obligation to my adoptive parents than their natural children did *because* they had taken me into their family. A part of me agreed with that sentiment, but another part of me felt that I had not received the loving and accepting family that the popular public image of adoption promised. I certainly never felt like the "chosen one," and I knew full well that I was not accepted as a legitimate member of the family. To a certain degree I felt that the adoption process had broken its promises to me, and I had already paid my dues to society and my family for my adoption. True and unconditional love cannot be coerced or sustained by guilt. Still, the severity of her illness and her need for support made me feel extremely guilty about not being there to help her. In the final analysis, my mother's comments had only rekindled my longstanding need to deal with my feelings about being adopted into the Smith family. Those feelings were never going to just fade away.

I tried to resolve my torn feelings about the situation as best I could without involving Barb. I wanted to visit my adoptive mother, but my limited vacation leave, unanticipated job search, financial constraints, and my obligations to my current job, my fledgling consulting business, and my own family, made it virtually impossible for me to drop everything on such short notice. We had also agreed to host a high school foreign exchange student from Germany that year and couldn't travel that distance without her. To compound matters, a few of my adoptive relatives contacted me to convey how much my adoptive mother needed me and how important it was for me to be near her—as if I wasn't already aware of it on my own. None of them seemed to understand or care that I didn't have absolute control over every aspect of my life at that point in time. I did my best to keep in close contact with my adoptive mother and to be as supportive as I could be during her time of need. Fortunately, the surgery and chemotherapy treatment were successful, even though it was a very traumatic experience for her. Before we decided to leave LaGrange, her recovery from the treatment was well underway.

As my adoptive mother recovered, my life became even more complicated and stressful. I had already come to the realization that my move to LaGrange was a serious mistake, when I received a call from my youngest sister, Anita. She had just returned to college in New Hampshire after transferring briefly to a college in Massachusetts and then dropping out for a semester, and she seemed to want some moral support from me. However, at one point during our conversation, she revealed that she and Daphne were upset with me for the problems I had allegedly caused my adoptive mother. In fact, they accused me of causing her cancer because my "persistent" requests that she visit us made her life stressful. I was stunned and angered by the accusation. After all, I hadn't pressed that subject for years, and I wasn't even aware of her cancer until she was ready to begin treatment. If I had been informed about the situation at the start, I would have been able to do more for her. Anita's accusation reminded me of how I felt in 1991, when I realized why my adoptive mother first refused to visit us during Michael's birth (largely because she didn't want to condone our move to Georgia). This time, though, I had several years to think about the problems with my adoptive family relationship, and I wasn't going to just punish myself. I decided that it was time to clear the air with my adoptive family and lighten the load of problems that I had to bear.

I knew immediately that Daphne was the source of the allegations (which Anita confirmed), so I called her and a bitter argument ensued. For the first time in my life, I defended myself against her seemingly eternal list of petty accusations. I finally told her how she had made me feel over the years and that I was tired of being blamed for everything that went wrong in her life. I also told her that I was aware of her longstanding jealousy of me and that I was prepared to do something about it. Daphne never tried to apologize to me. She only denied that she had blamed me for Mom's cancer, until I revealed to her that Anita had said otherwise. So, I said that I never wanted to speak to her or any of my sisters again. Although my response might seem extreme to the casual observer, I had no regrets. I was never able to view myself in a positive light through Daphne's eyes, and I knew that her attitude towards me would never change. I also knew from this incident that she was actively poisoning the water with my other sisters. My reaction to her was not based solely on our final argument. It was based on a lifetime of hollow accusations and jealous attacks that refused to end, even when I had moved out of her way. Even Barb was aware of that, so she had no objections to my decision. The rift between Daphne and I that began in the early 1970s with her angry childhood rejection of me had grown into a canyon that could never be bridged.

Although I did my best to maintain my relationship with my adoptive mother, my refusal to speak to my adoptive sisters was impossible for her to accept. In reality, it was much easier for her to suppress our combative tendencies when we were children. But as we became adults, her ability to control or manage the complexity of our strained relationships gradually diminished. I was not about to let their refusal to discuss and resolve long repressed feelings about the past destroy my chances for happiness in the future. Although we made a trip to visit my adoptive mother and Barb's family in September 1995, our relationship would never be the same, and it would only continue to erode with the passage of time. My adoptive family was finally coming apart at the seams. In many respects, I was surprised that it took that long to happen.

As my relationship with my adoptive family faltered, I began to spend more time thinking about what I really wanted to achieve from my own life. The mistake I had made in accepting the LaGrange job was a setback to my professional ambitions, but it made me realize that I needed a clearer direction in my career. When I started working at the East Alabama Regional Planning and Development Commission in April 1996, I was determined to restore my self-confidence. Fortunately, the job became one of the best I ever had. I enjoyed working with the staff, and the agency had an outstanding reputation with the communities it served. I was soon involved in a wide range of interesting and rewarding projects with the local governments.

We also managed to find our first dream home in suburban Oxford, Alabama only six miles from my office in downtown Anniston. It had a truly beautiful setting located between two heavily wooded vacant lots (one of which we bought with the house and the second we bought one year later) and on top of a ridge with a commanding view of Coldwater Mountain. Having grown up in the northern Appalachians, Barb and I both loved to admire the graceful, forested mountains and hills surrounding Anniston. Our house also had a large front porch with a hanging porch swing that we frequently used to enjoy peaceful evenings. My attachment to the place was quickly reinforced when I heard a whippoorwill from the porch for the first time since my childhood. Our new home quickly became our sanctuary from the chaos that had been our life in Georgia, and it gave me the peace of mind and clarity of thought I needed to focus my self-reflections.

As I began to feel more comfortable with my new direction in life, I began to spend more of my spare time reflecting upon my past and trying to deal with the skeletons that I had carefully tucked away in the back of my mind. Invariably, the path of my thoughts led back to my adoption and the unresolved questions surrounding it. It did not take long for me to realize that many of the life-changing decisions I had made in the past were either caused or influenced by my reactions to being an adoptee in the Smith family. I realized at a very early age that I had a very different personality and appearance from my adoptive family. My awareness of these differences became the initial source of my low self-esteem, inability to fit in, and the eventual deterioration of my relationship with them. I wanted to understand whether they were caused by genetic influences or my own perceptions. The veil of secrecy surrounding the circumstances of my adoption left me with the feeling that I had been rejected by my biological family or that my past was a source of shame for them. These feelings also contributed to my poor self-image and made it harder for me to implicitly trust family and friends.

I also didn't like the thought that I might have been erased from my biological family's memory and knowledge. I had no way to know if any of my biological relatives (other than my birth mother) even knew that I was born. I could accept the fact that I would die someday, but it was very unsettling for me to think that my surviving blood relatives would never remember me or even know that I had existed. Finally, I still had concerns about my unknown medical history and how it might affect Michael's future. I could not achieve a sense of closure regarding these issues without searching for my biological family, but I had no experience or guidance upon which to conduct a successful search.

While these thoughts occasionally ran through my mind, I did not find the motivation to actively pursue my final search until late in 1997. That September, Barb attended her parents' 45th wedding anniversary. Her grandmother's health was deteriorating, and Barb felt it might be the last chance she would have to see her. Unfortunately, Michael had just begun kindergarten at the time, and we didn't have enough earned vacation time to plan a family trip. So, Barb decided to fly alone to Vermont for the weekend to attend the planned anniversary celebration. Although Michael and I stayed behind in Alabama, Barb took recent pictures of us with her to share with her family.

One Friday evening, a month or two later, Barb's mother called. I was cooking supper at the time, but I answered the phone anyway. I had to use the speakerphone because the handset had been left in another room. When I realized who was calling, I called Barb to the phone. She took the cordless handset into the bedroom where she could talk without being distracted by the cartoons that Michael was watching on the television. I was busy in the kitchen tending the meal I was cooking, so I wasn't able to turn off the speakerphone when Barb picked up the handset. As a result, I accidentally overheard the first part of their conversation.

Barb's mother first thanked us for the gift and the pictures that she brought to the anniversary. Then she talked about how the whole family had looked them over and compared the three of us. Their conversation caught my attention when I heard her say, "Now please don't say anything about this to David, but we were all amazed by how much Michael looks like you and your brother, but not at all like David." Her observation hit me like a brick wall. It was confirmation of my own initial impression that Michael didn't resemble me as much as I'd hoped he would. This time though it wasn't just my own observation; it was coming from Barb's family. Once again, my personal insecurities were being confirmed just as it happened in high school.

At first, I was only disappointed. Later, after I thought about it some more, I felt insulted. I realized that Barb had a distinct advantage in being able to identify similarities between Michael and her family. She knew all of the genetic traits that had been passed through her family and could recognize family features in Michael that she didn't even possess, but her relatives and ancestors did. I only knew how I looked. My physical traits never came from my adoptive family, so I couldn't look to them to find similarities between Michael and other members of my own lost family. It occurred to me that Michael may not look a lot like me, but he might still possess some of my biological family's physical traits that I simply never inherited. I had no way to know for sure because I had no knowledge of what my biological relatives looked like. Once again, my adoptee status made me feel different—only this time it had an impact on my ability to feel connected to my son rather than my adoptive family. That was the final straw! I was tired of feeling isolated by my adoption. I was now determined to find the answers to all my questions. All I needed was a new opportunity to begin the search.

## *The Final Search*

During the early months of 1998, Barb and I began the lengthy process of redecorating the interior of our Oxford home, room by room. The original owners had used dark colors and wallpaper throughout the house, and we decided to use some lighter colors to make the house a little brighter and airier. We repainted all of the walls in the living room, main stairwell, dining room, sunroom, and eventually the downstairs recreation room. In the process of redecorating the rec room, I installed a new computer and telephone line so we could access the

Internet.  We established our first home Internet account in the first week-end of May.

Although I had used the Internet as part of my work in LaGrange, I never really had an opportunity to explore it.  Once we obtained our own Internet account, I spent a lot of spare time conducting searches on a wide range of topics that were of personal interest to me.  At one point, I conducted a search on the topic of adoption and quickly discovered a large number of websites devoted to the subject.  Some of these websites contained information for adoptees on how to conduct biological family searches.  Finally, I had found a source of information to guide me in conducting my next determined search.

At first, I was stunned to find so much information for adoptees. Although I knew I wasn't the only adoptee who wanted to search for his biological family, I had no idea that so many adoptees were conducting searches.  I found a number of websites offering guidance on search techniques and sources of information.  I also found scores of adoptee search registration sites on the Internet.  These sites typically provided an Internet bulletin board for both adoptees and birth families that were trying to locate blood relatives who had been lost to adoption.  Each site allowed searching adoptees and biological families to post information they knew about their lost relatives (birth dates, physical features, birthplaces, dates of adoption, and other distinguishing information), in the hope that the lost person or family would see it and respond.

Some of the listings included personal messages to the lost person or family.  I remember reading one message from a birth mother who was seeking the son she had lost to adoption roughly 25 years earlier.  In the message, she explained how difficult it had been for her to place her son for adoption.  She felt forced by her circumstances and the prevailing social attitudes at the time to relinquish her son even though she knew she would later regret it.  Throughout the years she hoped that he had done well, that he would understand her reasons for relinquishing him, and that he had been given a good family.  Then she revealed that she needed to find him soon because she had important medical information for him.  Her physician had told her that she had only two to six months to live.  I was reading her unanswered message nine months after it had been posted.

That birth mother's desperate and haunting plea to find and possibly save her lost son strengthened my own resolve to search.  It made me think about how I would feel to find a similar message that had been left for me years ago by my own birth mother.  After all the years I spent thinking about my birth family and wondering how to find them, I would have been devastated to discover that they had been looking for me all along, and I found them only after it was too late to know them. Suddenly, I realized how my own adoptive father must have felt when he finally learned the truth about his own biological father only after he had died. I tried desperately to search every adoptee registration listing I could find on the Internet, but there were just too many of them. I needed to find a better way to organize and conduct my search.

I continued to digest all of the available on-line information on adoptee searches. I was so relieved to find that many other adoptees shared the same basic desire to know about their hidden pasts. It made me feel less selfish and guilty to know that I was not the only person who had experienced an unpleasant adoption and who was trying to find answers to the fundamental questions of where he came from and who he was. Eventually, I found a couple of specialized mailing lists that allowed adoptees and birth parents to exchange messages and guidance on searching techniques. One was called the Adoptee's Internet Mailing List or AIML. It was operated out of St. John's University in New York and served adoptees and birth families across the country and around the world. The second mailing list was devoted to adoptees that lived in or were born or adopted in Alabama. It was called BAMAdopt, and it was managed and operated by a birth mother and an adoptee that also organized the Birmingham and Mobile chapters of "Truthseekers," a voluntary counseling group for searching adoptees and birth families. I quickly registered for both mailing lists, and I also joined the Birmingham Truthseekers.

The support and help I received through these Internet sources were crucial. I met and exchanged thoughts with literally hundreds of adoptees like me who were desperately trying to uncover the mysteries about their hidden pasts. Every week at least one member of the mailing lists would find his or her biological family and post the story on the Internet. Most of the reunions resulting from these searches were successful, and they only served to inspire me onward.

However, a part of me knew that my own search might not have a happy ending. Some adoptees—but not as many as one might think—find birth mothers who can't accept the fact that they gave birth to an unwanted child and work obsessively to hide the truth from the people around them. Although at some level deep inside they may truly regret their actions, their fears of shame or of being exposed compels them to deny any connection or relationship to the adoptees who find them. When a search ends in denial, it can be a crushing blow to the adoptee, who may have struggled for years to find his lost family only to face a bitter and cold second rejection. In some cases, searching birth parents are rejected by their children, who are not able to overcome their resentment of the initial relinquishment or who believe that the reunion would hurt the feelings of their adoptive families.

Although my initial desire to search was triggered by a need to answer some basic personal questions, I quickly began to realize that I was motivated by even deeper needs that I did not even recognize during the early stages. In the past, when I had discussed my desire to search, many of my friends whose lives had never been touched by the adoption process could not understand why I would even want to search for a mother who had once rejected me. Of course, they never knew what my adoptive family environment was really like. Even so, their casual attitude regarding my relinquishment never broke my resolve. At some intuitive level I knew that my biological mother could have chosen to abort me, but she didn't. I was alive today because she cared enough about me to give me a chance for a better life than she believed she was capable of providing. After all, she had no way to know what would actually happen to me. All she could do was to put her faith in the unwritten promise of the adoption process. I just refused to believe that she would have no concern for me.

Eventually, I realized that I really wanted to thank her for giving me my life. I thought that by finding her I might actually be able to make her feel better about the difficult decision she had to face. Perhaps easing her pain would make it easier for me to face my own insecurities. Just the knowledge that my biological mother could still feel an attachment to me after all these years would make it easier for me to believe that I was an inherently valuable person. My childhood experiences with my adoptive family never instilled in me that basic sense of value and worth, and I was beginning to fully realize how desperately I needed to accept it before I could ever successfully rebuild my own self-esteem. In one sense, my biological mother's acceptance was the real Holy Grail that I sought.

Conversely, I guess the knowledge that I could be rejected again was the demon that made it so difficult for me to fully acknowledge my motivations for searching. During the initial phase of my search, I met a number of adoptees and birth parents whose searches ended in bitter disappointment. The lingering fear of a similar conclusion to my own search haunted me throughout the process creating an emotional roller-coaster ride. Every new clue or bit of information I uncovered along the way brought me initial joy and enthusiasm. However, the initial excitement often faded when I realized that I was getting closer to learning whether I would be accepted or rejected by the family I sought. It was this constant struggle to temper excitement and subdue fear that made my search so emotionally stressful, as it is for every searching adoptee and birth parent. If not for the persistent support and guidance I received from my fellow Internet searchers, I might never have mustered the strength to persevere the ride. Every time one of us felt defeated by obstacles, dead-end leads, or our own fears, the others would step in and provide encouragement. I truly owe my own success to each and every one of them.

Following the guidance that I obtained from the Internet, I began my search by collecting and compiling all the information I knew about my birth and adoption. I prepared a detailed list of every documented or known fact I could find regardless of how significant it appeared to be. From my amended birth certificate, which my adoptive parents had once tried to hide from me, I learned that I was a single birth and that I weighed nine pounds, thirteen ounces. The amended certificate also listed the name of the attending physician. Suddenly, I realized that my amended birth certificate gave me the name of a person who was with my biological mother at the time of my birth!

Armed with his name, I used an Internet telephone directory to locate him. Fortunately, he had an unusual last name, and I was able to find the address and telephone number for his retirement home in Maine. For days I tried to decide how to ask him for any information he might have kept about my birth or my birth mother. My fellow adoptees on the Internet warned me against revealing that I was an adoptee because I would be quickly rejected by all who could help me. I didn't like the idea of lying, but ironically, I knew it was the only way I could learn the truth. In all reality, my amended birth certificate contained false information about my parents, so I didn't feel too unjustified about lying to uncover the truth.

I needed to concoct a story that would give me a reasonable justification to request information about a mother that I never knew without revealing that I had been placed for adoption. That's not easy to do, since the only people who know nothing about their biological mothers are adoptees. I eventually created a complicated story that seemed to work, but was admittedly hard to believe. Actually, it sounded rather like the plot of a soap opera, but I couldn't think of anything better. It was inspired, to some degree, by my adoptive father's family circumstances.

I decided to say that I was going through some personal papers of my recently deceased father when I stumbled across some old letters he had received from the woman he married around the time I was born. I had always believed her to be my true mother. One of the letters I would allege to have found was her response to his proposal of marriage. In it, she accepted his offer and agreed to accept and raise me as her son and never reveal the truth about my real mother, who was never mentioned by name. That letter along with other documents I allegedly found made me realize that she had married my father several months *after* I was born. I soon realized that my real mother was a woman that he had known in a previous relationship and had abandoned to marry another woman with whom he was having a secret affair.

It now appeared, from my contrived body of evidence, that my father and his lover may have stolen me from my real mother to give his new wife a baby that she would not otherwise be able to bear. The woman I was led to believe was my mother died fifteen years earlier in an automobile accident, so I could not confront either of my known parents to learn the truth. To further support my story, I decided to say that recent blood tests revealed that my father's wife could not have been my biological mother. Although I did not have an official birth certificate, I had found a box of old receipts containing records of payments that were made to the attending physician at the time of my birth. I decided to call him to see if he could check his records from that time and find out the name of my real mother, so I could find her.

Having constructed the story I intended to use, I decided to call the attending physician the following Saturday afternoon. When I finally heard his voice on the phone my heart leapt with anticipation. For the first time in my life, I knew I was hearing a voice that my biological mother once heard, and I realized how tantalizingly close I was to the prize I had sought for so many years. I explained my fabricated story to him as convincingly as I could, but I knew my voice was shaky. I am not a very confident liar. After I finished my explanation, he paused for a moment and then asked if I had been adopted. I said no, but I knew he could see through my facade. Clearly, I had wasted my time trying to create such a complicated story. At any rate, I knew the moment he asked me that he would not be willing to help. He told me that he no longer had access to his records and that his office in Portsmouth closed nine years ago when he retired. He expressed his sympathies and recommended that I call the Portsmouth Hospital, which would have all of the records I needed.

Although I was disappointed, I was determined not to give up. A week later I called the Portsmouth Hospital and tried to use my story again to get them to release my mother's name from their medical records, but they refused to cooperate. They said I would have to file a written request and send them all of my supporting documentation before they would research their archives. The direct route I had taken was another dead end. I would have to find a different path to obtain my answers.  At least I was reassured that the efforts my adoptive parents had made to keep the information on my birth certificate hidden from me had not hindered my efforts to find my biological family.

Fortunately, the guidance I received from other adoptees on the Internet mailing lists helped me discover other ways to search.  Several fellow adoptees told me that I had a legal right to request non-identifying social and medical information from my adoption case file.  So, I contacted the New Hampshire Department of Health and Human Services which oversees adoption cases throughout the state.  I spoke with a caseworker who acknowledged my right to certain non-identifying information, and she agreed to send me the appropriate release forms that I had to submit.  She also sent me additional information on adoptee searches, which made me feel that she at least understood my need to search.

Another adoptee advised me to obtain a copy of my final adoption decree.  The decree is the final document issued by the court to certify that the adoption has been approved.  In some cases, it is possible to glean additional information from that document.  However, I could only get my final decree from my adoptive mother.  It was then that I called her and told her of my intentions to search for my biological mother.

I tried to discuss it with her calmly and sensitively explaining my reasons for wanting to know about my heritage and my medical history.  Her reaction was sharp, direct, and immediate.  She chastised me bitterly and accused me of being insensitive and unappreciative of everything she had done for me.  I asked her politely for the final decree and any information she knew from the adoption process.  Although she resisted at first, she eventually agreed to send the final decree (which provided no new or immediately useful information).  However, she asserted that she had never been given any information about my biological family or me.  I knew that my relationship with her and the rest of my adoptive family was now jeopardized, but I agreed to let her know what I found.

Although my adoptive mother insisted she was never given any information about my birth family, I knew she was lying.  Many years earlier, Great-Aunt Sue had told me in one of her letters that I had been named "Glenn" by the foster mother with whom I was placed shortly after my birth.  She got this information from my adoptive parents, who had stopped by her house on their way home from their trip to take custody of me in Portsmouth. After speaking with my adoptive mother, I called Great-Aunt Sue to see if she knew any additional information that might be helpful.  She was supportive of my need to know, but she knew very little about the circumstances surrounding my adoption. She reconfirmed her knowledge that I had been named Glenn after John Glenn, the astronaut. She also thought she had been told that my birth mother was very young when I was born, but she wasn't certain. However, she was able to confirm that my adoptive mother was lying. She clearly remembered being told that my adoptive parents had been given more information, but that they were going to forget about it because, "I was *their* child now." That attitude made me feel more like a piece of property than a human being.

Roughly one week later I discovered that my adoptive mother was working behind my back to cover her tracks and make my search more difficult. When I revealed that my mother had lied to me about her knowledge of my birth family and the circumstances surrounding my adoption, one of my search assistants suggested I try talking to some of her best friends from that period in time. She felt that my adoptive mother might have been more willing to talk openly about my adoption with her close friends than with any of her relatives. Perhaps they might even know more of the story than my great-aunt Sue. Fortunately, I knew the names of several of her close friends from the early 1960s. I decided to call one of them that I knew she hadn't seen very often after she moved away from North Georgetown in 1986. This particular friend knew me well and had always seemed to be open-minded. If any of them would be willing to help I felt certain she would. However, when I finally managed to contact her, she was reluctant to even discuss the issue. As I tried to explain my reasons for searching, she broke down and revealed that my adoptive mother had visited her only two days earlier and made her promise not to discuss the issue with me. Her response was proof that my adoptive mother knew much more than she had ever revealed and that she would go to great lengths to block my search efforts. I decided not to discuss my search with my adoptive mother again until it was completed. I did not want to give her any information that would make it easier for her to interfere.

On a more positive note, I met Stacy over the Internet. She was a Vermont adoptee who had received help with her search from a volunteer search assistant in New Hampshire. His name was Larry Maurice. Although he was not an adoptee or a birth parent, he knew the adoption system in New Hampshire well and had considerable experience with New Hampshire searches. Stacy gave me his e-mail address and advised me to contact him for help with my own search.

Larry was a breath of fresh air in my search process. He was eternally optimistic and very supportive, but his optimism was always tempered with a good dose of realism. Larry had been involved in over 300 adoptee and birth parent searches of which roughly 95% resulted in some form of successful contact. While his success rate was encouraging, he was careful to warn me that there are no guarantees of success. Some of his searches took years to complete while others were resolved in only a few days. Throughout my early e-mail correspondences with him, Larry was warm and understanding. His unwavering support gave me confidence that I could succeed as long as I refused to give up.

To improve my chances of success Larry gave me a number of good suggestions on how to collect additional information. Unfortunately, one of his suggestions was to request information on my birth records from the hospital, which I had already tried and failed. I told him that I had applied to the state for release of my non-identifying medical and social information. I also planned a weeklong vacation trip to New Hampshire at the end of June to meet the caseworker personally and receive my non-identifying information. Another adoptee had suggested I do so because it increased my chances of getting complete information. Fortunately, my caseworker agreed to meet me during my trip. I then arranged to meet Larry and his friend, Annie, with whom he worked on adoptee searches. He had planned to take some time off from work during that week, and he offered to help me conduct my search while I was in the area. I arranged to meet with Larry and Annie immediately after I was scheduled to receive my non-identifying medical and social information from the caseworker, so that I could devote the maximum amount of my limited vacation to my search. Although I would be in New Hampshire for only three-and-a-half days after receiving my non-identifying information, the knowledge that Larry and Annie would be there to help gave me all the confidence I needed.

I spent most of the month prior to my vacation trip trying to collect as much information as I could to aid me in my search. I met a birth mother in Mobile who told me how she had managed to access information on adoption cases at the local probate court. I decided to use her technique at the probate court that handled my adoption case, if my non-identifying information was not helpful. I also consulted my local doctor concerning my irregular heartbeat. Several adoptees on the Internet had suggested that I document my medical condition, as it might give a sympathetic probate judge good cause to open my adoption records. I was outfitted with a heart monitor for several days and was given an electrocardiogram at the regional medical center in Anniston. Unfortunately, the tests showed no abnormal or life-threatening condition. The results didn't establish that I did or didn't have an irregular heartbeat; they only confirmed that it was not persistent or serious enough to constitute an immediate health problem.

I also continued to monitor the numerous search notices I had posted on various adoptee Internet registries. For the first two weeks, my listings went unanswered. Then on May 31, I found a simple message attached to one of my listings. It read simply:

*If you would like some help with this search for Birth parent, please contact me at the e-mail address.*

*Regards,*

*Laura*

I responded immediately to the mysterious message and told her my story. Her name was Laura Simms, and she was both an adoptee and a birth mother. She lived in Florida, but had considerable experience with New Hampshire adoption cases, which is why she responded to my posting. In fact, she had worked with Larry and Annie on many tough adoption cases. As a registered nurse and a private investigator, she had considerable expertise regarding sources of information and search strategies. She had worked with over 700 adoptees and birth parents as part of an underground network of search assistants in Florida. When I told her I was working with Larry, she immediately offered to help.

As a fellow adoptee, Laura knew my feelings intimately. I talked to her over the phone several times prior to my trip to New Hampshire. She sent me several poems written by adoptees that helped reassure me that many others shared my feelings about adoption. Laura encouraged me to prepare a brief, but heartfelt letter to my birth mother that I could use to introduce myself to her and explain my reasons for searching. She said she would use the letter as an initial contact for my birth mother when we found her. She also said it would give me a good outlet to release my feelings about searching, which I had harbored for so many years. That sounded simple and logical, but it wasn't going to be easy for me to do. The first draft I wrote was awkward and unemotional, so she told me to rewrite it.

I found it very difficult to satisfy all of Laura's instructions. She told me that the letter needed to be short, not over one page in length. Yet I had to explain my feelings and why I wanted to find my birth mother. She didn't want me to make it too personal because it might make her feel that I was pressing her to give me more than she was capable of giving. It also might scare her off. My letter had to be heartfelt and reassuring–but not smothering. The instructions seemed contradictory in many respects, but I knew it was something I needed to do. After struggling with the words for days, I wrote the following message:

*June 20, 1998*

*Dear Birth Mom:*

*I have waited with anticipation for a long time to speak with you and, now that I have the opportunity, I find it difficult to know how to begin. So many thoughts are running through my mind that it is hard for me to sort them out. I guess I should begin by telling you that you are a very important part of my life, even though I can't remember meeting you. On February 14, 1962, you gave me my life. I have never had an opportunity to express my appreciation for that. Thank you. I want you to know that I have carried you in my thoughts for years. We have been together in spirit, if not in person. Now we have an opportunity to break through the barriers that have kept us apart. I welcome the chance to meet you, and I hope that you will as well.*

*Although I have led a rewarding and satisfying life, I have always felt that a part of me was missing. There is a bond between us that time and distance can never erase. My adoptive parents have helped me build a life and a future, but they can never give me my lineage or my past. These are the emotional voids in my life that only you can fill. When I look at my reflection in the mirror and my son's face, I know that I am seeing your features. I just can't recognize them. More than anything else, I want to see your face and learn about you and your life. I want to know that you have been well and that you remember me. I also want to learn about my lineage and the people who helped make me what I am today.*

*I also would like to help bring closure to what must have been a very difficult period in your life. We cannot change what has happened in the past, but we can make it easier to live with in the future. I want you to see that I am satisfied with my life and to tell you about my achievements. I want to show you pictures of my wife and son, your grandson, and tell you about them. I hope that by meeting you and telling you of my life, I can bring you some emotional peace and security. I believe that we both need that.*

*I truly hope that you will be willing to meet me. I appreciate all the difficult choices and personal sacrifices you made to ensure that I would have a happy life. I believe that you have always wanted that for me. I now ask only one more gift of you to make my life complete—an opportunity to meet you and to thank you personally for everything you did for me. It is my final hope that this meeting will be the beginning of a new chapter in our lives—one that will bring us both greater happiness. As I said at the beginning of this letter, you have always been a part of my thoughts. I would now like to give you an opportunity to be a greater part of my life. I will do everything I can to make that possible for you. I only hope that you can find the courage to try. Thank you for all you have done.*

*Thinking of you always,*

*Dave*

Laura liked my second draft, so I decided to bring a copy of it with me on my trip to New Hampshire. If I was successful in my search, I wanted to be able to give it to her. I decided that it expressed my feelings more clearly and concisely than I could in spoken words, and I didn't want my first meeting with her to be a disappointment. I wanted her to know how I really felt, but I didn't feel confident that I could express my feelings properly at our first meeting. I also decided to compile a photo album of my family as a gift to my biological mother should she decide to meet me in person. I didn't want to let my expectations get out of control, but I also wanted to be fully prepared for a successful outcome. Although I have not always been satisfied with my planning career, I have always been a planner by nature.

Two days before I was scheduled to leave on my trip, I attended my first meeting of the Truthseekers group in Birmingham. It was my first face-to-face meeting with other searching adoptees and birth parents. At that point, I was no longer seeking new sources of information or search strategies. All I wanted was moral support. I met one adoptee who accidentally found her biological mother while they were attending the same college course at a local university. I also met another adoptee who was coldly rejected by her biological mother when they first met. The personal stories I encountered ran the gamut from complete acceptance to complete rejection. Although the stories I heard did not give me the emotional boost I had wanted as I approached my final search, they did help me temper my expectations. It was also comforting to talk with others who shared my plight. In hindsight, it was probably better that way. To date, none of my previous search attempts or strategies had brought me any closer to my goal. Now I was traveling over 1,400 miles to obtain one final piece of information that represented my last hope for success, and I would have less than four days to discover where and how far it would lead me. In hindsight, there was absolutely no way for me to be adequately prepared for the adventure upon which I was about to embark.

## *49 Hours*

My trip to New England began on June 29, 1998 with a flight from Atlanta to Hartford, CT. When I arrived in Hartford, I rented a car and decided to make a brief trip to the University of Hartford campus. Although I had not visited the campus in more than ten years, I thought the experience would help me recapture some of the self-confidence I had first gained during my early years as a student. I wanted to visit some of my former sociology professors to reminisce about the past and tell them all about the fantastic direction my life had taken. In my mind, their approval of my decision to search would further validate my quest. However, I quickly discovered that only one of my former professors remained and even he was not in his office. All of my other former professors had either retired or moved on to other positions. Most of the current faculty and students were on summer break, so the campus seemed like a ghost town. As I drove around the nearly deserted campus, I was surprised to see so many new classroom buildings and dormitories that had been built in the intervening years. It seemed that everything I once knew had changed, just like me. I realized that I had lost the familiarity and security of my first real home, but the experience reminded me that change in life is inevitable, and it was time for me to move on and to seek the security I needed in new places. If I couldn't go back, at least I could move forward.

After my tour of the university, I drove to the New Hampshire home of my adoptive cousin, Maria. Her house was an easy drive from Concord, where the final, decisive leg of my journey would begin. Maria was Carl's older sister and a member of the family I could trust. As an art teacher by education and experience, she had an open mind, a tolerant personality, and a positive attitude about life that I always found refreshing, if not entirely unique within the family. I felt that Maria could accept and understand me better than my parents or sisters—perhaps for no other reason than her willingness to listen. She also understood the dark side of my adoptive family, so I felt comfortable seeking her counsel and support. I had discussed my plans with her in early June, and she graciously agreed to let me stay with her during my search.

When I first arrived at Maria's house, I was concerned that, by staying with her during my search, I was placing her in the middle of the increasingly volatile relationship between my adoptive mother and me. Although I had little confidence that I could salvage any meaningful relationship with most of my adoptive family, I didn't want my actions to interfere with her family relationships. However, Maria was a true free spirit, and she possessed a level of self-confidence that I envied. As long as she felt I was searching for the right reasons, she wasn't going to be influenced by what the rest of the family thought about it. In fact, she helped put my mind at ease by openly discussing her own perspective on my adoptive family. I soon discovered that she had a good basic understanding of the various character flaws in my family, even though she never knew all the specific incidents that occurred in my life. We spent most of that first evening sharing stories about my adoptive family. It was reassuring to know that I was not the only one who could see through the cloying veneer that they worked so hard to project. I could have spent the entire night talking to her, but I wanted to be well rested for my morning meeting with the caseworker.

***** *****

The next morning, I awoke at the crack of dawn. I was too nervous about the meeting with my caseworker to sleep comfortably. My mind churned with questions that I wanted to ask her to ensure that I got as much information as I could. I had prepared a handwritten list of questions the day before my trip, which I continued to edit and expand until the moment I got into the car for the thirty-minute-long drive to Concord. Although I knew that I had everything I needed with me, I was gripped by fear. What if my adoptive mother had called the state and tried to influence my caseworker? What if I was given bad or incomplete information? What if my biological family had been killed years ago in some tragedy? The cloak of secrecy placed on adoption cases by our legal system always makes it easy to project the negative outcomes of a search, which in turn, makes it harder to believe that the positive outcomes will occur. Perhaps that's one of the real reasons why it was incorporated into the adoption process. All I knew was that this meeting represented my last chance to obtain the information I needed to complete my search. I did not want anything to go wrong.

I arrived at the office about twenty minutes early. I spent the first few minutes in the car reviewing and editing my list of questions one last time. Then, I gathered my courage and entered the massive edifice. Everything about the building made it clear that I was entering a bureaucratic environment. The walls were heavy, blank, and painted in neutral colors. A glassed-in reception station that looked like a bank drive-through window blocked access to the main offices. An armed security guard, who escorted lost and confused people to the reception window, patrolled the foyer. A row of cold, stiff, plastic chairs lined the outer wall of the foyer. I announced my arrival to the receptionist, signed in, received a visitor's pass, and obediently took a seat along the wall. It seemed like an eternity before my caseworker came to the reception area to greet me.

The caseworker received me with a warm smile and a surprisingly firm handshake. Her name was Cindy, and she didn't look at all like the image I had formed in my mind from her voice. She stood about five feet, ten inches tall with dark, graying, shoulder-length hair and strong facial features. Her size and imposing presence were a stark contrast to her soft and lilting voice. I had also expected her to be younger than she appeared. Although I am not a good judge of age, I would say that she was actually between 50 and 55 years old, even though her voice made her sound much younger. After a brief introduction, she led me into an open, two-story, central atrium, which was partitioned into a dozen or so large cubicles, each equipped with a small round meeting table and molded plastic chairs. A huge central skylight that spanned the length and width of the partitioned area lighted the atrium. I followed Cindy to the first vacant cubicle and sat down on the opposite side of the table from her. She was carrying a soft leather tote bag, which she placed on the floor beside her as we began to talk.

"So, how was your trip?" she casually and pleasantly inquired to open the conversation. She was obviously well practiced with these meetings. Even her relaxed body language conveyed her comfort and assurance.

"Oh, it was fine. I flew into Hartford early yesterday afternoon where I rented a car and drove up to New Hampshire. The only delay I ran into was a traffic jam in downtown Springfield, Massachusetts. Otherwise, I made pretty good time."

"You told me over the phone that you had a wife and son. Did they come with you?"

"No, my wife just started a new job in March, so she couldn't get any time off. We figured that Michael would get bored having to sit through my meeting, so he stayed home with Barb to keep her company."

"And you're staying with your adoptive family?" As she asked that question, she looked directly and firmly into my eyes as though she was searching deep into my soul to find the answer for herself.

I could tell from the tone of her voice that she was trying to feel me out, so she could judge what I hoped to gain from my search and how it would affect my relationship with my adoptive family—especially my adoptive mother. Fortunately, my Internet friends had warned me to expect that, so I tried to put my situation in the best possible light. If I could convince her that my adoptive family was supportive of my need to know, then she might be more forthcoming with information and also might be more willing to help me contact my biological mother. This was, in all reality, the make-or-break question that would forever define and dictate the rest of our brief relationship.

"That's right," I responded calmly to put her concerns to rest. It wasn't a lie because Maria was a member of my adoptive family. It was just a different interpretation of her question from the one that I knew was on her mind. Without a moment's hesitation, I continued, "When Barb and I originally planned this trip last year, we were going to spend our vacation visiting both of our families, but Barb's recent job change made that impossible. We talked about canceling it altogether, but I decided it would be a good opportunity for me to answer some personal questions I've had for years. Back when I was in college, I learned that I had an irregular heartbeat. I've also had some blackout spells that no one has been able to explain. When I learned that my son was born with a venous murmur, and we knew there was no history of heart problems on my wife's side of the family, I began to wonder if Michael might have inherited a genetic heart condition from my biological family. At first, I talked about it with my adoptive family, but they knew nothing about my former family's medical history. I recently learned that I could obtain non-identifying medical and social information from my adoption case file, so I decided that I needed to see if it contained any answers. My adoptive family fully supported me when I told them I was going to do this. They really want to know as well." Now I was beginning to lie, but it was necessary to ensure that the door between us remained open.

My explanation and the rather casual demeanor with which I managed to convey it seemed to put Cindy at ease. I was a little nervous about lying to her, because I didn't know whether or not my adoptive mother had tried to call the agency and block me from getting my information. However, Cindy's reassuring smile and nod in response to my story quickly assured me that she knew nothing about my adoptive mother's real reaction. I had passed the test and, in doing so, gained the additional reassurance I needed.

Cindy reached into her tote bag and removed a white business envelope. Her demeanor became more professional as we transitioned into the purpose for our meeting. As she slid the envelope across the table to me, she said calmly, "The information in this envelope is all I have to give you from your adoption case file. I know you probably have a lot of questions that this information won't answer, but please understand that we have to consider your biological mother's feelings and wishes. Just remember, if you don't find the answers you need, I can try to locate her for you and serve as an intermediary to help you get some additional information or, if everyone can agree, possibly even contact. So, why don't you open the envelope and see what it says. If you have any questions, just ask me."

My heart was racing as I carefully opened the envelope. I tried to project a calm, non-emotional demeanor. I didn't want to appear desperate or overly eager to see what was inside, but it was hard to mask my enthusiasm. I was holding in my hands the only information about my past and my heritage that I had ever known. My hands were trembling slightly as I removed the document and unfolded it. It was three typewritten pages long. Clearly, it was a photocopy of the original document that was placed in my file. All identifying information in the document had been concealed by whiteout. I began reading it immediately as fast as I could, as if I was afraid it would be snatched from my hands at any minute. This information had been elusive throughout my life, and it didn't seem real that it was finally in my possession. I wanted to digest it all as immediately as I could. Perhaps no non-adoptee can truly understand how it feels to first possess intimate information about yourself and your past that has been locked away by a public department of the state—an agency whose basic purpose is to help people and serve or support their most basic needs. Was that really an irony or just a sad joke?

The first page was titled, "ADOPTIVE HISTORY," and it contained a description of me and a brief summary of my health history, up to the point that I was placed with my adoptive family. It listed my name as "Baby Boy Glenn," which immediately proved that the story Great-Aunt Sue had told me about my name was true. My original first name was spelled with two "n's" instead of one, just like John Glenn's last name. In all instances I have ever encountered, the name Glen is spelled with one "n" when it is used as a first name. As I read the body of the narrative, I discovered that it discussed my delivery, my weight and length at birth, and some general observations about my behavior and reactions to various stimuli. However, the standard psychological tests were waived "*in favor of early placement."* The report noted that the foster mother, with whom I was placed, was caring for five small children.

The second page of the report contained a background description of my biological mother and her family. The month and day of her birth were blotted out, as well as her birthplace. However, the remaining information did reveal that she was born somewhere in Massachusetts in 1937. It listed her religion as "Protestant" and her marital status as "widowed." She was described as approximately five feet two inches tall, with shoulder length, light brown hair, and large brown eyes. The only medical information it contained was my mother's statement that she had never had any health difficulties and an observation by the caseworker that she *"appears to enjoy better than average health and to be of a strong constitution."*

The report further indicated that my mother left school in the seventh grade. She was released from school on the basis of a doctor's statement that she was needed at home to care for her own mother, who was sick at the time. Her only work experience was a job in a shoe shop that she held before her marriage and for a short time afterward. The caseworker also noted that, *"Although Mrs. XXXX's education is limited, we found her to talk quite rationally about surrender and appeared to have well thought out reasons... [She also] approached adoption realistically. She realized that the social security benefits were barely adequate to care for the three children she had already and that to keep this child would be taking from them. She also realized that this child would be receiving a mother and father by adoption who would be able to care for it financially. In short, she saw adoption as the best for the sake of her three children, herself, and the coming child."* It went on to say that my mother had refused to see me at birth or to know my sex. She had only asked to know my birth weight, for comparison with her three other children, who had all been of normal weight and size. The report also contained a passing reference to her "twin" brother, indicating that she was born with a fraternal twin.

The third and final page contained some general information about my father and my maternal grandparents and siblings. It indicated that my father's first name was John and that he was approximately 35 years old. My mother had described him as being roughly five feet ten inches tall and having dark brown hair, blue eyes, and a medium complexion with a husky build. The report contained no medical history for him and stated that little was known about the "alleged" father, as my mother maintained that she went out with him only once and didn't even learn his last name. My mother did indicate that she was impressed by his seeming knowledge on a wide variety of things and recalled that he appeared to speak with authority. As a result, she thought that he had at least completed high school and may have even attended college. The report further noted that my mother had been introduced to my father by her deceased husband's brother, who was a serviceman stationed in the area. Clearly, my birth mother was not the "dockside hooker" that my adoptive mother had alleged.

The report also contained some basic descriptive information about my mother's immediate family. It stated that my grandfather was 58 or 59 years old and that he had worked with a city as a garbage collector for the previous 35 years. My mother didn't know how much formal schooling he had received, but she recalled that he always joked about his education *"consisting of entering school through the front door and going out through the back door."* My grandmother had a similar educational background and had been employed by a local shoe shop for the past eleven years.

My mother was one of eleven children in her family, six of whom were girls. She and her twin brother were one of two sets of twins in the family. All of her brothers and sisters had left school somewhere between seventh grade and the first year of high school. Two of her sisters (one of her older sisters and the youngest) dropped out during their first year of high school, while one of her brothers attended trade school for a short time. My mother felt that they had achieved the highest level of formal education. None of her brothers or sisters had ever been committed to "state schools," however one child had attended a "special class."

The report further stated that all of her brothers and sisters had been regularly employed after they left school. One of her brothers worked at a can company, while the other four were employed by the city. One of her sisters worked at a Western Electric plant and another worked at a Hytron plant. All of her other sisters had worked at the shoe shop with her mother, although some of them had married and were no longer working.

I flipped through the pages several times just to make sure that I understood everything it contained. At first, I was just amazed to see so much information. It appeared that I would have a good base of information for my search. I had been searching for months with much less information. Although all of the names (except my father's first name), important dates, and place names were obscured, the report told me a lot about my mother's family and her background. I retrieved my list of hand-written questions and began filling in all the answers that I could glean from my adoption history.

As I pored over the report for the second time, I came to the realization that my mother must have experienced a hard life. She was born into a very large family that must have lived on the margins of society. After all, it was not very common for both parents to be employed in the 1950s and early '60s. My mother clearly came from a working-class family. Although her parents apparently did not stress the need for a good education, the fact that all of her brothers and sisters (and even she) had secured steady employment suggested that the family did have a strong and healthy work ethic.

However, her hardships obviously did not end there. Her husband had apparently died before I was born, leaving her with three children. Her lack of education and work experience obviously made it difficult for her to take care of the children, and her husband's family was clearly trying to help her find a new husband. While I was excited to learn that I did have some brothers or sisters, I could easily understand the difficult choices she must have faced when I was born. My only disappointment with the information I received was the lack of any meaningful background medical information.

Cindy sat quietly and patiently as I read the report and jotted down some notes. I could sense her watching me closely, waiting to see my reaction—even though I was too focused on the report to look at her. I tried to show as little emotion as I could. I did not want her to think that I was determined to find my mother, as I was afraid she would try to discourage me or block me from being able to speak with her. I felt like I was taking a tough final exam for which I hadn't studied with the teacher watching over my shoulder to see if I was trying to cheat. I felt nervous, excited, and scared all at once, but I had to maintain complete control and composure. The curtains had not yet closed on the play.

I also felt that my own privacy was being violated. After all, the information I held in my hands was a part of my own life that had been taken away from me without my consent. Granted, I was only an infant then, but once it was taken away, I never got it back—even when I became an adult. I had never been given the opportunity to know any of this information about my biological family and myself, but the stranger in front of me knew it all and more. My history was an open book to her, but to me it was a 36-year mystery. What made it even worse was the knowledge that she controlled my access to it, and I had to plead with her to get it back. It was immediately apparent to me at that moment how different it felt to be adoptee, and I hated it with every fiber of my being. More than anything else, I wanted to be a whole person again—a normal, decent person with a past and a heritage as well as present and a future—a person with some dignity, rather than a big, shameful government secret—a person who could recognize the features in his reflection—a person who could know what medical conditions he might have inherited—a person who could, for once in his life, feel like everyone else.

When I finished taking notes I looked up at Cindy. She smiled reassuringly and asked, "How do you feel?"

"Well, I don't know. I had written down a bunch of questions I wanted to ask, but I'm at a loss to know where to begin. There really doesn't seem to be a lot of information on my family medical history. Is this all you have?" I tried to keep the focus of my interest on the medical history because I knew that would be less threatening to Cindy.

"I know and I'm sorry about that," Cindy replied. "You see, back in 1962, it wasn't common to ask a lot of medical questions for adoption cases. We ask for more information today, but I know that doesn't help you very much."

"Did either of my biological parents ever submit an update to my records or file a release form to give me free access to my records?" This is an important question to ask because birth mothers sometimes feel guilty after relinquishing their children, and this is one way they can submit additional information that might help their children find them. I knew the state would not offer that information without my asking.

"No." That was the only question she answered without any elaboration.

"Can you tell me my mother's first name? I don't think that would be identifying?"

She gave no direct answer to that question. She just hesitated for a moment then said, "I understand that it may be hard for you to accept what happened, and I'd like to try to help." As she said those words, the first image that popped into my mind was the smile my adoptive grandmother gave me after I apologized for suggesting I wanted to find my biological mother so many years ago. "I've given you all the information I can right now. If you feel you'd like to learn more, I can serve as a confidential intermediary for you. That would allow me to try and locate her to see if she would be willing to answer some questions about your medical history or even allow you to have some contact with her. Obviously, I can't promise anything. We don't even know if she can be found, but I would be willing to try."

"Well, I really don't want to impose myself on anyone, but I would be interested in talking to her, if she wants to talk to me. I would really like to know more about my family medical history, especially if there was any history of heart problems. Do you think there's a good chance that she would want to talk to me?"

"That's always a difficult question to answer. I always want these situations to work out for the best, but each case is different." Cindy slid her chair closer to me and picked up the papers she had given me. She turned the pages and pointed to a specific statement. "What concerns me is the statement here on the second page that your mother didn't want to see you or know your sex. It also says here that she clearly understood what she was doing when she placed you for adoption. That, combined with the fact that she already had three children from a previous marriage, suggests that yours may be a difficult case. I often find in a lot of cases like this that the mother is reluctant to have any contact. That wouldn't mean that she doesn't care about you; it's just a common sign that she may have decided to rebuild her life for the sake of her remaining children. Of course, I'd be willing to do the best that I can to help you, if you want me to try. I just don't want to guarantee anything."

Although she tried to appear sympathetic to my feelings, I really felt that she was trying to interpret statements in the record in a way that would dissuade me from searching. Some of the statements I read in the report demonstrated that my mother had deep concern for my well-being, but Cindy didn't point to those. The report also contained some obviously derogatory comments by the original caseworker about my mother's appearance and lack of education. I felt that those unnecessary judgments were deliberately placed in the report to project a negative image of my mother that would discourage a future search.

"I understand, but I would like you to try." I really didn't want her to be my search intermediary, but at the same time, I wanted every chance I could get to find my family, and I didn't want to make her realize or even think that I would be searching on my own. "How long do you think it will take?"

"That's also hard to answer. We do have some resources that I can use, but if she's remarried or moved out of state, it's going to take longer. Why don't you give me a week or so to see how it goes? I'll plan to call you then. Just let me know where you can be reached."

"I'll only be in New Hampshire until Friday. By next Tuesday, I'll be back at work. If you've got the business card I sent with my application, then you have my number."

"Yes, I left it in my office. Do you have any other questions?"

I asked her a couple of other questions about my parents, but the only bit of additional information that she would reveal was that my mother was living in New Hampshire when I was born, which was basically self-evident. By the time that we finished talking, it was nearly 10:00, and I had planned to meet Larry and Annie in downtown Concord at that time to begin my search. It was time to put the information I had received to good use. I thanked Cindy for her help, picked up my belongings and headed for the state library–the home stretch of my life-long quest. For once in my long search, I felt that I was making some progress.

Parking a car in downtown Concord, NH is the ultimate test of perseverance and creativity. I was very fortunate to find an on-street parking space in a nearby neighborhood that was within walking distance of the state library. Even so, I arrived about fifteen minutes late. Unfortunately, I had never met either Larry or Annie before, so I really didn't know who I was looking for. I scampered quickly about the main reading room trying to find a man and a woman who appeared to be watching out for someone else. Fortunately, the woman at the main desk near the entrance to the building saw me and asked if she could help.

"Well, I don't know," I responded. "I was supposed to meet someone here who was going to help me conduct some genealogical research. Unfortunately, I've never met them before."

"Oh, you must be David," she said in a matter-of-fact tone. "Larry said you'd be looking for him. You'll find him and Annie in the archive room on the right." It was obvious that Larry and Annie spend a lot of time at the state library.

As I entered the archive room, I saw Larry and Annie sitting at a large, antique wooden table in the middle of the room. Several books and files were stacked on the table between them, as they were obviously conducting research on some of their other cases to pass the time. Larry looked up as I approached the table and immediately recognized me from the pictures that I had sent him earlier.

"Hello, David," he greeted me warmly. "It's great to finally meet you." He jumped up from his chair and firmly shook my hand. Larry was in his late forties, a little shorter than me, and quite stocky. He had dark, thinning hair, a very friendly round face with a wide, reassuring smile that almost seemed to stretch from ear to ear. "Let me introduce you to Annie. I believe you've had some telephone conversations with her.

Annie was about my age and height. She had very fine, wavy, shoulder-length, blonde hair, and a slender face. She wore plastic rim glasses and large earrings. Like Larry, she was very friendly and polite.

"Yes, it's a pleasure to meet you both," I said. "I just got out of my meeting with Cindy, and I've got all of my non-id."

"Well, let's take a look," Larry replied eagerly as I handed him the papers. He unfolded the document and showed it to Annie as he flipped through it. Then he looked up at me with a slightly puzzled look on his face. "Is that all? Did she give you anything else?"

"No," I replied with a hint of surprise and disappointment, as I struggled to figure out what I had forgotten to request from her. "She said that was all she could give me. Is there something else I should have received?"

Annie took the report from Larry's hands and started to flip through the pages as she responded, "Well, the information you have here is the standard adoption history. Most of the adoptees we've helped receive five pages of information. A three-page adoption history like this and a two-page summary of the background check and interview conducted on the adoptive family. I'm just a little surprised she didn't give that to you as well, since it wouldn't be expected to have any identifying information. However, sometimes the background check report will contain some casual statements about the biological family or the circumstances surrounding the adoption that can be helpful. We've dealt with a number of Cindy's cases, and she's usually quite consistent. Don't worry, though, it's not a big loss; it just seems a little odd." Ironically, that would not be the only odd situation surrounding my adoption case.

Once Annie had a chance to read my adoption history carefully, she noted the reference it contained to the waiver of my psychological evaluation, "*in favor of early placement.*" She had read hundreds of adoption records in her work with other adoptees and that was the first time she had seen a statement like that. She felt that it was a little strange because she couldn't understand why an early placement could be so important that it would serve as cause to waive standard procedures. It wasn't as though they were overly inundated with demand to place adoptive children during that era. There were far more children awaiting adoption than adoptive parents seeking to take them. I didn't realize it then, but the statement was also strange to me because I could remember my adoptive mother saying that they had taken me to a psychologist who advised them to let me scribble on the walls, if I wanted to express myself that way. My adoptive parents always thought that was funny. Yet, it made me wonder why the psychological assessment was waived during my adoption process especially when one was conducted after my adoption by the Smiths. These little wrinkles seemed odd at the time, but they were only distractions to the primary purpose of my search. I would not learn the potential significance of these "irregularities" until much later in the process.

"Well, I really didn't know what to expect from Cindy," I conceded. "I read the information she gave me very carefully, and it seemed pretty good to me. There's a lot of descriptive information on my mother's family in there. What do you think?"

Larry looked over Annie's shoulders, as they studied the document for a few moments. When they finished, they looked at each other for a second and then Larry turned to me. "Well," he carefully began, "you're right that it contains a good description of your family, but we've come to expect that much information. It's also good that it is a photocopy of the original report. Since it was prepared on an old typewriter, the letters are not proportionally spaced. That means we can use the words and characters in lines directly above and below the whited-out names, places, and dates to figure out how many letters were in the missing words. That will help us a lot. I guess it's pretty good information to start with, but we were hoping it would be a little better."

"In what way?"

"Well, you came from out of state, and in the past, Cindy has been very forthcoming with information in those situations," Larry explained. "For example, I remember one woman from West Virginia, who met with Cindy a couple of years ago to get her non-identifying information. To our surprise, the documents she got actually revealed her mother's name. Forty-eight hours later, we found her mother, and they were able to sit down together for dinner that afternoon. Of course, that was a really rare event. But Cindy has worked there for about 30 years, and she's getting close to retirement. We've seen her soften over the years, and we just thought she'd leave you with a little more to work with than she did. That's all."

"When I talked with her, she seemed really intent on serving as my confidential intermediary. Once I saw that the report had virtually no background medical information, I told her that I would like to see if we could get more from my biological mother. She immediately offered to help, but she also made a point of showing me statements in the record that suggested to her that my mother might not be open to contact. I told her I wanted her to try anyhow. I really don't want her to be the one to find my mother, but I was afraid she'd realize that I was going to search on my own, if I declined her offer."

"That was probably a good reaction," Larry reassured. "But she should know not to put too much stock in statements your mother made over 30 years ago. Many of the birth mothers we work with regret their decisions for years, and most welcome contact when they are offered the opportunity. A caseworker asking a frightened, young, expecting mother if she knows what she's doing in placing a child for adoption is a little like a principal asking an elementary school student if she likes going to school. What else would you expect her to say? If she doesn't know how she's going to take care of her child before she goes to the caseworker to place a child for adoption, she's certainly not going to know afterward. Although we won't know how your mother will feel about it until we contact her, I wouldn't let this report discourage you."

"Oh, I'm not discouraged. This is the first time I've made any real progress in my search efforts, and it'll take a lot more than Cindy's concerns to stop me now. I'm fully determined to complete my search. I do a lot of research in my professional work, and I'm a determined worker. I just got the feeling that she was trying hard to persuade me to let her conduct the search. The only thing that worries me now is that she'll find my mother first and talk to her in a way that will reinforce her own preconceptions of my mother's attitudes and damage any chances I may have of talking to her. I've also got my own adoptive mother out there trying to block my access to information. For all I know, she may have talked to Cindy and that's the real reason why she wanted me to allow her to be my intermediary. I've just been dreaming about this for so long now that I don't want to be the last one across the finish line. I sense a real urgency to complete my search as quickly as I can."

Annie looked at Larry for a second and then turned back to me. "Well, let's not worry about the outcome now, because we don't know what it will be, and we can't do anything about it. But at the same time, we can't get our hopes up too high. Many of these searches take years to complete, and we're just getting started. Let's go over our strategy now and then we'll pick this report apart and see what we can get out of it."

Annie's work schedule only allowed her to assist me with my search on Tuesday and Wednesday mornings. Larry was on vacation, so he was willing to spend more time with me, but he had to return home by 2:00 that day. We decided to review the report first, then Annie and Larry would give me some assignments to finish for them that afternoon. I was to call Larry in the evening and report what I'd learned, and we'd decide how to proceed on Wednesday morning. The game was afoot!

Larry made three photocopies of the report—one copy each for him and Annie and a third for Laura. My first assignment was to fax Laura's copy to her after we finished our work at the state library. The next step was to scrutinize the information that had been whited-out. First, we counted the spaces in each blank space to see how many characters were in the missing words. My mother's last name at the time of my birth contained six letters. Upon close inspection of all the obscured references to her in the report, it was evident that some traces of the last letter in her name had not been completely whited-out. Cindy had obviously done a rush job. That letter appeared to be an "r." The same was true of her hometown and birth city. It was nine characters long and appeared to end in an "l." The only other missing piece of information was my mother's birthdate. We knew she was born in 1937, but we couldn't read the month or day. However, the blank space immediately preceding the year was eight characters long. Assuming one blank space between the month and day, and two spaces between the day and year for a comma and a space, the birthdate had to be either a three-letter month with a two-digit day (May 10-31) or a four-letter month with a one-digit day (June or July 1-9).

Once we had deciphered as much of the missing information as we could, Annie started preparing a rough family tree from the background data and a list of follow-up questions for me to ask Cindy over the phone later in the afternoon. Larry started to compare my information with some old birth parent files he brought with him to see if there were any commonalities. I was given the task of compiling a list from an old Rand McNally atlas of Massachusetts towns and cities that consisted of nine letters. I was instructed to write them down and circle the ones ending in an "l." The task reminded me of my early childhood geography research that had first led me towards the field of planning.

The resulting list that I compiled contained roughly 50 cities and towns. However, only three of them ended in an "l"—Haverhill, Pepperell, and Sand Hill. I went back to the information in my adoption history to see if I could narrow the list further. The first thought that struck me was that my mother's birthplace had to be a fairly large city. The background information on my mother's immediate family stated that her father had worked for the city as a garbage collector for 35 years and that four of her brothers had also worked for the city. The fact that it was consistently referred to as a "city" implied that it was a fairly large community. My experience working with city governments made me realize that only a large city could afford to offer its own garbage collection services for such a long period of time. I also realized that it would have to be a fairly large city to be able to employ five people (her father and four of her brothers) from the same family without facing public scrutiny and criticism for nepotism. Even so, it did seem strange that even a large city would employ five people from one immediate family.

Nevertheless, I went back and looked at the population of the three most likely communities. Haverhill had a population of just over 50,000 people, while Pepperell had a population of only 2,350, and Sand Hill had only 1,800. What's more, the town of Sand Hill was located on the south shore roughly twenty miles south of Boston and more than seventy miles from Portsmouth. It was not likely that a large working-class family could afford to live in an expensive and exclusive seaside community like Sand Hill. Both Pepperell and Haverhill were in the right location (northeastern Massachusetts), but in my mind, Pepperell was just too small to be realistic candidate. It was my belief that Haverhill, Massachusetts was my mother's birthplace.

I approached Larry with my conclusions. We then scrutinized the report again to see if my hunch could be further supported. Larry pointed to the statements that my mother, her mother, and at least four of her five sisters all worked in the same shoe shop. Larry had once worked in Haverhill, and he was well aware of the city's history as a shoe manufacturing center. He also knew that there was a large Western Electric plant in a nearby town. My adoption history noted that one of my mother's sisters was employed by Western Electric.

I immediately went to the reference section of the library to find an Industrial Directory for Massachusetts. An Industrial Directory contains general information on large manufacturing employers in each city within a given state. In my work as a planner, I had used such directories in other states to compile background information for my planning studies and reports. I quickly scanned the directory for Haverhill and found that it did list a number of shoe companies and one aluminum can manufacturing plant. My adoption history also stated that one of my mother's brothers was employed by a can company. The directory also revealed that a company by the name of Hytron (a business name that appeared in my Adoptive History) operated a plant in nearby Amesbury, Massachusetts. Amesbury was less than 10 miles from Haverhill, but it was more than 30 miles from Pepperell. It appeared quite likely that my mother was born and raised in Haverhill. Annie wanted me to keep an open mind, but she had to agree. Haverhill was to be the first focus of my search.

By now it was nearly noon, and both Larry and Annie had to leave. Annie gave me a rough diagram of my mother's family, based on the information in my adoption history. It would serve as a handy reference chart to build upon as we discovered more information. She also gave me a list of additional questions to ask Cindy. She wanted me to try asking specific questions about my mother's first name to see if Cindy would offer any more clues. She also suggested that I ask about the special school or class my mother's sister once attended. If Cindy were to reveal the name of the school, it might help us confirm Haverhill as my mother's birth city. Annie also wanted me to ask Cindy about the ages of my three older siblings and the name of the military base where her husband's brother was stationed. There were two military installations in Portsmouth at that time, Pease Air Force Base and the Portsmouth Naval Shipyard. Annie believed that my biological father either worked or was stationed at the same base.

Since I had the rest of the afternoon to myself, I decided that I was going to Haverhill to conduct some research there. We decided that I should try to get my grandfather's name from city hall. If he had worked for the city for more than 35 years, someone working there today might remember him. If I was able to get a name, I was instructed to go to the public library and look it up in the 1938 edition of the Polk Directory. The Polk Directory contains an annually updated list of every resident of the city, including their street addresses, occupations, and the names of any other persons over the age of 18 living at the same address. The 1938 edition would contain information collected in 1937, the year my mother was born. The information is indexed both by the name of the head of household and by street address. Once I knew the name of my grandfather, I could look it up in the Polk Directory and confirm his occupation, get the name of his wife (my grandmother), and find out exactly where they lived when my mother was born.

Annie also suggested that I look up my possible grandfather's last name in the local phone book. It was quite possible with a family as large as my mother's that some of her siblings would still be living in Haverhill today. As we learned the names of other family members, we may find one for which we could get a current telephone number. However, she warned against calling anyone until we had spoken to my mother first. We had no way to know if any of her siblings were even aware that I was born, and revealing my existence to others prematurely might frighten or embarrass my mother, making it less likely that she would be willing to speak to me.

When I was finished with my research, I was instructed to return to my cousin's house and call both Larry and Laura to tell them what I had learned. Larry would be able to check my grandfather's name on the Social Security Death Index. This index is a public record that contains information on every deceased person who had been issued a social security number. From it we could learn his social security number, his date and place of birth and death, and the name of his primary death beneficiary. Larry would then call Annie to discuss search strategies and decide how we should proceed on Wednesday morning. It sounded to me like a well-conceived plan of action.

As we parted company, my heart was filled with anticipation. I was amazed to realize how much I had learned over the past few hours. Although I didn't want my hopes to be dashed, I couldn't help but feel that we were very close to finding my long-lost family. After all the years I had wondered about them, I was finally on the verge of getting answers to my questions.

After leaving the state library, I went to a downtown print shop on South Main Street. There, I found a fax machine I could use to transmit a copy of my adoption history to Laura. I also found a pay phone there, which I used to call Cindy with my follow-up questions. I told her that I was back at my adoptive family's home, and we were looking over the information she had given me when we realized that we had some questions about it. Once again, she refused to answer any of them. She insisted that I let her handle my search and that I remain patient. She said she was concerned that I might make a mistake that would scare my birth mother and make it more difficult, if not impossible, for me to get the information I wanted. I didn't push the issue with her, because I didn't want Cindy to locate my mother first. It was the last time that I would call her.

After our telephone conversation, I began my drive to Haverhill. I had never been there before, although I had driven past it a number of times on the Interstate. While I was driving, I thought about the information I had learned. I was a little concerned about how Laura would react. When I first talked to her about my desire to know my birth family, she had warned me not to expect too much from a reunion. She had helped many adoptees in the past, and while most of the initial reunions were very positive, they tended to change over time. Some of the adoptees she helped reunite eventually tried to take advantage of their birth families and the same was true of some birth families. Laura and I had developed a strong bond during my search, and she had already expressed her fears that I might fall into the latter category. Given her initial concerns, I was afraid that the information I had uncovered about my mother's background would only reinforce her initial fears.

As for myself, I had already considered a wide range of possible search outcomes before I made my final decision to proceed with it. I met one adoptee at my first Truthseekers' meeting who was rejected by his biological parents because they feared the reaction and "judgments" of their high society friends, who never knew about his adoption. I had also heard the story of a Native American adoptee whose biological father was a prominent liberal U.S. senator from a Great Plains state. He had pressured her biological mother to place their baby for adoption, because he didn't want the scandal to ruin his marriage and his political career.

I knew from these and other stories that I could be easily rejected by my own biological family simply because they might be embarrassed by what they had done or because they feared the impact my sudden reappearance might have on their social status. I certainly did not want to be judged that way by my biological family, so how could I look down on them just because they might not travel in the same circles that I now did? There was no way for me to know what I would find even though most people automatically assume that a child given for adoption would be placed in a "better" family. I guess people outside the adoption process will always believe that misconception as long as state governments are allowed to seal adoption records from public view. In my own mind, I had long since decided that I would accept whoever I found as part of my legitimate family no matter what they were like. After all, isn't that why people always say—that you may be able to choose your friends, but you can't choose your family? Even as one of the supposedly "chosen" adoptees, I knew that. I just didn't want Laura to prejudge my biological family, just because they had led a hard life. Sometimes, adversity does help build integrity. At least, I felt that was the case for me, and I hoped that it would be the case with my birth family.

On my way through Methuen, I stopped at a local restaurant for lunch. While I was eating, I tried to concoct a story that I could use as an excuse to ask the city for my grandfather's name. It needed to be simple, but convincing, as I knew that city officials were often reluctant to divulge personal information about former employees. The story I finally devised seemed clever enough, but I didn't know if it would work. I decided to say that I was helping to coordinate my grandparent's 50th Wedding Anniversary party. According to my story, they were raised in Haverhill and lived there until they were married, when they eventually moved away to Chelsea, New Hampshire. All of the grandchildren were trying to locate and invite as many of their former long-time friends from Haverhill that we could find. My assignment was to find one of my grandfather's next-door neighbors and good friends, who we didn't know by name. However, we did know that he had worked for the city as a garbage collector for more than 35 years. If they couldn't remember him by his long work tenure, then I would add that I knew several of his sons had also worked for the city. All I would need from them was his name. It was the best story I could devise on such short notice. I decided to give it a try.

By the time I found Haverhill City Hall and parked the car, it was nearly 2:00. Fortunately, I noticed that the public library—my next research stop after completing my initial work in city hall—was right across the street. As I climbed the steps to the massive city hall, my heart began to race. I gathered my courage and entered the main lobby. On the opposing wall from the entrance, I found a directory and a bulletin board. I approached the directory to determine where I needed to go, but my attention was temporarily diverted by a solitary job notice that caught my eye. The city was seeking a new planning director, which was the very same position I held at the East Alabama Regional Planning and Development Commission. The irony of the situation was somewhat reassuring. Maybe it was a good omen.

My first stop was the public works department, which I assumed would oversee the city's sanitation services. I walked up to the receptionist's desk and asked to speak with the director. I had to wait nearly half an hour before he was able to see me. I distinctly remember swallowing my heart four of five times during that wait. When he finally emerged from his office, I told him my story as casually as I could. He listened patiently to me, although I was gripped with fear that he would see me sweating or notice that my face was turning three shades of red.

After I finished with my story, he pondered it for a minute and then asked, "What year did you say this man worked for the city?"

"I'm not sure when he started or left the city, but my grandparents left Haverhill in 1962, and I remember being told that he had been working for the city for at least 35 years prior to then."

"Well, I hate to tell you this, but the city didn't provide its own collection services until much later than that. During the early years, it was a contract service. There's no way the person you're looking for could have been a city employee. If your grandfather really knew him as long as you say he did, then he should've known that. I'm afraid I can't help you." Having said that, he turned abruptly and walked back into his office.

My heart sunk. I didn't even know what to say. I turned to look at the receptionist, but she had already resumed her paperwork. Dejected, I left the office and walked down the hall to an empty bench. "Now what do I do?" I asked myself. My mind scrambled for an answer. It seemed impossible that Haverhill might not be the right city. But if it truly was the correct city, why didn't my mother know that her father couldn't have been employed by the city as a garbage collector? The only reasonable conclusion I could draw was that her father was the city's contractor, and she mistook his contract with the city as a city job. Maybe my grandfather actually operated his own private sanitation business. That might explain how he was able to secure employment for four of his own sons without violating city policies against nepotism. It was a long shot, but I was already in Haverhill for the afternoon, so I decided to follow this new thread and make sure it wasn't right before giving up. After all, all I needed to do was go to the city clerk's office and ask for the name of the contractor that had provided garbage collection services during the early 1960s. I didn't need a fancy excuse to get that information, because I knew that all such contracts were a matter of public record.

I walked downstairs to the main administrative offices and asked to speak to the city clerk. When he emerged, I simply asked him if he could tell me the contractor's name. He asked me to wait a minute, while he checked his files. A few minutes later, he re-emerged and told me that the contractor was Capriani Waste and Transportation Services. I decided to see if I could engage him in a casual conversation to get more information.

"You said Capriani Waste and Transportation Services. Was that John Capriani?" I inquired, throwing out the first common name that came into my head in a desperate attempt to get his real first name.

"No, John was his brother. Tony ran the business back then for years. He inherited it from his father in the late 1930s, and he turned it over to his oldest son, Frank, when he retired around 1970. They dropped the waste collection services about 25 years ago, but they still operate the buses for the city schools. Frank ran the business for a couple of years and then sold it to a local accounting firm, O'Leary and Associates."

"My mother told me that the Caprianis were a big family. Didn't several of Tony's sons work for the company?"

"Yeah," the Clerk replied. "I think four of five of his sons worked for him from time to time, but Frank was the only one who stuck with it. I know he had several daughters, too, but I don't know how big the family was."

"Do you know where the current owner's office is?"

"Yeah, it's down on Briley Boulevard, but I don't know the street number. You can look it up in the phone book, though."

I finished scribbling my notes and thanked him for his help. Everything he had said lifted my spirits. Perhaps this Tony Capriani was my grandfather and his son Frank was my uncle. The pieces were starting to fit again. I learned that Tony had a fairly large family and that several of his sons worked for his company. I also knew he had contracted with the city for years. I rushed across the street to the library to continue my research.

My first stop in the library was the reference librarian's desk. She directed me to the genealogy room on the second floor where the old Polk Directories were kept. I searched through the stacks and found the 1938 volume. I fumbled through the pages, until I found the Caprianis. There were nineteen listings under that name in Haverhill. Among the listings, were Anthony Capriani and his wife, Nardina. She might be my grandmother. Tony's occupation was listed as "truck driver," which made sense, because I had learned that his business provided both garbage collection and school transportation services. Scanning through the other listings, I found one for John Capriani (Tony's brother) and several other names that I had not heard. I was excited when I saw the occupation "shoe worker" listed next to several of the names. There certainly were enough Caprianis to account for a large family. I photocopied the page from that edition then looked up and photocopied the Capriani listings from the 1963 edition.

Finally, I asked the genealogy librarian if I could borrow the current phone book. She gave it to me, and I looked up the name Capriani. Sure enough, several names were listed, including Frank. Unfortunately, I did not see a listing for Anthony, Tony, or Nardina. Perhaps they had moved away or died. I photocopied that page as well then looked up the address and phone number for O'Leary and Associates' business office on Briley Boulevard. Then I sat down for a while to clean up and organize my notes. I was really confident that it would all end the following day. By the time that I had finished rewriting my notes, it was 3:55 PM. I wanted to avoid Boston's legendary rush hour traffic, so I picked up my belongings and began the nearly two-hour drive back to Maria's house. I couldn't wait to tell her what I had learned on my first day.

To celebrate my good fortune and to thank Maria for allowing me to stay with her, I treated her and her boyfriend, Bart, to a seafood supper. I showed them all the information I had compiled and told them about my adventure. I was eager to call Larry, but I knew that I couldn't reach him until 8:30 or 9:00. When we returned from the restaurant, Maria went off to bed, while I immediately called Larry and told him what I had learned. He said he would check the Social Security Death Index for Anthony and Nardina Capriani to see if we could get any more information. He also said he would talk to Annie then call me back around 11:00 PM to explain our plans for Wednesday.

I couldn't just sit there and wait for Larry to call, so I called Barb and Laura to explain everything that had happened. Barb was excited, but cautious. Laura felt that we had made good progress, but that it was too early in the process to draw any conclusions. As soon as I had finished talking to them both, Larry called. He said that the Death Index showed that Anthony Capriani died on September 4, 1982. His wife, Nardina, was listed as his beneficiary. That was all of the information we were going to collect that day, but it was more than enough. Larry asked me to pick him up at a park and ride lot south of Concord, so we could drive down to Haverhill together. Annie was going to meet us at the public library at 9:00 AM, so we could all work together until noon when she had to leave for work. Now that we knew the day that Tony died, we could try to get a copy of his death certificate. We could also look for a death notice in the Haverhill newspaper from that day to see if it listed the surviving children. If we had the right family, the newspaper death notice might reveal my mother's name. Larry and I would stay for the rest of the day to finish our research. Perhaps Wednesday would be *the* day. After all these years, could it really be that easy?

It was nearly midnight, but I couldn't go to bed right away. I was far too excited. Too many thoughts, aspirations, and memories were racing and swirling through my mind. I decided to reorganize my information and jot down some reminders for my search the next morning. It was almost 3:00 AM before I finally felt exhausted enough to turn in for the night. I had been awake for more than 21 hours that day, and it was going be another long day on Wednesday. I had to wake up in about three hours to shower, dress, eat, and get back on the road to meet Larry.

***** *****

When I met Larry the next morning, he was guardedly optimistic that we were on the verge of a big discovery. However, he wanted to caution me that, whenever a search nears completion, it becomes important to find as many independent pieces of confirming information as is possible. The more information sources that confirm a find, the more confidence you can have in your conclusions. That confidence is important when contacting a potential birth mother, not only to know that you're contacting the right person, but also to assure her that the match can be confirmed. Larry wanted to make sure I understood that before we drew any firm conclusions.

We arrived in Haverhill around 8:30 AM and parked at the library which didn't open until 9:00. To kill the extra time, we decided to take a quick walk over to O'Leary and Associates' office on Briley Avenue. It was only a few blocks away, and perhaps the agency's Chief Executive Officer, Brian O'Leary, could give us some insights on the Capriani family. We really didn't know what to ask, but we knew we'd think of something. Unfortunately, when we arrived at the office, the secretary informed us that Mr. O'Leary was on vacation that week. However, during our informal chat with the secretary, we learned that she had been Frank Capriani's secretary back when he owned the business. Although she didn't know the entire family, she was quite certain that only three—not four—of Tony's sons had been employed by the company. It was the first hint that something might be wrong with my assumptions, but Larry was not too concerned at this point. Sometimes, the adoption records contain mistakes. Sometimes the birth mothers lie about their family backgrounds. We didn't know the sources of the information that appeared in the report. We decided to check all of the information sources available to us and let the body of the evidence drive our conclusions.

By the time Larry and I returned to the library, it was open and Annie had already arrived. We went straight to the genealogy room, where Annie had set up shop with her husband, Charlie, who was a computer whiz. Larry told her what we had learned from O'Leary and Associates, and we began our research. I could sense Annie's unspoken concerns about the complexity of the assumptions that were driving my conclusions about the Capriani family.

Annie asked me to find a copy of the September 4, 1982 issue of the Haverhill paper in the library's microfilm archives and see what Tony Capriani's death announcement said. She and Larry were going across the street to city hall to obtain a copy of Tony's death certificate. Annie's husband was going to search through the computer records that were available to them to see if he could uncover any additional information. Like a well-coordinated army, we immediately set out to work.

It took only about fifteen minutes for me to locate the newspaper microfilm archives and the reel containing the issue I was seeking. Scanning through the September 4 issue, I found a brief article announcing Tony's death. He apparently had died from injuries he received in a car accident. The notice indicated that he left behind his wife, Nardina, and nine surviving children, four of which were boys and five girls. Suddenly, another inconsistency presented itself. My adoption record clearly said that my mother was one of eleven children in her family, five of whom were boys. The intense optimism that I awoke with in the morning was beginning to falter under the weight of a heavy dose of reality. However, it was possible that two of the children had died sometime between 1962 and 1982. Trying to maintain my composure, I decided to wait and see what additional information Annie and Larry were able to acquire before drawing any firm conclusions.

Annie and Larry were gone for more than half an hour. By the time they returned, I was concerned. They had been successful in obtaining Tony's death certificate, but it had taken much longer than they anticipated. We sat down together with the document and studied it carefully.

The death certificate showed that Anthony Capriani was born on August 27, 1918. That birthdate was consistent with his age, as reported in the death announcement. However, it created another problem. My mother was supposedly born in 1937, when Tony was just under nineteen years old. That alone might not be a problem, but my records also indicated that my mother had at least one older sister, maybe more. Once again, we couldn't rush to conclusions because we had no way to know how many of my mother's siblings were older than she was or how much age difference there was between her and her oldest sibling. If my mother was the second oldest child and was only a year or two younger than her older sister, then Tony could have been the father. However, there was very little room for a large difference in age. We needed more detailed information on the Capriani family to be certain. The most critical documents were a marriage certificate and birth certificates for their children. In New Hampshire, we would have great difficulty accessing that information. But this was Massachusetts, and both Larry and Annie knew that we could access those records at the vital statistics office in downtown Boston. Annie did not have the time for a trip to Boston that day, so she suggested that Larry and I go by ourselves, after we had completed our research in Haverhill.

Larry and Annie went back to the Polk Directories both prior and subsequent to 1962, to look for names of any additional Caprianis who could have died between 1962 and 1982. Annie's husband was unable to find any additional information in the available computer databases. We also spent some time reviewing old high school yearbooks. We looked for pictures of Capriani children who were graduating from high school at about the same time I graduated. We wanted to see if there were any physical similarities or resemblances between pictures of my son, the Capriani children and me. We found several photos of Capriani graduates, but there was little similarity. The Capriani kids all had dark black hair. Both Michael and I were blondes. Also, the shape of the faces, chins and noses (which were the most striking characteristics in me) were all quite different. Finally, none of the Capriani children were wearing glasses. That was considered somewhat odd because my records mentioned that my mother had eyes that appeared to cross, and I was severely nearsighted. By the time that Annie had to leave, we were finding more inconsistencies than consistencies with the Capriani family.

It was noon before Larry and I left the Haverhill library on our way to Boston. I did not like the idea of driving in Boston traffic, so I suggested we park at the Alewife transit station in suburban Cambridge and ride the "T" into downtown Boston. We grabbed a quick lunch at a hot dog stand in the station, while we waited for a train. My spirits were beginning to spiral downward, and Larry had to work hard to keep me energized. I had experienced the highs and lows of searching before, but never like this. I was tired from lack of sleep and emotionally and mentally drained by the intensive research. But I knew I had to keep going. My return flight to Atlanta was scheduled to depart the Hartford airport in just about 56 hours, and we still had a long way to go.

After arriving in downtown Boston, we walked several blocks to the vital statistics office. Larry had been there many times and even knew some of the regular employees. He explained to me that we were going to research the birth list or index. This list is a catalog of all births by year. We knew my mother was born in 1937. All we had to do was look in the index for 1937 to see if Tony and

Nardina Capriani had given birth to a child in that year. Once we found the correct birth listing, the index would give us the book and page number of the birth certificate, and we could ask to see it. Then we could compare the information on the child's birth certificate with the information from my adoption history to see if they matched. The office maintained a similar index for marriage licenses. Larry thought it was best for him to check the marriage index because we had no firm evidence as to when Tony and Nardina were married.

Larry started me off with the birth index for 1937. He instructed me to check that book thoroughly. If I could not find a birth record in that year, he suggested I check the 1936 and 1938 indexes just in case my adoption history was off by a year. I went through all of the Haverhill birth listings for 1937 and found nothing for the Caprianis. At that point, I was really becoming nervous. Every new piece of information we uncovered seemed to contradict my adoption history. I did discover that Nardina had given birth to twins in 1938, but they were identical male twins. They had no children in 1936. After reviewing the marriage index for a number of years, Larry learned that the Caprianis were married in January 1937, not more than six months before my mother could have been born (assuming that she was born between May 10 and July 9, 1937). What's more, we knew that at least one of my mother's siblings was older. If Tony and Nardina were her parents, then their first child would have been born out of wedlock and prior to 1936 at that. At this point, Larry and I both had to admit that my mother was not a Capriani. We had the wrong family!

It was about 3:30 PM when we finally decided that we needed to regroup, reconsider all of our initial assumptions, and find a new direction for my search. Larry and I didn't talk much until we left the train at the Alewife station and got in the car. I was now more exhausted than ever, but my mind continued to churn, going over every assumption and every scrap of information from my adoption history, desperately trying to figure out what went wrong. The pieces were fitting together so beautifully, until we started following the Capriani family line. But, if the Caprianis weren't my mother's parents, who in Haverhill could be? According to the city staff, the Caprianis were the city's exclusive contractors for garbage collection services throughout my mother's lifetime, prior to my birth. None of Haverhill's city employees would have been involved in garbage collection, and the city's primary contractor would have been the only person who could have reasonably been confused as working for the city.

I was beginning to feel that Haverhill was the wrong city. But even that thought didn't set well with me. After all, Haverhill seemed perfectly consistent with many of the details from my adoption history. It had the right number of letters and ended in "l." It had a city staff large enough to employ several people from the same family (assuming that at least some of my mother's siblings were actual city employees), all of the occupations that my mother's family members held were available within the city or in the immediate area, and the city was only a short driving distance from Portsmouth. It seemed very hard to believe that another city in that part of the state could satisfy all of the basic constraints as perfectly as Haverhill did. All I knew was that I had very little time remaining to solve the puzzle. If I didn't find my family while I was staying in New Hampshire, it might take years for me to finish the search from Alabama. Certainly, Cindy would have ample time to complete her search first.

Larry did his best to console me on the drive home from the transit station in Cambridge, but I had failed too many times in the past, and my whole search seemed hopeless at that point in time. I didn't even feel like being optimistic. Then, Larry suggested something that I hadn't considered. What if my grandfather had been one of Tony Capriani's employees? Of course, it seemed unlikely that my mother would confuse one of Capriani's employees as an employee of the city, but what did we have to lose in considering it? We had already exhausted all of the other possibilities, and we'd never be completely certain that Haverhill was the wrong city until we had disproved it.

The only obstacle we faced was how to investigate it. We couldn't talk to Tony Capriani, because he was dead. We also had no legitimate story we could use to get the current owner to let us see the company's historic employee records–even if the company retained records from 1962. I finally suggested to Larry the only remaining avenue that we could use. Although Tony Capriani died in 1982, his son, Frank, who took over the business and eventually sold it to O'Leary, was still alive. Since he had worked with his father for many years prior to his father's retirement, he might be able to remember some of the long-time employees that worked for the company. In fact, it might even be easier for him to remember a family that would have provided five workers–my grandfather and four of his sons. Finally, I knew that Frank was still living in Haverhill. I even had his current street address and phone number. I had collected that information Tuesday afternoon, when I photocopied the Capriani telephone listings from the Haverhill directory. Since we could be back in Haverhill before 5:30, we might just be able to pay a quick visit to Frank Capriani's home and see what he could tell us.

Larry had to agree that talking to Frank was our only realistic chance of determining whether or not my grandfather had worked for the Caprianis, but he was very reluctant to recommend it. First of all, it involved talking to someone who might know my biological family well, thereby revealing who we were seeking before we could find my mother. In the adoptee search business, that was a serious potential disaster. Second, Larry knew that Laura and Annie would oppose that strategy, and we needed their help and cooperation to ensure our success. In all reality, we might never complete my search by ourselves. Larry didn't have the time, and I lived too far away. He thought that Laura might be able to access the company's records through her computer. As a licensed private investigator and registered nurse, Laura had discovered and used databases that Larry and Annie didn't even know existed. But we couldn't be sure that Laura could do that for us until we abandoned our opportunity to speak with Frank.

Still, Larry did not like to dictate search strategies to adoptees, especially those who were actively participating in their own searches. Although he was not an adoptee, he knew that I was the person who would forever bear the pain of failure whether it occurred because we were never able to find my family or because our search efforts were discovered and made public before we had a chance to talk directly and privately with my mother. Since it was my potential pain to bear, he thought I should make the decision. He just wanted to make sure that I thoroughly understood the risks and potential ramifications.

From my perspective, it seemed as though the difficult decisions would never end. My analytical nature made it easy for me to rationalize my search strategies to death. Thus far in my search, I had taken the cautious, safe, and time-tested approaches at every step of the way. I had lied and manipulated the truth wherever I could to achieve my objectives. I was also extremely tired, emotionally drained, and frustrated by circumstances and influences beyond my control. Then, to top it all off, I faced the very real possibility that I might have to start over from scratch and do it all again. Given those circumstances, my choice was clear. No guts, no glory–no pain, no gain. I told Larry that I wanted to give it a try.

To minimize the potential for a disaster, I agreed to let Larry talk to Frank alone. Larry had much more experience dealing with delicate conversations like this one, and I think he knew that I was at the end of my rope. If, for some reason, our strategy didn't work, Larry would prefer to break the news to me in his own way, rather than let me face the disappointment directly. I agreed to wait for him in the car.

Using the telephone listing I had copied and a street map of Haverhill I had purchased the previous day, we managed to find Frank Capriani's home. It was just after 5:30 PM, when I parked the car across the street from his house.

To our surprise, Frank was sitting on the front porch as Larry got out of the car. It was his habit to watch and greet his neighbors as they returned home from work. Larry walked up to him and started a conversation. I sat patiently in the car as they talked. As the time passed, I could feel my anticipation build. After nearly twenty minutes of waiting, I decided I just couldn't take it anymore. I got out of the car and approached the house.

Larry was visibly concerned to see me walking up the driveway, but he played it like a pro. Before I could say anything, he introduced me to Frank as the person he was helping with his genealogical research. That tipped me off to the approach he was taking in his conversation with Frank. Frank rose from his bench to shake my hand then gingerly collapsed back onto his seat. He was a very friendly and soft-spoken man with gray hair and brown eyes. His smile was warm and engaging even though he was missing a few teeth. He seemed genuine from the start. I liked him immediately.

Larry explained that Frank remembered several large families that had worked for his father over the years. All of them had several sons who had worked for the company periodically, but he couldn't remember them all. I scanned Larry's notes for a moment then looked up at him.

"Larry, I respect and appreciate what you're trying to do, but let's just tell him what we really want." After all, none of the lies and stories I had concocted and told had done any good, so why not use the truth for once and see what happens. From my perspective, I had little left to lose. Then I turned back to Frank. "Mr. Capriani, my name is David Smith, and I'm really trying to find my biological family. My friend, Larry, is trying to help me. You see, my mother placed me for adoption in 1962, and I've come here from Alabama to find her. At first, we thought that my mother might be one of your sisters, but we've since determined that she wasn't. Now we believe that my mother's father and several of her brothers may have worked for your father around the time that I was born. You're our only hope to find out who they were. Would you be willing to help us?"

"Oh my! That is interesting." His eyes widened and seemed to glow with intrigue. "Sure, I'd be willing to help you, if I can; but you know what you really need to do? You should go on that TV show—Montel Williams. He helps people like you find their families."

"That might be a good idea, if this doesn't work out for us," I chuckled. "But first, I'd like to ask you to do something for me. You gave Larry a list of about five or six large families that worked with your father back then. One of them might be my mother's family. I'd like to ask you to take a minute and look at my face very carefully. Don't say anything right away; just study the features of my face. Once you've had a chance to think about it, please tell me if you think that I strongly resemble any one of the families you mentioned."

Frank leaned towards me and studied me carefully. I turned my face slowly from side to side just to give him a full perspective. I could feel the penetration of his eyes as he examined me closely. I could see his mind working, as he compared me to the people he had known so many years ago. After a minute or two, he leaned back on the bench, and a smile came to his face. "Woodward!" he said emphatically. "You look like you could be a Woodward!"

Just as Frank declared his observation, his wife emerged through the front door. She had gone into the house to prepare a drink for Larry when I got out of the car. Although she didn't hear the question I had asked, her face responded immediately to her husband's statement. "Oh, my goodness!" she chimed. "You're right. He does look a lot like the Woodwards."

That was all I needed to hear. I looked at Larry and smiled. Then, I turned back to Frank. "Thank you so much for your help, Mr. Capriani. That was just what I needed to know. Now, did one of the Woodwards work for your father a long time?"

"Yes, that would be Charles Woodward. He started working for my father when I was a little boy. And yes, several of his sons worked for my dad, too, but I don't remember how many. I do know that Charles had a large family. He was a good man and a dedicated employee. My father liked him a lot."

"Well, we really do appreciate your help. Of course, I must ask you to please not say anything to the Woodwards until Larry and I have had a chance to check it out. We don't want to start any rumors. We've got to do some more research before we can say for sure if there's any connection between the Woodwards and me. I've got your address and phone number, and I promise to let you know what we learn. Thanks again for all your help."

"No problem, son. I sure hope it works out for you. Come back and visit me anytime."

"Thanks for the offer. I just might do that." I said as we started down the driveway towards the car.

Larry looked at me with a sly grin on his face. "I can't believe you *did* that!" he said as we opened the car doors. "But I'm sure glad you did."

As we left Haverhill for New Hampshire, Larry reviewed our notes and outlined our strategy for Thursday. Larry said he would check the Social Security Death Index for Charles Woodward when he got home and call me later with the results. He would also let Annie know what we learned, although he wasn't quite sure of how to explain it. My approach really could not be described as proper adoptee search procedures. I must admit, I was truly lucky that it worked. Skill and foresight had little to do with it. Exhaustion and frustration were far better motivations. Even though I had managed to get a name, we still had to prove that Frank Capriani's hunch fit the profile of my biological family. My search was hanging by a single thread like the fabled sword of Damocles, and I could sense the weight of the blade over my head.

When I finally returned to Maria's house, I was beginning to get my second wind. The look of recognition and familiarity on Frank's face when he made the connection between the Woodwards and me immediately restored my hopes that we could be on the right track. I had a good feeling about it, and I had a hard time waiting for Larry's call. Once again, I spent the time reorganizing my notes from the day, explaining the turn of events to Maria, and talking to Barb over the phone.

By the time Barb and I talked, it was nearly 8:00 PM, and I had managed to get less than six hours of sleep over the previous 48 hours. Barb was growing concerned about the time I was spending on my search and my lack of sleep. I had to admit that I felt exhausted, but I still found it impossible to rest until I was able to know in my own mind that I had made the most of my opportunity to search. I had never been this close to answering the questions that plagued my mind throughout my life. Although the four days I was spending in New Hampshire were thoroughly exhausting and nerve-racking, they were still only four days out of my entire life. If I could sacrifice just four days of my life to answer some fundamental questions about myself that I had carried for more than 25 years, it was time well spent. In fact, I'd have a hard time living with the knowledge that I hadn't done everything I could in the time available to me just because I wanted to get a good night's sleep. It was my nature to be so tenacious. There was just too much at stake this time around. From my perspective, I could find plenty of time to sleep when I returned home.

Once again, Larry finally called just after 9:00 PM. Of course, Annie was not too happy with what I had done, but she wasn't going to give up on me *this* time. That was my warning. Larry said that he found Charles Woodward in the Social Security Death Index. The records showed that he was born on January 7, 1903 and died in April 1969–although no specific date was listed. His primary beneficiary was his wife, Charlotte. Larry said that he would research her background information in the morning. Since we didn't know the exact date of Charles' death, Larry suggested that I begin my research at the Haverhill public library. He asked me to go through the newspaper archives for the month of April 1969 and find a death announcement. That would give us his precise date of death so we could request a copy of his death certificate from the city. He also reminded me to write down the names and number of all surviving children and family members. When I had finished with that, he wanted me to check the Polk Directories to find out which of his children were living in Haverhill at the time of his death and during the year I was born. He also instructed me to determine what their occupations were. We could then compare that information with the family employment information in my adoption history. If I had any time left over, he suggested that I try to find pictures of Woodward children in the high school yearbooks to see how much Michael and I resembled them. While I was completing my assignments, Larry was going to the vital statistics office in Boston to research birth certificates and a marriage license for Charles and Charlotte Woodward. He said he would meet me at the Haverhill library when he was finished.

Larry's enthusiasm was more restrained this time than it was the night before. I knew that he didn't want to get my hopes up, as we were both well aware of just how fragile each promising house of cards was. In thinking about his distribution of work assignments, I realized that he probably decided to go to Boston alone because he wanted the chance to break any bad news to me in his own way. He had loaded me up with busy-work tasks to help keep my mind occupied, prevent me from taking any more careless risks with my search process, and provide an outlet for my unbridled energy. Little did either of us realize at the time, I had very little energy left to expend.

After my conversation with Larry, I prepared a list of tasks and little reminders to guide my work on Thursday morning. I packed up my notes and went to bed around midnight. Once again, I just couldn't get to sleep right away. My mind wouldn't stop re-evaluating every step I'd taken and every assumption I'd made along the way. By now, I had practically memorized my adoption history. I didn't have much time left to make more errors. I had to make sure I was right.

I tried to console myself with the knowledge that even if I could never find my biological family, at least I knew something about them. But it wasn't good enough, and it never would be. A part of me always knew that, even if I didn't want to admit it. Perhaps I just wasn't the type of person who should have been an adoptee. My life never seemed better just because the Smith family tried to give me a lineage and a heritage that was not my own. I always felt empty or incomplete because I couldn't know the people whose blood coursed through my veins. Some people might feel that it was selfish of me to think that way. After all, the Smiths were only trying to give me a family that I no longer had— regardless of the difficulties and problems it caused them. We had all become victims of the circumstances we created, but that we couldn't control. But whenever I listened to others talk about their genealogies or their ancestors with pride, I immediately realized what I lost by virtue of my adoption. If it's so unreasonable for me to want to know my own true heritage, then why do so many people conduct their own genealogical searches these days? My search for my birth family was only different from any normal genealogical search because I was an adoptee, and the government decided that it was wrong for me to know my true heritage. Why does that make it wrong? Would that reason make it easier for anyone else to abandon his or her own genealogical search?

These thoughts and a number of other issues ran through my mind until around 2:00 AM, when I finally passed out from exhaustion. It would be another short night's sleep for me. I wanted be awake before 6:00 to make the most of my third day in Haverhill. With my return flight scheduled to leave Friday evening, it would probably be the final day I would spend there for quite a while, regardless of the outcome.

***** *****

When the desk clerk unlocked the front doors to the Haverhill public library at 9:00 AM sharp, I was already waiting in the doorway. I wasn't so much excited about searching this time around as I was antsy with anticipation about getting it done. I guess my fatigue was finally catching up with me. I knew I couldn't go on much longer. I was losing my edge. It was going to be a struggle to force myself to take my time and be diligent.

Now that I knew where all of the search records were kept, I went straight to the newspaper microfilm files and selected the April 1969 roll. As tired as I was, I just knew that Charles' death announcement would be in an issue at the far end of the roll. Well, almost. Roughly 45 minutes later, I found it in the April 22, 1969 issue. The announcement stated that Charles had died of Hodgkin's disease after spending a week in the Haverhill Hospital. It mentioned that he was survived by his wife, Charlotte, and eleven children. Yes, it said eleven children! I had to read it twice to make sure I wasn't dreaming. The announcement was short and no names were mentioned, but the size of the family matched the number of children in my mother's family. The announcement said that the funeral services were to be conducted on April 24.

My attention now piqued, I quickly scanned ahead to the April 25 issue. I knew that it would contain a short article on the funeral service. Sure enough, there it was, and it listed the names of the surviving children. Charles and Charlotte had five daughters–Harriet, Carolyn, Sylvia, Wilma, and June and six sons–Walter, Donald, Charles Burton, William, Everett, and David. Everything sounded good, but I had to make sure. I tore through my papers until I found my adoption history. Then it hit me. My mother was one of eleven children in her family, but my records said there were *five* boys and *six* girls. Charles had *six* boys and *five* girls. The number of children was right, but the distribution didn't match. I slumped forward onto the table. "Here we go again," I said to myself, projecting defeat. "Is it *ever* going to end?"

I just sat there, dejected, with my head on the table for at least ten minutes, while my thoughts swirled and faded from fatigue, until the Reference Librarian tapped me on the shoulder and asked if I was all right. I wanted desperately to leave right then and there, but I knew I had to wait for Larry. After all he'd done to help me, I wasn't going to just abandon him. Besides, I really needed some comforting reassurance. I rewound the microfilm roll and returned it to the cabinet. Then I slowly climbed the stairs to the genealogy room, where I knew he'd be looking for me when he arrived. I was certain that it would be the longest wait of my life no matter how long it was.

As I plodded my way into the genealogy room, the woman at the front desk looked up at me. She had seen me spending a lot of time there over the past two days and she immediately recognized me, even though we had never spoken to each other. As I laid my portfolio and papers on the table, she spoke to me.

"Are you David Smith?"

Her question startled me. It's not the kind of question you'd expect to hear from someone you've never met. "Yes, I am. How did you know my name?"

"I've seen you here several times this week. Your friend, Larry, called about five minutes ago. He said you'd be back this morning, and he gave me your name. He said he wanted you to wait right here for him. He's on his way back from Boston."

"Did he say what he wanted to tell me?"

"No, he didn't say. He sounded in a hurry, and he just asked me to tell you to wait right here until he arrived."

I guessed that Larry was in a rush to catch me before I got too involved in my research and discovered for myself what we both already knew—the Woodward family was another false lead. Well, at least I knew how long I'd have to wait for the bad news. The Haverhill library was a 45-minute drive from downtown Boston. He'd be here by 11:00 AM. Then I'd have the rest of the day to decide what I was going to do next.

I just sat at the table for a few minutes pretending to work on my notes. I didn't want the librarian to question me about my work primarily because I didn't want to explain it. It was quite depressing enough just to think about it. I was no longer tired, excited, or frustrated. I felt completely melancholy just as I did when I attempted to commit suicide almost nineteen years earlier. Not even that realization scared me now. I was completely drained, and I had no capacity left to feel anything.

As the minutes passed, other people filed into the room and started working on their own research. Eventually, I stopped pretending to work because I felt more invisible. Instead, I started watching the other people in the room wondering with envy what it must be like to be able to research and learn about their own family histories. It might seem a little strange to the casual observer for me to be so obsessed with something like that. But stop for a moment and imagine how strange it would actually feel to know nothing about your real family or heritage, even though a state agency knows it all and refuses to tell you. Then imagine further that you were raised by another family that didn't fully accept you, but made you feel guilty and ungrateful whenever you wanted to know your blood heritage. That's what it was like for me as an adoptee. It's hard to put yourself in someone else's shoes especially when they're several sizes too small.

The longer I sat and waited for Larry the more tense I became. It was like waiting for my own execution. I had to do something, so I requested a decade's worth of Haverhill High School yearbooks from 1976 through 1985. I decided to look for pictures of graduating Woodward students to see if I could understand why Frank Capriani thought I looked so much like them. I found nearly a dozen Woodward pictures in the yearbooks. Several of the pictures did look similar especially in the chin and lips. I was still examining the yearbooks when Larry finally entered the room.

I looked up as he walked through the door. He scanned the room and saw me in the far corner. However, as he approached my table, he began to smile. In fact, the expression on his face was so unexpected and counterintuitive that it almost frightened me. What was he going to say? Then, when he finally stood directly in front of me, he reached over, grabbed my hand, and shook it. All he said through his smile was, "Congratulations Mr. Conner, we've found your family!"

I was so stunned by his words that I was speechless. Here I was expecting to be sensitively consoled over our failure, and he was telling me that we had succeeded. Then again, what did this "Mr. Conner" business mean? I thought we were investigating the Woodwards. I was in shock! Larry almost laughed at the puzzled look on my face, as he led me to an isolated table in the opposite corner of the room. There, he set his notebook on the table, opened it and began to explain his findings.

"We did it, Dave; we really did it! Look, when I got to the vital statistics office, I started scanning the birth index for any children born to Charles and Charlotte Woodward in 1937. Sure enough, they had a set of fraternal twins born on May 11, 1937; that date precisely fits the empty space for your mother's birthdate on your adoption history. Your records also said that she had a twin brother."

"I pulled copies of the birth certificates and they showed that their names were Wilma and William Woodward. Then, I tracked Wilma Woodward forward in the marriage index figuring that she would have married sometime between 1953, when she would have turned 16, and 1961, the year before you were born. That's when I discovered that she married David Paul Conner on November 6, 1956. The name Conner has six letters and ends in an "r." Again, it's a perfect match to your adoption history."

"Then, just to be absolutely certain, I went back to the birth index to see if Wilma and David had three children between the year they were married, 1956, and the year before you were born, 1961. Look here! I found Rosemary Anne

Conner, born on August 19, 1957; David Paul Conner, Junior, born on August 22, 1958; and William James Conner, born on December 4, 1959. They are your three half-siblings. They had no other children."

"Finally, I called Annie and asked her to run a quick check on the Social Security Death Index for David Paul Conner. Your records said that your mother was widowed when you were born. She discovered that David P. Conner died in August 1959, but the records didn't give a day. We should be able to find his death announcement in a newspaper issue from that month. Don't you see? Everything fits perfectly. Annie said she'd call Laura right away to get a second confirmation, but I think this is it. We've finally got a match! If Laura confirms our find, she'll track your mother forward in time to find her current address and telephone number."

It was just too hard to believe. My entire body was shaking like a leaf, as he recounted his findings. Without saying a word, I walked over to the other table and picked up the copy I had made of the article about Charles Woodward's funeral. Yes, it had listed Wilma as one of his surviving daughters. However, there was still the issue of the number of boys and girls in his family. It simply didn't match. I showed Larry the information.

"Well, I wouldn't worry about it," he said. "We often find little mistakes in the adoption histories. They aren't always 100 percent correct. This isn't a major inconsistency when you consider all the matching facts we've found. The truth is in the body of the matching evidence. I've done this for years, and it's hard to find information that matches as well and as completely as this does. I'll tell you what, let's go to the newspaper archives and see if we can find out when David Conner, Senior died. That might be useful information in the final confirmation, but I don't think that anything will change."

We started looking through the old newspapers from August 1959. We found the article we were looking for on the front page of the August 22, 1959 paper. According to the article, David died by accidental drowning when he fell into the Merrimack River on the night of August 19. He had been seen drinking heavily at a local bar that night, and he apparently fell off a bridge on his way home. His body was discovered two days later when it finally washed ashore. The article mentioned that he left behind a wife and two children, but our records showed that his third child was not born until after his death. Once again, everything was consistent, and we finally decided to close my search at 11:00 AM on July 2, 1998–roughly 49 hours after it began. We were only one hour off Larry's record time!

I was so excited about our find that I had almost forgotten to call Barb. I had promised to let her know when we found my family. I rushed outside the library to the pay phone on the street and called her at work. I was so overcome by the story I had to tell her, that I had to wipe tears from my eyes as I talked. As I was reading the information to her, Barb interrupted.

"When did you just say your mother was born?"

"May 11, 1937," I repeated.

"And why does that date sound familiar?"

I couldn't believe it. My own birth mother was born on the same month and day that we were married! I was so excited about the find that the significance of her birthdate hadn't even occurred to me. After I shared the news with Barb, I treated Larry to lunch at a restaurant he once frequented up the hill from the library. I now had all the information I was seeking, but it would take some time for the reality of it to sink in.

After lunch, Larry returned to New Hampshire. I decided to spend the rest of the afternoon touring downtown Haverhill and taking pictures. I just wanted to absorb the experience of being in the city where my mother was born and raised. I had never seen Haverhill before my search, and suddenly, it was part of my true heritage. In fact, I went back to the library and checked the 1938 Polk Directory to find out where Charles Woodward lived when my mother was born. The address it listed was 145 Forest Avenue. I was able to find the street, but the city had obviously renumbered all of the houses many years ago, and I couldn't tell which one was my mother's old house. I took some pictures of the tree-lined street anyway.

I didn't leave Haverhill that afternoon until about 3:30 PM. The drive back to Maria's house was the most peaceful and pleasant trip I'd ever taken. All the way back, I reflected on my search and realized that I was a different person now than I was before. I now had a connection to the real world that had been missing for 36 years. For the first time in my life, I was my own person, not a creation of the state. All I needed was the final confirmation from Laura, and Larry said that she was going to call me at Maria's house around 8:00 PM. The excitement had returned; I could hardly wait for her call.

When I arrived at Maria's house, Bart was there. I told them about our success and tried to show them all my notes which had become quite disorganized by now. They were amazed at how well the pieces of the puzzle fit together especially after the disappointments of the previous day. I wanted to tell the whole world what I had found, but I knew that this was the most critical period of my search. The next step in the process was first contact with my birth mother. That was the potential turning point in my life-long journey. Either she would reject me (which would be the end of the road), or she would accept me, and we could proceed onward to actual reunion. If I was really lucky, I might get an opportunity to meet some of my original family. I had to wonder—did my adoptive father feel like this when he first met his biological aunt?

Of course, the issue of my biological father's identity remained. Half of my past was still missing. There was so little information on him that it would be virtually impossible for me to identify him from the records. My only realistic chance to find him was to establish contact with my birth mother. But for now, all I wanted to do was revel in the joy of my find. It was a truly remarkable day.

It was nearly 8:30 PM when I received Laura's call. Much to my relief, she confirmed that we had indeed found my birth mother. All of the information she was able to access from independent sources concurred with both the information that Larry and I had uncovered and my adoption history. There was no longer any doubt that my mother was Wilma Woodward/Conner. Laura was even able to track her forward in time. According to her information, my mother had remarried and her current name was Wilma Umling. Laura wasn't able to get a current physical description for my mother because she had never been issued a driver's license. However, she was able to establish a current address and telephone number for her. She was living with her current husband, John Umling, in Killeen, Texas. Her address was a surprise as I had expected her to be living in New Hampshire or Massachusetts. Obviously, I would not have to worry about rushing to first contact in order to meet her before I returned home. I would actually be much closer to her in Alabama than I was in New Hampshire.

Laura was able to find a current address for my half-brother, David Conner. She was able to get my mother's current telephone number by calling him. However, she warned me not to contact my brother before speaking to my mother because we had no way to know that my brother was aware of my existence. Laura also discovered that I had a younger brother, Timothy Scott Umling, who was born on April 25, 1963 just a little over a year after I was born. Laura felt that I probably was born out of wedlock to a man that my mother had a one-night stand with prior to meeting Timothy's father. That theory was consistent with my mother's statements to my original caseworker as contained in my adoption history. It also added substance to the belief that my mother might not be receptive to contact. That's why I decided to ask Laura to make the initial call to my birth mother to see if she would be willing to hear from me. If my mother was going to reject me, I didn't want to face it directly. I also felt that Laura's experience and understanding as a birth mother would be helpful in persuading my mother to talk to me.

Laura also managed to find some information on my mother's current husband, John Umling. The records showed that he had retired from the Air Force during the 1960s. He probably met my mother while he was stationed at Pease Air Force Base. According to his current driver's license, John Umling was born on July 9, 1923. The license described him as 5' 10" tall, weighing 160 pounds, and having brown hair and brown eyes. As she read the description, I realized that it sounded very familiar. I frantically flipped through my adoption history to find the descriptive information on my birth father. According to my records, my own father's first name was John, and he was described as being 5' 10" or 11" tall, with dark brown hair, brown eyes, and a rugged, husky build. His age in 1962 was reported to be "approximately" 35 years. The man that Laura was describing would have been 38 years old when I was born. Finally, the fact that he was a serviceman was consistent with my mother's statement that her deceased husband's brother (who we learned from David Conner's death notice had been stationed at Pease Air Force Base) had introduced her to my father. The coincidences between John Umling and the limited information I had on my birth father were astounding.

However, Laura was extremely cautious. While she couldn't deny that the two descriptions were very similar, her extensive experience with adoptee searches told her that the chances of a match were slim. After all, at least 90 percent of all adoptees are either from broken families or casual relationships (one-night stands or heat-of-the-moment encounters) that never develop into lasting relationships. Many are teenage pregnancy cases, and most of the fathers were never told that their "girlfriends" were pregnant. Furthermore, the thought that my mother's current husband could also be my father didn't make any sense. If she had married my father or even had another out-of-wedlock child so soon after I was born, what reason could she have had to relinquish me for adoption? However, this wasn't the first potentially odd situation associated with my adoption case that we had encountered during my search. Unbeknownst to us at the time it also would not be the last. Despite Laura's reservations, I remained hopeful that John Umling would be my father. It was an outcome that I could have only dreamed of before.

After my conversation with Laura, I felt relieved and, for the first time since I began my search in mid-May, truly relaxed. At last, my heart could stop racing. I asked Laura not to contact my mother until after I returned to Alabama. I didn't think that I could handle the stress at the time, and I wanted a chance to fully absorb everything I had learned. It was an amazing and unique feeling to finally learn my roots at the age of 36. Until that moment, my background and perspective on the world had been completely different. Suddenly, it had all changed in the span of a few hours. People that I never knew and places I had never visited were now part of my heritage. It was a life altering experience and another rebirth for me. All of a sudden, I felt that I could understand how the Native Americans must have felt shortly after the first Europeans arrived. Everything they thought they understood about the world around them instantly changed just as it did for me—albeit on a much smaller scale. I just couldn't imagine what I might learn next.

By now, my exhaustion was catching up with me. In the 75 hours that had passed since I first arrived at Maria's house, I had managed to get only 10-12 hours of sleep. At least I knew that I could sleep late the next morning. My work in New Hampshire was done. I had successfully suffered my way through the hardest, most stressful, and most gratifying vacation of my life.

***** *****

When I awoke on Friday morning, the house was already bathed in sunlight. I wasn't even roused by Maria when she awoke, prepared for work, and left. The house was totally quiet, and I finally felt refreshed. It was 9:00 AM, and I had slept for eleven straight hours. Fortunately, Maria and I had said our good-byes the night before, so I didn't need to worry about missing her before I had to depart.

My return flight was not scheduled to leave Hartford until 7:30 PM, so I had plenty of time to kill. I decided to visit my great-aunt Sue in Laconia to share my news with her. She had tried to help me during the early phases of my search, and I wanted to show her the information from my records that confirmed her story about my original name.

Although we exchanged letters regularly, I had not seen my great-aunt in nearly three years. It was good to talk to her again. As always, she was supportive but totally surprised by all the information I had found. She even asked me to give her a copy of the rough family tree I had sketched so she could keep it with her genealogical records. It felt good to know that at least some of my adoptive family members had enough room in their hearts to accept both my biological family and me. To me, that's what adoption really should be all about.

I also decided to stop one last time in Haverhill on my way back to Hartford. I wanted to visit the library and photocopy the yearbook pictures I found of the Woodwards. I had forgotten to do so in all the excitement of our find. I even bought a copy of the Haverhill newspaper that had been so helpful in my search to keep as a memento of my visit. I then drove to the airport for my return flight.

As my plane taxied down the runway later that evening, my mind began to shift gears and focus on first contact with my mother. What would I say to her? What questions should I ask? I knew that I had to get as much information as I could because there was no way to know if she'd ever be willing to speak to me again. I might never have a second chance. It was an ominous step, indeed.

As my plane climbed into the air, I looked out the window at the skyline of downtown Hartford. What had seemed like a big city to me in 1980 now appeared distant and tiny from my window—just as my tortured childhood was growing smaller and more remote to me now. I was mesmerized by the view and its greater meaning to me, as I watched the firm outline of the city softly fade away into the summer evening haze. It was ironic to realize that I was finally leaving behind the city of my rebirth to face a vast and uncertain destiny full of possibilities with no certainty of success or failure. Perhaps, I would be born yet again and reunited with my biological family. Even if that never occurred, I knew that things would never be the same for me again. It was a surprisingly comforting thought. Change was the only thing in my life that was familiar to me. This change would be different, though. I had reached out and plucked it off the tree myself—fresh and sweet. I finally felt that I had gained control of my own life and destiny. It was a wonderfully fulfilling and encouraging feeling.

## *First Contact*

Although I was truly excited about finding my birth mother, I was hesitant to contact her right away. I had her telephone number, but I wanted Laura to arrange my call. The information I had obtained through my search gave us mixed signals about her willingness to acknowledge me. Regardless of whether or not her husband was my real father, she had several possible good reasons to reject me. If John Umling was not my father, then I was the son of some other man with whom she had become romantically involved just prior to meeting John or during her relationship with him. On the other hand, if I was her husband's son, then I might have been an early out-of-wedlock "accident" that he might not know about and that she would not want to explain after 36 years. In either case, I would represent a potential embarrassment to her that she might not wish to face. In addition to those possible outcomes, there were the statements in my adoptive history that Cindy had emphasized. Perhaps she knew something more from the rest of my sealed records that I didn't know. While there were several potential outcomes that would lead to successful contact, the most realistic and simple scenarios were stacked against me. Although my conversations with Laura clearly showed that she was trying to keep an open mind about my first contact, I do believe that she privately shared my concerns. The emotional roller coaster ride was not done. I was just waiting through an intermission.

I tried to divert my growing anxieties about first contact by focusing on the story of my successful search. After I had called Barb from Haverhill with the news of my success, she immediately called my office and told the receptionist about it. All of my co-workers at the agency had been highly supportive of my search long before I made my decisive trip to New England. In fact, my story had become the agency's exclusive little soap opera with many of my co-workers requesting regular updates. They had watched adoptee reunions on a number of television shows, and they were excited to have one of their very own that they could watch unfold step by step. By the time I returned to work the Monday following my vacation, the news had spread to all corners of the office, and I received many requests to tell the story. Even people I worked with outside the office wanted to know all the details. Since I wanted everyone to understand the plight of all adoptees who are denied basic information about themselves, I was more than willing to honor their requests. Although I had to repeat the story many times, I never tired of telling it, and it helped take my mind off my fears of first contact. I was just relieved and pleased to know that everyone I talked to about it was supportive. Not one person felt I had done anything wrong.

Some people I talked to asked me which family I thought was my *real* family. To me, that question was impossible to answer, and in some respects, it was even improper to ask. *Both* families, regardless of my personal feelings about them or how their actions shaped my life, are essential parts of my being. My biological family gave me my genetic make-up. That essential link could never be severed or altered by the adoption process. It forever dictated my physical health and many of my genetic traits before I was adopted. My adoptive family gave me my childhood environment. Regardless of whether it could be judged good or bad, it still made me what I am today. Sometimes the ends don't justify the means, but I couldn't simply remove or rewrite those environmental influences any more than I could simply ignore them. Can a divorcee ever really ignore or forget all the good and bad memories from a lengthy marriage? If so, is that really a good indication of emotional security and health?

Although I didn't *like* many of my childhood experiences and I would never *choose* to relive them, they did motivate me to become a better and more self-reliant person. They even motivated me to search for and find my biological family. For those results, I was grateful, even as I struggled to deal with the experiences that fostered them. But to ask me which of the two influences was more important to me was like asking me to choose which limb I wanted to have amputated. I needed both basic influences to make me who I am. Moreover, I had no power to change them even if I didn't want them. I just didn't like the idea of being denied an understanding of one fundamental part of who I was—namely, my biological family—simply because I was adopted. People who were never adopted have the luxury of knowing, understanding, and taking for granted both elements that make them who they are. They have only one mother and one father who contributed *both* their genetic heritage and their childhood environment. They can never really know what it's like to have one of those fundamental influences permanently taken away without any recourse at all— without even an explanation as to why it was done. For adoptees, those elements are forever divided into two sets of parents—one biological and one adoptive—and one can never truly substitute for the other. Therefore, I couldn't answer that question, and I really didn't appreciate being asked to choose. It was just another reason for me to feel like I was different from everyone else just because I was an adoptee.

Another co-worker asked me if I might consider changing my name. That idea sounded much too complicated and too extraordinary to consider. Even if I wanted to consider it, there was no way for me to know for certain what my original last name would have been. Woodward was my mother's maiden name. Conner was my mother's and my legal name when I was born, but I knew that David Conner was not my biological father, and it was not even my mother's current name. What's more, there was already one David Conner in that family. I could just imagine the awkward situation that would create for William when introducing his two Conner brothers— "Hi, I'm Bill; this is my brother Dave; and this is my other brother Dave." Finally, I had no firm evidence to support my belief that John Umling was my birth father. In fact, there was no way to be certain at this point that I would ever know who my real father was. I also knew that Barb and Michael would have a hard time accepting any name change, and I didn't want to explain it all as often as I knew I would.

When I told my story to my executive director, his only response was, "Well, now that you know who all these people are, what do you plan to do with them?" It was a curious, but valid question. Assuming my first contact with my mother *was* successful, what then? I hadn't even begun to think that far ahead because I was more concerned that my first contact might fail, and I didn't even want to think about that. Even if I did have a successful conversation with my birth mother, I was more focused on the basic questions I wanted to ask her than what role I wanted her to play in my life. I had never really seriously considered how I would incorporate my biological family into my life. How would I refer to them? Would my mind accept a woman I have never seen or known to be my mother? What about my brothers and sister? How would I relate to them, and how would they view me? Could they just accept me as their brother? It's not something that's easy to think about, but it was necessary to have some idea of what I wanted my birth family to mean to me and, conversely, what I wanted to mean to my birth family.

After thinking about my situation, I finally concluded that my introduction to my birth family was actually no different than meeting my wife's family for the first time. It just *felt* different because I knew in my mind that these new people were genetically related to me before meeting them. But in all reality, I didn't know any of them any better than I knew Barb's family when I first met them. In fact, I wanted to make a good first impression on my biological family in just the same way I did when I met Barb's family. As long as I was conscious of the similarity, I felt that I could force myself to treat it the same way. There was plenty of room in my crazy life for a "second" set of in-laws. So, I decided that I would try to approach them the same way and see what happened. If a better and closer relationship developed naturally, then I would be all the better for it. I just didn't want to go into my first contact *expecting* that I would naturally fit back into my birth family as though my adoption had never happened. Interestingly enough, having made that conscious decision actually eased many of my anxieties about first contact.

However, shortly after I returned to work from my vacation, an incident occurred that gave me a new sense of urgency to pursue first contact. On Tuesday morning, July 6, I received a call at work from my New Hampshire caseworker, Cindy. As she had promised me when we met one week earlier, she was calling to tell me the results of her efforts to locate my birth mother. Of course, she had no idea that I had already found her, so I just played along. Once again, her voice was very soft, practiced, and soothing, as she told me that they had conducted a very thorough and exhaustive search, but they were unable to find her. *Of all the stupidity...* I began to think, as she gracefully and sensitively apologized for her failure. *Here they are with all that information about my biological mother right in front of them, and they can't even find her after searching for an entire week. It only took me 49 hours.* I received it like a sick joke.

When Cindy had finished her polished and practiced apology, I decided to have some fun with her. My search had finally put me in command because I knew something about myself that she obviously didn't. I knew my mother's current name, location, and telephone number. I decided to use my response to see how much she really enjoyed being in my shoes.

"Well, I appreciate all your kind efforts, Cindy. I can certainly understand how hard it would be for you to find her. After all, I've learned that she remarried shortly after I was born and has since moved out of state. Don't worry about hurting my feelings, though, because I've already found her, and I have her current address and telephone number."

There was a long silence at the other end of the line. Finally, she realized she was no longer in control and didn't know how to respond. This revelation simply didn't fit into her carefully practiced script. For once the shoe was on the other foot, and I hoped it was a very tight and uncomfortable fit. It was hard for me to keep from laughing. Then she finally asked, "How do you know you've found her?"

"Well, I had a difficult time trying to figure out who she was on my own. So, I found a private investigator working with an underground network of professionals in Florida that helps adoptees with their searches. I just gave her my information, wrote her a check, and within 48 hours, she told me everything. Here, I'll prove it to you. My mother's maiden name was Wilma Woodward. She was born on May 11, 1937 in Haverhill, Massachusetts. She married a man by the name of David Paul Conner in 1956 and had three children by him: Rosemary in 1957; David Paul, Junior in 1958; and William in 1959. Her husband died in August 1959 just before their third son was born. It was shortly after that when she met my father, who was stationed at Pease Air Force Base, resulting in the person with whom you are speaking. Does any of this sound familiar to you?" I was very careful to not reveal any information that would make it possible for Cindy to know my mother's current name or whereabouts.

Once again, there was a long period of silence over the phone. I covered the mouthpiece with my hand. By now, it was virtually impossible to contain my laughter. When she did finally respond, her tone changed to one of deep concern. "Have you tried to contact her yet?"

"No, not yet," I replied, casually. The fact that she even asked confirmed once again that we had found the right person. "But I will. I just want to wait a few days and think about what I want to say to her."

"I thought you agreed to let me be your intermediary. I'd still like to help you. Will you tell me how to contact her?" she pleaded.

"No, Cindy, I don't think I want to do that. I can handle it on my own, but I really do thank you for your help. I couldn't have done it without you. Maybe I'll give you a call to let you know how everything turns out. Would that be okay with you?"

She agreed, and I ended our conversation. I had to get off the phone quickly to avoid laughing out loud. I know it wasn't a very polite thing to do, but it was the most gratifying part of the whole demeaning experience. And, after everything I had been through, I felt I deserved some personal satisfaction. However, the gratification I received didn't last for long. Less than 24 hours later, Cindy called me again at work. This time, she said she had located my birth mother, and she still wanted to serve as my confidential intermediary.

It shocked me to learn that she could locate my mother in less than a day armed only with the information she had when she had failed to do so after a full week of searching. That meant one of two things to me. It meant that she had either deliberately lied to me about knowing my mother's whereabouts, or she had only pretended to search just to have an excuse to dissuade me from believing that my mother could be found. Either way, it clearly indicated that she was actively trying to prevent me from having any contact with my birth mother. Moreover, it proved that she now had the ability to talk to my mother before I was prepared to do so. My response to her request was direct, clear, and firm.

"Cindy, I don't know why you are doing this to me, but I do *not* want you involved in my case anymore. I will not permit you to contact my mother on my behalf under any circumstances. If you attempt to do so, I will fight you to the greatest extent that the law will allow. I have all the help I need right here with me. I ask you to please respect my wishes. You had your chance, and now it's my turn. I will handle the situation by myself. Is that clear?"

I could easily detect the disappointment in her voice, but she politely consented to my demand. I only heard from her one other time at the end of the month when she called to ask if I had tried to contact my birth mother. Several months later, Larry informed me that Cindy had suddenly left the agency just a month or so after my final conversation with her. Although she was expected to retire sometime within the following year, her sudden, unexplained, and unceremonious departure was a surprise to Larry and Annie. After all, she had worked at the agency for many years. Yet it was just another in a long line of odd, seemingly coincidental, occurrences surrounding my case. The possible reasons for these mounting irregularities and strange coincidences would only become clear through contact with my birth mother.

After my disconcerting conversations with Cindy, I decided that I was ready to pursue first contact with my birth mother. I called Laura that evening and asked her to proceed. She called me back one week later to tell me that she had talked to my mother and arranged a time for me to call her. But before she gave me the specific date and time, she had some more information to tell me. I decided before she even asked that I had better sit down to hear what she had to say.

First, Laura told me that I had two additional sisters that she did not find in the records–Katherine and Carolyn Umling. Carolyn was the youngest in my birth family, born in 1967. Katherine, on the other hand, was born on March 22, 1961–only ten-and-a-half months before me! The fact that Laura had not discovered Carolyn was not odd. Given the frequency of births that my mother had established, Laura had stopped searching for additional children when she found none born in 1965 or 1966. The fact that Katherine's birth was not discovered was somewhat more disconcerting. For some strange reason, she did not show up in the records at all. The number of strange circumstances surrounding my case continued to compound.

Laura also told me that my mother had confirmed that her husband was my birth father. Of course, that conclusion had suddenly become almost self-evident by virtue of the fact that my older sister and two younger siblings all bore the Umling name. But it did raise the intriguing question of why I had been placed for adoption in the first place. My birth family was completely intact, and I was a middle child. No other children had been placed for adoption. Yet, I grew up within an entirely different family for no apparent reason. Unfortunately, Laura had no answers. I would have to find out what had happened from my birth mother.

My mother had agreed to talk to me, but only reluctantly. She told Laura that none of my brothers or sisters had known of my adoption, and she wasn't sure that she was ready to tell them about it. Laura arranged a time for me to call at 8:00 PM on July 17 so that my mother could arrange to be alone in the house when I called. Again, she expressed her concerns about my mother's receptivity to me, and she reminded me that she would be there to console me if things didn't work out well. That was good to know, but it could do little to allay my concerns and trepidations. I wondered if Cindy had called and tried to intervene. I had three days to plan what I was going to say, and whatever I decided to say would have a lasting effect on my ability to develop a future relationship with my entire birth family. I tried to keep my expectations at bay. "If I could only keep her on the phone for an hour," I said repeatedly to Barb "I could get some answers to my questions. If I could have nothing else, at least that would give me some peace of mind and satisfaction that I could live with." Of course, I was only trying to find a comfortable way to let myself down before I had to face what might be the ultimate disappointment.

In preparing for my first contact call, I reviewed the original introduction letter that Laura had asked me to write before my trip to New England. I read it several times before I decided that my wording was too personal. According to Laura, my mother was hesitant to reveal my existence to the rest of my birth family. I concluded that any strong expression of emotion in my initial conversation might cause her to back away in fear. I couldn't say anything that might make her fear that I would intrude on her life, if she didn't want anyone else to know about me or even if she didn't want any further contact with me at all. Of course, I hoped that she would change her mind, but that wasn't likely to happen, especially if I came on too strong during first contact. I decided that I needed to say something that would give her the opportunity to freely express her feelings towards me without making her feel pressured or obligated to respond in a certain way. It reminded me of the difficulties I experienced meeting women through blind dates. At the same time, I needed to clearly express my receptivity to her. The constraints were beginning to sound even harder to satisfy than the directions Laura had given me for my introductory letter. I continued to wonder if *anything* about my search would ever be easy.

After considerable thought on the subject, I decided to introduce myself to her by simply stating my name, birthdate, and birthplace; then I would ask her if she knew who I was. If she used any possessive or endearing terms in her response, it would be a sign that she might be willing to give me a chance to know her. If she answered the question in an impersonal or dispassionate way, it would be a signal that she wanted to maintain some distance between us. Either way, I could gauge her receptivity to me before exposing my own feelings towards her. I felt that approach might benefit both of us. I could avoid placing myself in an emotionally compromising or vulnerable position before I had a sense of her feelings, and she would have the freedom to express her own feelings without any pressure from me. It seemed to be the best I could do.

I also carefully prepared a list of questions I wanted to ask her. I wanted to know about her life, my medical history, and my cultural heritage. I decided not to ask her why I was placed for adoption. Although a part of me really wanted to know, I was afraid that the question might be a sensitive issue for her, and it also might make her feel some sense of resentment from me for what she had done. I had already come to terms with the fact that I had been relinquished, and I could never change that. Still, if she wasn't willing to tell me about it, it would become a significant void in my life to live with, especially given all the curious unanswered questions surrounding my adoption. I just forced myself to believe that she did what she felt was best for me at the time, and that was all anyone could expect of his mother.

Finally, I decided that I wanted Barb to secretly monitor my conversation on another telephone. I asked her to listen carefully to everything I said and give me a hand signal if she felt I needed to soften my tone or express myself more clearly. I didn't want her to reveal her presence, as I was afraid it might make my mother nervous to know that our conversation was being monitored. But I did want both of us to take notes on what my mother said. If I wasn't able to write everything down, I might be able to fill in the missing pieces from Barb's notes. This call might be the only chance I would ever get to speak directly with my mother. I didn't want to miss anything.

Having decided how to handle my first contact call, all I had to do was wait for the appointed time. Of course, I didn't know if Cindy had honored my request. As the time passed, I grew more and more concerned that she might try to interfere. Once again, I could feel the stress of the situation building inside me. Then the fateful evening arrived.

I waited until 8:10 before dialing the number. I decided it was better to call a little late just to make sure she had enough time to get some privacy and to relax, if that was possible. I certainly couldn't relax at all. It was the most important telephone call I had ever made in my life. I felt like I was calling the White House to speak with the President. My entire body was trembling as I dialed the number. After a few rings, she answered the phone.

"Hello, may I speak to Wilma Umling?" I asked just to make sure.

"This is Wilma."

"Hi," I began, my voice cracking with fear. "My name is David Smith, and I was born in Portsmouth, NH on February 14, 1962. Do you know who I am?"

"Yes, I do," she said with a hint of eagerness. "You're my son!"

She had called me her *son*! It may have been a simple response to my carefully prepared question, but that word meant everything to me. She could have just said that I was the child she placed for adoption or even nothing at all, but she didn't. Just the reassuring tone of her voice washed away my initial fears and caused tears of relief to well in my eyes. After my long and arduous search, I had a reason for hope. I had a chance for the relationship that, until that moment, I could only dream of.

"I'm so relieved to hear you say that," I responded. "You don't know how long I've waited to hear it."

"It's okay," she reassured. "I always knew you'd find me someday. I even told my friends, 'You just wait and see; he's going to find me when he's in his thirties.' I always remembered you on your birthday. Every February 14, I'd wake up and tell your father, 'Well, I don't know who he is, where he is, or how he is, but he's another year older today.' I'm just glad to know you're all right."

I felt another wave of relief wash over me, as I listened to her words. Her statement that she had always remembered me on my birthday immediately reminded me of the day in 1978 after my 16th birthday when I tried desperately to find a message from her in the Portsmouth Herald. All the disappointment I felt that day was dispelled by the knowledge that she was thinking about me then, even if she hadn't tried or wasn't able to find me.

"That means a lot to me. I've thought of you all my life, too. I even tried to search for you when I was much younger. I was just afraid that you might not want to talk to me. When Laura told me that I could call you, she felt that you might not be ready to accept me. I just wanted you to know that I don't want to impose myself on you, but I would like you to be a part of my life, if you'll allow it."

"Well, when I got the call from Laura, I didn't know if it was true or why you were trying to find me. None of my other kids knew about you, so I wasn't sure that I wanted to tell them. But after thinking about it some more and hearing your voice, I think it might be time for them to know."

At this point in our conversation, it was becoming clear that my reunion would be successful. I was overjoyed, and all my anxieties subsided. We talked for a full hour. My mother asked many questions about me and my career. Eventually, she asked questions about Barb and Michael, and Barb was able to join the conversation. She also answered many of my questions about my medical history. She even told me some information about my father.

My father was born in Ellwood City, Pennsylvania where he was the oldest of five surviving children (two boys and three girls). When he was a child, his family spoke only German, so he didn't understand English until he began attending school. My father was a veteran of World War II and the Korean War. He had served in the Air Force for 22 ½ years before he retired. She also told me about all my brothers and sisters and her 21 grandchildren—not including my own son. I learned that I also had another half-brother, John Gary Umling, who was born on July 13, 1957 and lived with his former wife and two sons in Maryland. He was my father's son through a previous marriage. In fact, I learned that my father had been married to seven previous wives, but had fathered only one other son. His marriages never lasted long because he was transferred quite often during his military service. One of his earliest wives was simultaneously married to several other men. Since his wives rarely agreed to follow him, the marriages never survived.

Although I didn't ask her about the circumstances surrounding my adoption, she volunteered the story. As I had suspected, my mother had a very rough childhood. My grandmother suffered a nervous breakdown while my mother was in the seventh grade and became unable to care for her eleven children. She took my mother out of school to care for the family while she recovered. My grandmother decided to sacrifice my mother's education, because she believed that my mother would never amount to anything anyway. That statement instantly reminded me of my adoptive father's assessment by his stepfather. My mother said that, during the most difficult times, she would go to the bowling alleys in town to collect broken pins for the family to use as firewood. By the time she was nineteen, she had no formal education beyond the sixth grade, and she had little work experience. When she left home, she married David Conner and had three children by him. After his death in 1959, the only means of support she had to care for the children was her husband's Social Security death benefits.

David's brother, Robert Conner, introduced her to my father after David died. They were both stationed at Pease Air Force Base, and my father often drove her brother-in-law back to Haverhill on the weekends. Robert felt that my father wanted to settle down and build a family, so he encouraged John to date my mother. Shortly after my mother began dating him, she became pregnant with my older sister, Kathy. My father had often talked about marrying my mother, so she settled on the idea even though he never popped the question. My mother did not press the issue, as she was concerned about scaring him off. However, when she learned that she had become pregnant with me only six weeks after Kathy was born, she felt she could no longer wait for him to ask. She already had four children to care for with a fifth on the way. My mother moved to Portsmouth to be closer to my father and to avoid revealing to her parents that she was having out-of-wedlock children about which she knew they would disapprove.

However, when she eventually confronted him on the issue of marriage, my father finally revealed that he was still married to a woman in Maryland with whom he already had a son. He met his wife while stationed in Maryland, but like so many of his previous wives, she refused to accompany him when he was transferred to Portsmouth, New Hampshire. Many years later we learned that she, too, had been unfaithful during my father's absence. That secret affair was one reason for her unwillingness to accompany him during his transfer. My father wanted to divorce her and marry my mother, but he had not found a good opportunity to discuss it with her. My father never revealed if he suspected or learned about her affair.

My mother was devastated and frightened. She knew that she couldn't take care of five children on her own, and she feared that my father might never divorce his wife to marry her—especially if it meant that he might lose contact with his only son. So, she had Kathy placed in a foster home in New Hampshire. Although the state contacted her on several occasions to sign papers authorizing an adoption for Kathy, she couldn't bring herself to do it. She had already grown too attached to her daughter. Since I had not yet been born, my mother decided to place me for adoption at birth. She felt it would be easier to part with me, if she never held me or knew anything about me. That's why she told the nurse that she didn't want to know anything about me when I was born. However, the state did later confirm to her that she had given birth to a son, as she had suspected all along.

Several months after my birth, my father returned to her. He was now divorcing his wife in Maryland, and he wanted to marry my mother. She accepted his offer, but had to tell him that she had placed his daughter in a foster home. She also told him that, while he was gone, she had given birth to his son, but he had been placed for adoption at birth. My father was determined to get both of his children back from the state, so he instructed my mother to call her caseworker and demand that they be given custody of their children. Since my mother had never signed an adoption petition for Kathy, the state immediately agreed to release her to my father.

However, unbeknownst to my mother, the state had already promised me to another family—the Smiths. In order to avoid breaking the adoption placement they had arranged for me, the caseworker carefully and cleverly told my mother that she had already signed the papers placing me for adoption, so she had no legal right to custody of me. The caseworker also told her that the state would place me where she would never be able to find me. My mother and father were devastated, but felt they had no recourse. They accepted the caseworker's denial and tried to go on with their lives without me. My father retrieved Kathy from the foster home and subsequently married my mother on October 19, 1962—eight months after I was born and only five-and-a-half months after I was placed with the Smiths. My parents decided not to reveal or discuss the circumstances surrounding Kathy and me because they didn't want Kathy to feel that she was loved any less by virtue of her temporary foster placement. Before she could tell my other brothers and sisters about me, my mother knew that she had to explain the truth to Kathy.

Her story made it clear that I was a victim of extraordinary and unusual circumstances. I was never abandoned or unwanted as the Smiths had led me to believe. My birth was simply more than my mother could handle at the time. She loved all of her children, every last one. Even the one she could no longer know. She had remembered me through the years and even held out hope against all odds that I would find her someday. My search had fulfilled her hopes as well as my own. The natural bond between my birth mother and me that hardship severed in 1962 began to be restored that July evening in 1998. My search had ended in successful first contact. I was now moving inevitably towards full reunion with my birth family.

Before our conversation ended, my mother asked me to send her some pictures of my family and me. She promised to send me pictures of my father, brothers, and sisters. She also told me that I could call her anytime I wanted. My heart was filled with joy for more than a week after the call. I wrote a long letter to her that weekend and included lots of pictures from the photo album I had prepared for her. I knew it would soon be time for me to begin making plans to meet my birth family for the first time in my life.

Nearly a week later, I received another call from Cindy. She asked if I had attempted to call my birth mother. I told her that I had, and that everything had gone well. She also wanted to know how my adoptive family felt about it. That was a hard subject for me, as I had not yet talked to my adoptive mother about it. I was struggling to decide what I should tell her and how. I lied to Cindy at the time just to get her off my back. After all, she didn't deserve the truth. Her brief relationship with me was built solely on lies and deception. It was the last time I ever heard from her. She had no control over my life anymore.

I called my birth mother again eleven days later to ask if she had received my letter and pictures. She told me she received them over the weekend and thanked me for sending them. She said that she knew I was her son the instant she saw my picture because I looked so much like my father when he was my age. In fact, my father would have been roughly 37 years old when he first met my mother. I was 36. She said I also looked a lot like my brother Tim who was living with her at the time. His home in New Hampshire had been lost in a recent flood, so he and his family were staying with my birth parents until they could get back on their feet. Once again, my mother's mood was receptive, but she had not told anyone about me. She promised that she would break the news that weekend and send me a letter with some pictures of my family.

Based on her promise, I called a local florist and arranged for a bouquet of flowers to be delivered to her that Saturday. I wanted to show her my appreciation for the acceptance she had given me, but I didn't want to do it until I knew that she was prepared to reveal my existence. It might also gently prod her to do so. By the time I called her again the following Monday, she had received the flowers and had talked about me to my father, my younger brother, Tim, and my sister, Carolyn, who also lived in Killeen. The veil of secrecy had been removed once and for all. She had begun telling my family about me. It was a relief to realize the darkness surrounding my past that cast a pall over my self-image for so many years had lifted.

I was now beginning the process of meeting other members of my birth family. For the first time in my life, I spoke to both my father and brother. In another truly ironic twist of fate, I would eventually learn that Tim had married a distant cousin from my adoptive family in the 1980s. When we were all children, my adoptive sisters and I met and played with his future wife on a couple of occasions during family trips to our aunt and uncle's house. One of those childhood visits stood out in my mind because we found a large turtle in my aunt's back yard. Tim's wife also remembered that incident because she had asked to take it home with her and keep it as a pet. Consequently, that made Tim either my full brother by blood or a distant cousin in my adoptive family by marriage. If my adoptive mother was told basic information about my biological family when she took custody of me, she would've had good reason to know that both families were beginning to intermarry. My birth family's name is very uncommon and would not have been easy for her to forget.

What I never realized at the time was that by finally revealing my existence to the family, my mother had opened a floodgate. Three days later, Barb answered a call from an unknown woman who was so excited that she didn't seem to know what to say. I watched Barb struggle to understand who she was and what she wanted. After a few seconds, the woman frantically said, "I don't know what to say, I just learned I have a brother."

"Oh," Barb said with a smile. "Here, let me give you to Dave."

She handed the phone to me. It was my sister, Kathy. Our mother had just called her and told her the news. In fact, she had told her the whole story. Although the news that she had once been placed in a foster home was a complete surprise to her, she was not bitter or upset. Her excitement at learning she had another brother more than outweighed the shock she experienced upon learning of her own temporary foster placement. In fact, to her it was more of a uniting force between us.

Kathy had a warm and engaging personality that made me feel comfortable with her from the start. We were so close in age and so immediately compatible that we eventually began to refer to ourselves as "twins." In fact, I told many of my friends that Kathy was my "twin" sister born ten-and-a-half months premature. Kathy and I talked for over two hours that evening. It was almost as though we had never been apart.

By the middle of September, I had called or received calls from all seven of my brothers and sisters, two aunts, one uncle, and several of my cousins. In every case, my biological family accepted me unconditionally. In fact, a number of my new relatives told me how much of an improvement they had noticed in my mother's mood and outlook on life since my return. It was as though a great burden had been lifted from her shoulders. For the first time in years, she sounded truly relieved and happy to them. Later, my mother and two of my sisters, Kathy and Rose, sent family pictures. I couldn't believe how much I resembled my father and all of my full siblings. Several of my cousins felt that I also looked and sounded like my father's brother, Uncle Eddie. It was reassuring to realize that I had finally found a family that accepted me and to which I could feel so naturally connected. Finally, I had found the connection to society I had always wanted, but never knew.

My father's sister, Margaret (Aunt Peg), was very willing to tell me about my cultural heritage and ancestry. Of all my father's siblings, she was the closest to my grandfather and knew the most about the family history. Although I had determined that my roots were largely German, I learned that my family did not come to America directly from Germany.

My ancestors were members of an ancient Germanic tribe, the Saxons, who emigrated from Germany to Transylvania during the latter half of the twelfth century AD, long before Germany became the nation we know and recognize today. The Saxons who immigrated to England several hundred years earlier and mixed with another early Germanic tribe (the Angles) to form the Anglo-Saxons were from the same area of ancient Germany, but took a different cultural path. The Transylvanian Saxons left Germany to settle the virgin lands of Transylvania at the invitation of the Hungarian King, Geysa II. They were seeking freedom from persecution, excessive taxation, and cultural subjugation by the neighboring Franks. In exchange for Saxon allegiance and defense of his nation, the King granted the Saxons the "Golden Charter," which gave them the authority to elect their own mayors and clergy, essentially granting them cultural independence within the Hungarian state. In essence, it was an agreement for peaceful co-existence between the Saxons and Hungarians in Transylvania, and that symbiotic relationship became the foundation for a thriving society that lasted until the turn of the twentieth century. The great mass emigration of Saxons to Transylvania has been immortalized symbolically in Robert Browning's famous 1888 fable, _The Pied Piper of Hamelin_. At the end of the poem, the following lyrics can be found:

And I must not omit to say
That in Transylvania there's a tribe
Of alien people who ascribe
The outlandish ways and dress
On which their neighbors lay such stress,
To their fathers and mothers have risen
Out of some subterraneous prison
Into which they were trepanned
Long time ago in a mighty band

*Out of Hamelin town in Brunswick land,*
*But of how or why, they don't understand.*

I found the passages of his fable to be an ironic, yet comfortably prophetic analogy to my adoptee search. Like the children of Hamelin in that famous story, I had been led away from my biological family by the lilting "promise" of a better life and into a dark, secret underworld from which I would ultimately emerge 36 years later. Unfortunately, the Pied Piper's children never again saw their parents. I felt like the lucky one among the tribe.

I also learned that my grandfather, Johann Umling, Junior, was a first generation American. He was born in New Castle, Pennsylvania in 1902 a few years after his parents (Johann and Katharina Umling) emigrated to the United States to earn the money they needed to help support their family and rebuild their wine operation in Transylvania. From that humble beginning, an extensive line of American Umlings was spawned. My grandparents had five surviving children (three others died at birth or during childhood). My father had a total of five children. His brother, Eddie, had a total of twelve. His sisters, Margaret, Betty and Dorothy gave birth to five, two, and three children respectively. These people formed the nucleus of my father's side of my biological family.

Unfortunately, my mother was not as forthcoming in discussing her side of the family. Like my relationship with my adoptive family, her relationships with her parents and siblings had been strained by the responsibilities that were placed on her shoulders throughout her childhood. She still carried some resentment from it. Although she knew that she was one-eighth Blackfoot Indian by blood, she offered little more about her heritage. I decided not to press the subject. She would talk more about it when she was ready.

All of the Umling relatives I talked to answered each of my questions freely and taught me everything they knew about my biological family and cultural heritage. Within subsequent weeks, I made arrangements with my parents for a Thanksgiving reunion at my mother's home in Killeen. However, before I could focus my energies on my impending reunion, I had to sort through my own thoughts about everything I had learned and fulfill my promise to my adoptive mother. She could no longer interfere in my relationship with my birth family, and it was time to tell her what I had found.

# The Rest of the Story?

I may never know what really happened during my adoption, but the information I obtained from my search and my birth mother's explanation provided some insight into the odd circumstances that appeared to surround it. Before calling my adoptive mother, I wanted to see if I could finally understand what might have happened during that period of my life and come to terms with it. Now that I had found my biological family, I didn't want to fight or argue with my adoptive mother over events from the past that could never be changed.

Obviously, I was not the "unwanted" child that I had been led to believe that I was. It was also apparent that my adoptive parents knew much more about my background and the circumstances surrounding my adoption than they had ever revealed to me. Great-Aunt Sue knew how I was named even though she was not remotely involved in my adoption. The only way she could have known that information was through my adoptive parents. What's more, she remembered that my adoptive parents knew even more information about me. I now had good reason to believe her side of the story. My adoptive mother had taken great effort to make sure that her long-time friends wouldn't say anything to me, as though there was something unspoken to hide. I knew that my adoptive mother would never admit to her deception and lies, so I needed to see if I could understand the situation on my own.

The critical piece of information my birth mother provided was my father's efforts to retrieve both Kathy *and* me from the state. In a normal adoption process (as I have come to understand it), the state is responsible for obtaining a signed petition from *both* biological parents. Once both biological parents have signed the petition, their custody rights are legally severed and the adoption can be processed cleanly. If only one parent can't be located (as the state initially believed to be the situation in my case), the adoption can still be processed, but the adoptive parents cannot be awarded a final adoption decree until the "missing" biological parent has been given adequate notice and opportunity to reclaim the child. The final decree is a court order that legally severs the biological family's parental rights and confers full legal custody to the adoptive family. According to New Hampshire law, my biological father had a one-year period from the date of relinquishment within which to announce his parental rights and request custody of me before a final adoption decree could be issued to the Smiths.

However, when my birth mother called the caseworker to request custody of me, she was apparently never informed of my father's legal right to intervene in the adoption process. The state also never made any attempt to secure my father's signature on the adoption petition even though he had made his presence and intentions known by regaining custody of my sister, Kathy. My birth parents never knew that they had any right to stop the adoption process after my mother signed the petition, and they didn't have the financial resources to seek the legal counsel they would have needed to understand and exercise their rights. They simply accepted the caseworker's carefully worded statement, which was valid *only* for my biological mother. It was a clever and clearly intentional oversight that favored the state's control over my custody.

It is my belief, although I have no way to *prove* it, that the New Hampshire Department of Health and Human Services fully realized that my biological father's parental rights could compromise my adoption process. Since my adoption, there have been many high-profile cases of this nature throughout the country, including the now famous "Baby Jessica" case in the late 1980s and the more recent "Baby Sam" case decided by the Alabama Supreme Court in November 2000. In both of these highly publicized and embarrassing cases, custody of the adoptive child was eventually awarded to the biological parent, but only after a lengthy court battle.

I believe that the Department of Health and Human Services knew that such a battle could have been waged over my adoption in 1962. Therefore, I think that the responsible state officials may have undertaken extraordinary efforts to expedite the processing of my adoption case in order to issue my final decree *before* my biological father had an opportunity to understand his rights and intervene in my adoption proceedings. This scenario provides a possible explanation for the waiver of my psychological evaluation (and other standard procedures) as noted in my adoption history. It also might explain why I received no record of the background check on my adoptive family. In their efforts to expedite my case, the background check might have been waived or never fully completed. Finally, this scenario offers a simple explanation of why Cindy had gone to such efforts to dissuade and discourage me from searching, even though she had been more helpful in past cases. Larry referred to such "compromised" adoption cases as "black files." Cindy would have instantly known that my records were sealed as a black file and made every effort on behalf of the agency to make sure the irregularities in my case would not come to light. All along, she was protecting the *state's* privacy interests—not my birth mother's.

Furthermore, I believe that my adoptive parents were at least partially informed about the irregularities surrounding my case. My adoptive mother clearly knew how I was named as though she had talked directly to my foster mother. The foster mother might have known a great deal about my family, especially if she was the same foster mother who was caring for Kathy around the time that I was born. To me, it makes perfect sense to believe that she was. My adoptive mother obviously knew more information about me that she worked hard to keep secret over the years. The fact that she talked to her close friends about it suggests to me that it was more than just casual information. These friends also may have known the truth about her brother, which demonstrates her willingness to confide in them with her most personal and disturbing secrets. In fact, she may have eventually discovered that one of my brothers had later married into her family, which might have caused her concern that my biological family would be possible and perhaps easy to find, if I ever learned their name. Clearly, the information she sought to hide from me caused her some distress, or she wouldn't have taken such bold and deliberate steps to keep it secret and to talk about it only in the strictest of confidence with her closest friends. She also knew her knowledge would be very helpful in my search. After all, she did send my final decree to me, which clearly suggests that she was not concerned about giving me access to information that she knew would *not* be helpful in my search.

I also believe that my adoptive mother knew that my biological parents had tried to get me back. My adoptive mother was always afraid that strangers would kidnap me and my sister, Jeanette. When I was a young child, she was very reluctant to allow me to spend nights at my friends' houses and would not even consider letting me walk to the village school, which was less than a mile from home. I always attributed her overprotective behavior to a general paranoia of people. However, I began to rethink my position on the issue when my biological mother told me what the caseworker had said when she requested custody of me. According to my mother, the caseworker specifically told her they would place me where she would never be able to find me. That statement alone suggests to me that the caseworker feared that my birth parents might try to take me back. It also reflected the level of fear that they had over the looming custody battle that could arise. Perhaps the caseworker had also communicated that fear to my adoptive mother, thereby contributing to her overly protective and generally paranoid behavior during my early years.

I realize that many of my conclusions are based on circumstantial evidence and supposition regardless of how carefully I built them and how incredibly consistent they were with the emerging facts. As long as my adoption records remain sealed by the Department of Health and Human Services, I may never know the full truth about my placement. All I can say for certain is that there are many unanswered questions and suspicious circumstances surrounding my adoption case. I also know that my adoptive parents knew more information than they ever revealed, and they deliberately lied to me about many facets of my background and records. My conclusions represent my best effort to reconcile the unusual evidence I collected during my search with my birth mother's story, which she told me long before she knew about any of the irregularities I had discovered. Some of my conclusions may not be entirely correct, but I would be happy to entertain New Hampshire's side of the story, if it ever desires to set the record straight. Somehow, though, I doubt that it will *ever* choose to do so. After all, what possible benefit would that serve *them*?

## *Ultimatum*

Once I was satisfied that my reunion was secured and that I understood the circumstances surrounding my adoption, I no longer feared my adoptive mother's reactions or interference. It was time to fulfill my promise to her and determine what role *she* wanted to play in my future. On August 23, 1998, I called her for the first time since May, when my search began. Once again, I was nervous about making the call.

Our initial conversation was cordial, but not much more than that. I told her I had found my biological family and had made successful contact with them. Her voice over the phone gave no hint of her emotional reaction to my news. Her remarks were trite and formal, reflecting her overwhelming disappointment in me. Her lack of emotion alone was revealing, as it did not seem to surprise her in the least to learn that my biological family was completely intact. This reinforced my conclusions that she knew a lot more than she ever revealed. I also explained everything I had learned about my cultural and medical histories, but she seemed coldly disinterested. She never even asked me how I felt about it all. She listened patiently, but I could sense that she wasn't really receiving it very well. I'm sure she felt embarrassed by the full exposure of her previous lies.

About halfway through the conversation, I decided that I needed to make her understand my feelings about adoption, if I was ever going to convince her that there was room in my life for both of my families, biological and adoptive. I began by explaining why my medical history was so important to me. My search had revealed possible causes for virtually all of my known medical conditions, including my irregular heartbeat, my eye problems, and my blackout spells. I explained how I felt that this information was important for Michael's future health. She clearly understood and accepted the legitimacy of my need to know in that respect.

I also tried to make her understand my feelings about being the product of two different families. I told her how I felt that both of my families contributed different, but essential, elements of my being. Her contribution was my environment, which helped shape my perception of myself and the world around me. Of course, I avoided expressing any judgment on the quality of that influence. I also explained that the genetic contribution by my biological family was just as important to me as the environmental influences. My birth family gave me my appearance and health, both of which were critical to my existence and self-awareness. I finally revealed to her how, as an adolescent, my awareness of the physical differences between me and the rest of my adoptive family had made me self-conscious about my appearance. This revelation came as a complete surprise to her, as I had never mentioned it before. Virtually everything I said to her about my feelings was a surprise to her, because no one in my adoptive family ever openly discussed their feelings. Perhaps I had finally made her realize that she was not the only one who had felt hurt by all the circumstances surrounding my adoption.

At this point in the conversation, I could sense that my comments were beginning to affect her general attitude. She became more responsive and inquisitive, as I revealed my feelings and explained the source of my long-standing desires to know about my roots. I then asked her an important question. I wanted to know, from her perspective as a mother, if she felt it was truly possible for her to love all of her children equally, and if she expected each of us to feel equally loved by her. Without even hesitating to think, she said, "Yes, of course." I then asked her why she felt it was impossible for a child to love more than one set of parents equally. She had no answer to that question. At that moment, I truly felt I had finally reached her.

Having disarmed and frustrated her initial objections to my search, our conversation became gradually more interactive, even though she was still clearly reluctant to accept the legitimacy of my birth family. She didn't even want me to give her my biological parents' address or phone number. However, she did eventually begin to ask questions about the medical information I had learned. I answered them to the best of my ability and then gently turned the focus of the discussion to Jeanette and her son. I knew this would be a sensitive topic for her, given the volatile history of their relationship, but the need to know about Jeanette's medical history was much greater than my own.

Although my experiences in the Smith family were no picnic, Jeanette's experiences were many degrees worse, and they had even more tragic impacts on her adult life. While Jeanette did manage to graduate from high school, she was not emotionally or intellectually prepared to assume adult responsibilities. After her graduation, she decided that she wanted to become a cosmetologist. So, Mom and Dad sent her to a beautician's school in Manchester, New Hampshire, the state's largest city. In less than three months, she was failing her classes and threatening to harm other students. For some reason, she slashed the tires of several cars in the school's parking lot and then went to her cousin's apartment (who had agreed to let her live with her while attending school) and slashed all of her cousin's clothes hanging in the closet. Shortly thereafter, the school expelled her and Jeanette began a life on welfare, bouncing from one squalid downtown Manchester apartment to another. Her social circle consisted largely of drug users and alcoholics, and she soon became addicted herself. She was eventually caught shoplifting and given a suspended sentence.

Later, and without explanation, she suddenly moved to Littleton, New Hampshire, the town where she was born in 1963. I never knew the reason why she chose to move there, but I often wondered if she, too, had become curious about her biological roots years before I began my final search. Not long after she moved to Littleton, she was arrested, this time for drunk and disorderly conduct. Perhaps she experienced some of the same feelings of rejection and frustration from the impenetrable secrets surrounding her past as I had. Understanding her cognitive handicap and developmental immaturity as I did, it was a little difficult for me to accept that at face value, but I realize it's not beyond the realm of possibility. After spending a night in jail at the Littleton Police Department, she returned to Manchester.

Within a short time of her return to Manchester, she became pregnant and gave birth to her only son, Collin, in October 1983. Although she would never reveal the name of Collin's father, we all privately concluded that he was a pusher with whom she had traded sex for drugs. Where my own son knew at least one half of his family history, Collin would have neither. His mother was an adoptee like me, and his father was a disreputable ghost from Jeanette's drug circle.

After Collin's birth, Jeanette began to get desperate. She used her son as a tool to get additional welfare aid, which she needed to support her growing drug and alcohol addictions. Soon, Collin became malnourished and ill much of the time. Jeanette would suddenly send him to visit our adoptive mother whenever his condition became critical or the welfare caseworker was scheduled to visit. Jeanette did not want the caseworker to see his condition, because she feared that the caseworker would quickly realize that she was not using her welfare money as it was intended. She also did not want the state to take her son away, as they may have done to her when she was born. It sounded like the games my adoptive father's mother had played with his real father.

Once my adoptive mother nursed Collin back to health, Jeanette would always demand his return. Eventually, the drugs and alcohol got the best of Jeanette's marginal mental health, and she attempted suicide—not once, but twice. The state tried to place her in counseling, but she usually refused to attend and was generally uncooperative and abusive on the few occasions when she did. The counseling staff eventually gave up on her and dumped her back on the streets, where she resumed her pattern of petty crimes and misuse of welfare funds to support her addictions. She had been in and out of trouble with the law ever since.

During the worst period of Jeanette's dependency (if any one period can be objectively classified as worst) my adoptive mother began a determined effort to persuade Jeanette to relinquish custody of Collin. She considered Jeanette to be an unfit mother, so she wanted Aunt Brenda's son, Carl, and his wife to adopt him. Carl's wife also believed that she was unable to bear children, and my adoptive mother wanted to keep Collin in the family, so she could maintain her connection to him. At that time, she had no other grandchildren. She knew that if Collin was ever placed for general adoption by the state, she would lose contact with him forever, just as had occurred with my own biological family. Perhaps my adoptive mother even feared being treated the same way she always knew that my birth mother had been treated.

After months of constant pressure, Jeanette finally conceded to my adoptive mother's wishes. She signed the adoption consent form, allowing Carl to adopt her son. Custody of Collin was given to Carl and his wife on January 28, 1986, the day the space shuttle Challenger exploded during liftoff. Later, Jeanette got into trouble with the law again, this time for pick-pocketing. Embarrassed by her growing record of immoral and illegal activities, my adoptive mother eventually bought Jeanette and her best friend (who also happened to be her partner in crime at that time) one-way bus tickets to Minnesota in 1988 just to get them out of New Hampshire. After all, now that Collin was no longer in Jeanette's custody, my adoptive mother had no further need for her. I heard that she later married and bounced around to several Great Plains states, but I never saw her or spoke to her again.

Given Jeanette's history of mental instability and other emotional problems, I believed that knowledge of her medical and genetic history might someday be important for Collin or his future children. Using my own recently discovered medical history as an example, I tried to impress this need upon my adoptive mother. I tried to convince her that, if she really cared about Collin's future health, she would give me the basic information about Jeanette that I needed to begin a search for her biological family. Laura and Larry had already agreed to help me search, and I assured my adoptive mother that she would not have to reveal the information to Collin until it was needed or until he was old enough to understand it. To me, it seemed the only sensible, responsible, and morally right thing to do. At the time we talked about it, it appeared that my adoptive mother was inclined to agree. However, she said she wanted to discuss it with Carl first. I agreed to her terms, and she said she would call me back with an answer.

Overall, I felt that my conversation with her went very well. We had not argued, and she had agreed to call me. That made it feel like a double success. I couldn't remember the last time that my adoptive mother had called me. It was very rare for her to do so because she didn't want to condone our move away from New England. In fact, she even failed to call me or even send a card on several of my birthdays after we moved south. What an irony. My biological mother had always thought about me on my birthdays even though she had never seen me and didn't know who I was. However, my adoptive mother who supposedly "chose" to adopt me could neglect to call her only son on his birthday even though she had known me for all but a few months of my life. However, based on the evolution of our telephone conversation, I was actually beginning to think that I might be able to reach her in a new way. Perhaps my search had grabbed her attention in a way I had never been able to do before. Maybe I could really encourage her to change her ways and turn my search and reunion into a success on both sides of my strange and tenuous patchwork family.

I waited two weeks for her to call me before I finally decided to call her again. She said she had meant to call me, but it slipped her mind. That seemed rather hard to believe. At this point in our relationship, she would have to do a lot more to restore my trust. I asked her if she had talked to Carl about searching for Jeanette's biological family. She said she had and that they had decided against it. They felt it would be too damaging to Collin and their family, probably because they had never told him he was adopted and didn't want him to know. In the final analysis, they all decided that it was better to simply risk Collin's future health in order to prevent Jeanette's biological family from interfering in his life.

To me, their assessment of Collin's "best interest" was an indictment of my own search. In their jealous efforts to conceal Collin's past from him, they were condemning him and his heirs to a life without a potentially important medical history. As I knew from my own search experience, failing to search while Jeanette was still alive would effectively prevent Collin from learning that information in the future. My adoptive mother had obviously learned *nothing* from my previous conversation with her.

From my perspective, my adoptive mother had every reason to understand and sympathize with an adoptee's need to know his biological family. First of all, she had gone out of her way to arrange Collin's adoption by Carl, in order to keep him in the family and maintain her relationship with him. She knew that Jeanette couldn't or wouldn't care for him properly, and the state would eventually take him away. She also knew that a standard adoption by the state would make it impossible for her to be a part of his life, just as it had done to my biological parents and me. While she could understand how that loss of contact would affect her, she demonstrated no ability to empathize with my biological parents' loss, even though the circumstances were very similar.

Second, my adoptive mother knew firsthand how her own husband had benefited from his reunion with his biological aunt. She had witnessed a reunion very similar to mine that had no negative impacts on my adoptive father's relationship with his mother, even though it taught him that she had lied to him all his life. My adoptive father never knew his biological father or anyone on that side of his family. Yet only through his reunion with Aunt Sarah was he able to know the truth about his past and establish a rewarding and loving relationship with his father's only remaining relatives. In fact, my adoptive mother and siblings all benefited financially from the reunion, as we all received a share of Aunt Sarah's inheritance, something that they believed was rightfully theirs. Although my adoptive mother accepted that reunion and the inheritance that came with it, she objected to mine.

Finally, as if that wasn't enough, my adoptive mother's family had recently benefited from yet another adoptee reunion. Carl's older brother, Paul, had a daughter by his first wife in the late 1960s. Unfortunately, his marriage ended in a bitter divorce, and Paul lost custody of his daughter. I don't know all the details of that divorce because, as with all other sensitive subjects affecting our family, it was never openly discussed. I was told that Paul was unemployed at the time, and he never paid any child support. His ex-wife remarried a short time later, and her new husband eventually adopted Paul's daughter. Although Paul wanted to contact his daughter, he never had the courage to try.

At some point in the early or mid-1990s, Paul's parents (Aunt Brenda and Uncle Keith) received an unexpected call from their lost granddaughter. She had found them and wanted to establish contact with her father. Like me, she was concerned about her medical history, as she had developed a severe case of asthma, which was a condition she had inherited from Paul. Several months later, they were all successfully reunited and have remained in close contact ever since. In fact, Paul and his parents were all able to be present when Paul's daughter gave birth to his first granddaughter. It was a birth they would have never even known about, had Paul's daughter not decided to search for him.

Although my adoptive mother had all of these adoption lessons to draw upon, she flatly and jealously refused to accept my search and reunion. She didn't even want to hear me talk about my birth family, no matter how sensitively I tried to broach the subject. She felt that I had learned everything I needed to know, and now it was time to put it all behind me. She gave me an ultimatum—come back to her unconditionally or stay with my biological family. That attitude, combined with her refusal to help me research Jeanette's adoption records, made me angry. I was tired of being slapped in the face and manipulated by my adoptive family, and I wasn't going to take any more of it, especially after everything I had discovered about my own adoption process. I became defensive of my position, and my adoptive mother bristled. Our second telephone conversation soon began to degrade into a bitter argument.

At first, my adoptive mother tried to make me feel guilty about my actions, as she had done so many times before. She told me how she had done everything she could to provide a good home and life for me, but she concluded it just wasn't good enough. Of course, this attitude demonstrated little concern for my feelings, even though I had tried hard to explain them in our previous conversation. I was furious at her insinuation, and my legendary temper erupted again.

"No Mom," I responded mockingly. "It wasn't you; it was me. I just couldn't be the son you really wanted. I was an ungrateful and unappreciative child. No matter how hard I tried to please you and do what was expected of me, I just didn't have what it took..."

"Cut that out!" she interrupted angrily. She knew immediately what I was doing.

"Right back at you, Mom, right back at you! You've taken me on that guilt trip too many times in the past. I'm not going along for the ride this time."

"*Well!*" she said with a sneer of contempt, "I guess your biological mother should feel glad that she never had to face any real hardship."

"Oh yeah, that's right, Mom. My birth mother never had any hardship in her life at all. She was just forced to leave school in the seventh grade to take care of her family; lost her husband and faced having to raise three children on her own; lost one of her sons to adoption because she didn't think she could care for him; and lost three homes because she couldn't afford to keep them. No, she never had to face any real hardships like you did. In fact, I'm sure she'd agree with you completely, and that's probably the biggest difference between you and her. You see, she realizes that, despite everything she's had to overcome in her own life, there are many other people who've had it worse. I really don't think you've ever tried to think that way about your own life." Again, she had no response to that explanation.

I continued to lash out at her about my childhood frustrations. She had successfully tapped into my anxieties about the past, and I threw them back at her, one by one. By the time our argument ended, I was exhausted, disappointed with myself for letting her get to me, and finally convinced that my relationship with her could never be repaired. I had found my biological family, but only at the expense of my adoptive family. It was another strange twist of fate, considering all the fears I initially had that my reunion with my birth family would ultimately end that way.

That conversation with my adoptive mother was deeply disturbing to me. It consumed my mind frequently for more than a week. I was furious with myself for letting her make me feel guilty about searching. I had sincerely hoped that I would be able to salvage or even improve my relationship with her, but I knew that I could never accept her unconditional terms. She would never meet me halfway. Finding my biological family was the most rewarding and fulfilling event in my life, and I could never turn them away simply to serve my adoptive mother's irrational and selfish insecurities.

Nevertheless, I couldn't decide what to do about it. I still had a few supporters within my adoptive family that I didn't want to lose, even though I couldn't talk to my adoptive mother and sisters. In reality, those few relationships represented all that was left of my adoptive family. On the other hand, there was my flourishing new relationship with my biological family to consider. With every new contact I made, I was met with unconditional acceptance and support. Within the first two months of my reunion with them, I had spoken to everyone in my immediate family, and I was truly overwhelmed by their generous outpouring of affection, compassion, and support. In fact, I soon found myself in continuous daily contact, either by telephone, e-mail, or letter, with one or more of my biological relatives for a full eighteen months! I had never felt so valued in all my life, especially when I had done nothing of consequence to earn it. After all, they had no compelling reason to accept me, other than their own sincere concerns for my feelings. In my mind, I already owed my biological family a debt of gratitude that I felt I might never be able to repay.

For more than two weeks, I battled with my conscience to resolve the dilemma. I never wanted to choose between my biological and adoptive families. In fact, I really didn't know *how* to choose. However, my adoptive mother seemed to leave me with no alternative. She expected me to satisfy my curiosity then close the door on my biological family and return to her, as if they had never existed. I firmly believed that she would accept nothing less, but how could I even consider doing that in all good conscience? I couldn't be that cruel or inconsiderate to the only family I had ever known that had unconditionally accepted me as a legitimate member. I felt trapped within an adoptive family that never gave me any real sense of self-worth as they tried to tear me from a birth family that made me feel like a valued member. My mind eventually returned to the question my executive director asked me when I returned from my search. Now that I had found all these people, what was I going to do with them?

When I could no longer tolerate or resolve the debate that raged in my mind, I turned to the local birth mother who had counseled me during my search. Her name was Charlotte, and she had been my guiding light throughout my reunion. I needed to talk to someone who could understand my biological mother's feelings, and she was the best source of advice that I knew. I told her about my recent telephone conversation with my adoptive mother and the torment I faced because of it. She knew all about my reunion with my birth family and the strong bond that was beginning to form between my biological parents and me. Although I would not meet them until Thanksgiving, I had logged well over twenty hours in telephone calls with them within the first two months of my first contact call. We had also exchanged letters and photos on several occasions. As a birth mother who wanted to rebuild a relationship with the daughter she had relinquished, I wanted to know what Charlotte thought about my own birth mother's feelings. In other words, did she think it could be possible that my birth mother would truly want me to be meaningful part of her family again after all these years?

Charlotte knew my feelings well, and she could sense the full dilemma of my question. Although she had never spoken to my birth mother, she felt as though she knew her from all of the stories that I told her about our telephone conversations and letters. She knew intuitively that my birth mother would not have revealed the truth about the past to my brothers and sisters or maintained frequent contact with me, unless she truly wanted me to be a meaningful part of her life. Charlotte also reminded me of the comments I had received from several of my relatives regarding the improvement in my birth mother's mood and disposition that they noticed because I found her. She said she didn't know my mother personally, but she did know those feelings. She told me how she experienced the same feelings of relief and fulfillment when the daughter she relinquished finally found her. It was as though the missing piece of her heart had been returned to her.

"There's just something about the bond between a mother and her natural children," she explained, her eyes lost deep in her own thoughts. "I don't know how to describe it to you, but even if you think you understand it, it's still stronger than you realize. When I placed my daughter for adoption, I thought it was the best thing I could do for her. Her father would never acknowledge his relationship to her because it threatened his marriage and his position in society. I wanted to give her a better life–something I knew I could never do by myself. At the time, it seemed like the ultimate expression of love that I could give her. I never gave any thought to the emptiness it would leave behind. It was like I'd lost a part of me that could never be replaced. I carried that wound for years, and when she finally found me, I thought it would heal. My heart was filled with joy and anticipation." I caught the distinctive glint of tears pooling in her eyes, reflecting the humbling depth and wisdom of her experience.

She hesitated only for a moment as she blinked her tears away and struggled to maintain her composure and then continued. "But I soon learned that she was bitter with me for having sent her away. She just couldn't understand why I had relinquished her, but kept her sister and brothers. The gift I thought I had given her had become the source of her discontent and anger with me. Now she won't even speak to me anymore, and the wound I carried all those years has only grown deeper with time. If, as you say, you truly have room in your heart for your birth mother, please don't let her face the eternal loss I have to bear."

Charlotte knew from everything I had told her that my mother never wanted to let me go and that she was acting out of desperation and concern for my well-being when she placed me for adoption. She also knew how much my birth mother's acceptance meant to me, and she encouraged me to talk to her about it. She felt that my mother probably wanted me to be a part of her family once again, but that she wouldn't feel it was her place to ask me to accept her as my mother. Charlotte had faced the same dilemma with her own daughter. She had dearly wanted her daughter to accept her as her mother because that acceptance would be her absolution. However, Charlotte knew that the decision to place her daughter for adoption was hers and hers alone, so Charlotte didn't feel she had the right to ask. If her daughter had asked Charlotte to be her mother again, she would have accepted in an instant. But she never did, and now that opportunity was lost forever. Charlotte couldn't speak for my birth mother, but she firmly believed that my mother would eagerly want me back. All I had to do was tell her how I felt and ask.

Charlotte's advice meant a lot to me, and her guidance throughout my search had never been wrong. In fact, I suddenly began to realize that I had turned to Charlotte for advice as though she was my surrogate adoptive mother. The more I thought about it, the more I realized that I established a long track record of doing just that—using my older friends as surrogate adoptive parents ever since I left home for college in 1980. Dr. Ofslager, my undergraduate advisor, was only the first of many close friendships I had made with men and women at least twenty years older than me, to whom I always turned when I needed advice. When I attended the University of California at Berkeley, I turned to Allan Jacobs (my graduate advisor) and Kaye Bock (the graduate secretary for the planning department). Throughout my college and early adult years, I had sought advice and moral support from Great-Aunt Sue, who I often considered to be my surrogate adoptive mother figure. When I began work at the Lakes Region Planning Commission, I sought advice and moral support from Collin Morris, the agency's semi-retired transportation planner, and Jim Klinger, the agency's draftsman and Best Man at my wedding. After I moved to Vermont, I turned to Jan Miller, my next-door neighbor and Avi Fancher, one of the senior members of the Middlebury Area Singles club I established. In Macon, I developed a strong friendship with Bob Montague, a lieutenant colonel at Robins Air Force Base and fellow member of the Lake Wildwood board of directors. In LaGrange, I often turned to Lonny Newsome, the city's chief building inspector. During my long tenure in Anniston, I had several older friends I turned to for guidance, including Charlotte; Corine Dean (the Goodwater, AL city clerk) and her husband, LaRue; Remel Williams (president of the Cherokee County Chamber of Commerce); and Earl Chase (chairman of the Lincoln, Alabama Planning Commission). All of them knew of my search and reunion as well.

No matter where I had moved as an adult, I had sought the friendship and moral support of an older mother or father figure. I have continued to do so today. My sudden awareness of that consistent, historic pattern made me realize that I had subconsciously stopped regarding my adoptive mother and father as my parent figures after I left home for college. My adoptive family raised me, but it was not what I turned to for advice. I just never had the courage to acknowledge it—until now.

For the first time since my search began, I was seriously considering the idea of changing my name and rejoining my biological family. It was a difficult thought to consider, because it would require many changes. After thinking carefully about it for several more days, I approached my executive director to tell him what I was considering. I wanted to know how he felt about it, as I was afraid that some of the local officials we worked with might think it was strange or indecent. I was concerned that they might privately question my judgment or rationality, which could have a negative impact on the agency's image. However, he thought that should be the least of my concerns. He felt I should do whatever I felt was right, but he reminded me that it would be a lot of work to change my name on all of my records, and I might be working on it for years to come.

I knew it would not be an easy task, but I did feel it was the right thing to do. After all, I was bearing the name of a family to which I had never felt a strong connection. As long as I maintained that link, I knew I might never fully overcome the anxieties I harbored from my childhood. That name would serve as a constant reminder of a past that tormented me, but that I could never repair or resolve. My adoptive family would never want to acknowledge or discuss it. All they could bear to do was hide from it all.

It was time for my life to change yet again—to face the lingering guilt and put it behind me deliberately and decisively. Only this time, it would be the biggest change of all. Not only would my perspective on the world change, but so would my identity within it. However, before I could discuss the subject with my birth parents, I needed to ask Barb and Michael how they felt about it.

When I finally decided to discuss the idea with Barb, I fully expected her to hit the ceiling. She had already demonstrated considerable understanding, support, and encouragement throughout my search and reunion, but the thought of changing my identity to become part of a family I had never known almost seemed too much to ask of her. If I did decide to do it, both she and Michael would need to change their names as well. However, her actual reaction was much more reserved than I had anticipated. Although I had considered it privately for a few weeks, I think she had a good sense of the direction in which my life was moving. She now had a better understanding and appreciation of the strained relationship between my adoptive family and me, and she had already sensed its gradual demise. She also recognized the growing bond between my biological family and me, which became more and more apparent every day. There was no denying the acceptance I received from them and the peace of mind it gave me. In all reality, I was already becoming a part of my biological family, and it only grew stronger with every call, every letter, and every e-mail message I exchanged with them. I was now a part of my adoptive family quite literally in name only.

Barb's initial reaction was that it seemed unusual for a man to change his last name, but her main concerns about the name change were Michael's reaction and the uniqueness of my biological parents' last name. After all, Smith was a fairly common name. Umling sounded quite odd by comparison. While Barb took comfort in having a simple common-sounding name like Smith, I had always realized the problems it caused. I had never lived in a community (large or small) where there wasn't another David Smith, and I was forever receiving mail and telephone calls intended for another person who had the same name. I thought it would be nice for a change to have a name that couldn't be confused with anyone else. Of course, I also reminded Barb that Umling was the only name she would have known, if I had never been adopted. It just sounded strange to us now because we had never heard it before. To everyone else—aside from the friends who had known us for years—it would just be another different name. Having worked in as many different banks as she had over the course of her career, Barb had been exposed to many strange names, but she had never judged anyone based on the sound of a name. It took a few days for her to become comfortable with the idea, but she eventually decided she could live with it. After all, she knew how much it meant to me.

The issue of Michael's reaction was a different story. At the time, he was only six years old. The idea was quite a shock to him, even though I knew it would be easier on him to change his name before he advanced too far along in school. He was afraid his friends would laugh at him, because the new name sounded strange. I didn't want to force him to accept something he really didn't want, but I also realized that I had an opportunity to give him something that I never had— a family that fully embraced us and a heritage that was truly and rightfully his. Unlike me, Michael now had an opportunity to grow up knowing his roots and medical history. His only connection to my adoptive family was through my past experiences with them and our last name. They had never made any effort to spend time with him, and he had no idea who they were. When I showed him a picture of his adoptive grandmother, he couldn't recognize her or tell me who she was. How could he? After all, he had seen her only three times in his life and only once since he was six months old. After my last telephone conversation with my adoptive mother, I seriously doubted that he would ever see her again. To me, it seemed senseless for him to carry forward a last name that would have no meaning to him, but would forever remind him of my broken adoption. I at least wanted him to have the clarity of identity that I never had.

I eventually decided to seek his teacher's advice. I told her my story and what I planned to do. She agreed that it would be easier on Michael to change his name now than it would be when he was in the elementary grades. She told me that most of Michael's friends knew him by his first name only. First-graders were not required to write their last names on their schoolwork. To help reduce his anxieties, she agreed to discuss the issue of my adoption search, reunion, and name change in her class, so that his friends would understand why it was happening.

After the teacher's discussion in class, Michael's attitude was more receptive. He now knew that his friends wouldn't laugh at him, but he was still a little apprehensive about the new name. At first, we suggested that he could use a hyphenated last name (Smith-Umling). However, that seemed even more awkward and difficult for him to learn. Besides, everyone might assume that Barb's maiden name was Smith rather than Hitchcock. I also felt that it was inappropriate for him to keep my adoptive family's name, since it was contrary to my reasons for considering the name change in the first place. I also knew that my adoptive family would want nothing more to do with me or my family when they learned what I planned to do. After a few days of discussion with Michael about his feelings, he dropped his objections, although he still wasn't eager for the change. Fortunately, some sixteen years later, it is not something he even thinks about today. At that point, I decided it was time to discuss it with my biological parents.

On the evening of September 30, 1998, I called my birth parents to seek their approval of my decision to rejoin my biological family and assume their last name. As usual, my mother answered the phone. Following Charlotte's advice, I began by telling her how much her acceptance and support meant to me. I was careful not to discuss the gradual demise of my adoptive family relationship, because I didn't want her approval to be driven by any sympathy she might feel for my situation. I wanted to know that her acceptance was from her heart.

After talking with her for a few minutes, I came straight to the point. I asked her if she or my father would object to me changing my last name to Umling. I expected to hear a moment of silence, but her answer was immediate. She said she was proud to know that I wanted to restore my last name. In fact, she admitted that she and my father had recently discussed how they could ask me if I wanted to change my name. Her approval was a great relief to me and further validation that my reunion was a complete success. Of course, my father wanted to talk to Barb about it, just to make sure she was in full agreement. My parents recognized that this was a bold step. In fact, there was very little precedent for it in the scope of adoptee reunions. I told my parents that I would talk to a local attorney to see what would be involved in the process.

I contacted a local attorney who I had met through my work at the regional planning commission. She said that name changes for Barb and me were simple procedures that could be handled through the county probate court. However, she revealed that she was an adoptee as well, and she knew that certain states allowed adult adoptions. This provision of law made it possible for any adult to legally adopt another adult, as long as both parties consented. Although the idea of an adult adoption sounds odd or unnecessary, its primary purpose is to allow adult caregivers to adopt disabled or otherwise dependent adults who have no living relatives to care for them or to help them manage their finances. I never realized that adults could be adopted, but it sounded like an intriguing process. It was much quicker and simpler than a child adoption, and it might provide a way for me to be formally and legally readopted into my biological family, thereby effectively reversing or annulling my original illegitimate and failed adoption.

According to my attorney, an adult adoption had to be processed in the state within which the adopting parents currently reside. At that time, my parents were living in Killeen, Texas. We checked the Texas statutes and, sure enough, Texas law allowed adult adoptions. When I learned the news, I immediately called my birth parents and they both agreed. I was to be officially readopted by my biological parents.

To facilitate the process and file the court petition, I hired an attorney in Austin, Texas. He agreed to represent me, as I could not arrange a special trip to Texas for the final adoption hearing. The attorney helped my parents file the petition and, after a brief hearing before a local judge, I was officially readopted by my biological parents at 8:37 a.m. on December 9, 1998. My official name change was processed as part of my adoption. My life had now come full circle, and I was once again a legally recognized member of my original family. Ironically,

I became the only nonadoptee I have ever known who was adopted in two states. It was truly one of the greatest and most profound moments of my life.

Shortly after my readoption process was completed, we filed petitions at the Calhoun County Courthouse in Anniston to change both Barb's and Michael's last names. By early 1999, the transition was complete, and we have been known as the Umlings ever since.

As I had expected, the news of my readoption put an abrupt end to my relationship with my adoptive mother and sisters. Unfortunately, I had to accept the fact that I could never maintain a relationship with both of my families. Most of my immediate adoptive relatives were extremely bitter about my actions. In fact, my cousin Paul wrote me a five-page letter, printed entirely in bold-faced type, which accused me of being driven by blind emotion into an irrational and arrogant course of action that I would regret for the rest of my life. He chastised me bitterly throughout the letter and demanded that I retract the adoption and rejoin my adoptive family, as though that would somehow affirm their love for me. He even told me that, if I refused to comply, I should stay "dead" and never speak to any of them again. He also suggested that he would conduct a funeral service on my behalf to help my adoptive family deal with their grief. His strong reaction actually surprised me, since he was the one who had benefited from a similar reunion with the daughter he lost to adoption.

However, Paul's letter never bothered me. By that time, I had expected a harsh response from my adoptive family. Actually, I felt comforted by his plan to conduct a funeral service for me for two reasons. First of all, it might indeed be a good way for my adoptive family to deal with the grief and frustration I had caused them. I never wanted my relationship with them to end this way, but my adoptive mother left me no meaningful choice. Second, I felt honored by the thought, since Paul's mother (Aunt Brenda) had pretended for years that her own brother (Craig) was dead without ever giving him the dignity of a funeral. To me, his suggestion was the first sign of true respect and dignity that my adoptive family had shown for me in many years. When I calmly discussed it with him and reminded him of his own reunion with his daughter, his tone changed, and he actually became one of my supporters. We maintained contact for several more years after my readoption.

I can't say that I was pleased with the ending of my adoptive family relationship, but I was satisfied that I had done the best that I could to manage and salvage it. I had hoped that I would be able to have a relationship with both sides of my family, but my adoptive family refused to permit it. Needless to say, my biological family was stunned by my adoptive family's reaction. They never had any intention of interfering in my adoptive family relationship, but they also didn't agree that my continued relationship with my adoptive family was a legitimate reason to exclude them from my life. In the end, my adoptive mother's reaction merely created the scenario she had always feared the most. By demanding my undivided loyalty, affection, and attention, she inevitably drove me away from her.

Fortunately, at least four of my former adoptive relatives chose to maintain contact with me for several years after my reunion and readoption, including my cousin Maria, her brother Paul, and my great-aunt Sue. In fact, I continued to exchange frequent letters with my great-aunt Sue for another four years, as if nothing had ever happened. Over the passing years, our communications grew more infrequent, and we eventually decided it was best to end our contact. After all, they still had to live with the rest of my adoptive family and faced being torn between me and my immediate family, which would never truly understand or accept what I had done. The knowledge that those remaining relationships continued would also make it more difficult for my immediate family to put the issue behind them.

Our differences were ultimately irreconcilable, just as our often petty and bitter arguments had always been. However, to me, my ability to maintain a continued relationship with the more understanding members of my adoptive family—even if for only a few years—was proof that I had the integrity and determination to make my adoptive family relationship work, if they had only given me a fair chance. In the final analysis, my adoptive mother's stubborn refusal to accept my biological family and my decision to make them a meaningful part of my life forced me to make a choice that I never asked to make. Once I had made that choice, it was time to move on with my life, just as I had done so many times before. Sometimes, you just don't have the amount of control over the direction of your life that you wish you could have or feel that you should. As I have said many times before and firmly believe, your personal character should not be judged solely by the consequences of the difficult decisions you make in life, but by the integrity and responsibility you demonstrate by making difficult decisions in recognition of the potential consequences. I had demonstrated my personal integrity to the best of my ability. At least I didn't come up empty handed.

# Part V: A New Chapter Begins

My reunion with my birth family had a profound impact on my self-image and my outlook on life. Just learning that I shared so many behavior patterns and physical characteristics with my biological relatives made me feel more comfortable with those aspects in me. It was reassuring to know that the traits that once made me different from my adoptive family were the common threads that linked me to my biological family. That feeling of connection made it easier for me to accept those characteristics, where before they had been the source of my social isolation. It also provided a context for my son's features and appearance that made the connections with my side of the family more apparent. I soon found it easier to let go of the pain caused by my childhood memories, and I became a more relaxed and happier person. Finally, I had found a source of contentment in my life, and I was ready to let it consume me.

It was truly amazing to learn how many personality and behavioral characteristics I shared with my biological family. Of course, the physical resemblance was more than enough to make me happy. However, it was the little things that often took me by surprise. For example, in talking to my mother one day, I happened to mention that I had a life-long periodic interest in exploring Australia. My wife had heard me talk about it for years. After I mentioned it to her, my mother told me how she had always heard my father talk about his own desire to visit Australia. While many of these similarities may mean nothing more than simple coincidences to the casual observer, they were very comforting to me. I could look back at my adoptive family and find so many differences that it often seemed we had almost nothing in common. My wife has often noted that my adoptive family and I were like oil and water. It gave me a real sense of security and connection to see so many of my own traits and characteristics reflected in my biological family. Suddenly, I didn't feel so alone or disconnected anymore.

As my reunion with and eventual reintegration into my biological family progressed, I became increasingly comfortable with my new identity and perspective on the world around me. While I didn't start meeting my blood relatives face-to-face until October of 1998, I had introduced myself to 88 members of my biological family within the following year. I had also talked to scores of additional relatives over the telephone, including several distant cousins living in Germany. In fact, I have met or spoken to more relatives in my birth family than existed in my entire adoptive family, and I still have many more blood relatives to meet. I may never be able to meet them all. The enthusiastic acceptance we received with each new introduction also made it easier for Barb and Michael to accept our new relatives and feel like legitimate members of the family. After several years, I began to compile my family genealogy and managed to be the first person to discover and verify the connections between the American and German Umlings.

Ironically, my reunion was not an end to my search process. As I began meeting my biological relatives, I learned that I was not the only family member who had been lost to adoption. Eventually, I was asked to help find a lost blood relative from the other side of the adoption fence. For the first time since my reunion began, I was given an opportunity to return something of value to my birth family for all of the love and affection they would extend to me throughout my many introductions. Although I had decided what I wanted to do with my newfound relatives, I had no idea of where it would all lead. Oddly enough, I would soon learn that my new life would take me back to where it all began, 37 years earlier. That final journey back to New Hampshire would, in some small but meaningful measure, help me gain the personal redemption I had sought for years.

# Reunion and Beyond

During the earliest months of my reunion, contact with my newfound relatives was limited to telephone calls, e-mails, and letters. Our phone bill became astronomical, as I spent hours talking to them on the telephone. Although I was understandably anxious to meet my biological relatives, virtually all of them lived more than 500 miles away and most of them lived 750 or more miles away. Since I had used a significant chunk of my available vacation time in late June and early July to conduct my search, I couldn't just jump in the car and drive off to visit them. However, as I received more and more pictures of my biological relatives, I knew I eventually had to meet them in person. So, I made arrangements in early September for a Thanksgiving weekend trip to Killeen, TX to meet my biological parents and sister, Carolyn. I then began making plans to visit as many of my other relatives as I could.

I soon discovered that at least one of my blood relatives, Stan Umling lived within 150 miles of our home in Oxford. He was my first cousin and one of my uncle Eddie's twelve children. He lived in Alpharetta, Georgia, roughly 25 miles north of downtown Atlanta. Because he lived close by, I was able to arrange a trip to meet him over the Columbus Day weekend. As it happened, the day we visited him, October 11, was his birthday.

When we arrived in his neighborhood, it took us a while to find his home. Stan lived in a new subdivision, and many of the houses looked alike. We pulled into several driveways trying to locate his home. However, when I saw my cousin emerge from one of the garages as we were driving past, I knew we had found the right house.

Stan was about my height and possessed the same dark blonde hair as me. We both had husky builds, large hands, and similar facial features, especially the now infamous Umling nose. It was a trait I had seen many times in the family pictures I received. Some of my relatives had said that they knew as soon as they saw my picture that I was an Umling because of my nose. Never in my life had I experienced such an immediate feeling of familiarity in a person I had never met. It was a wonderful, reaffirming feeling. At that moment, I truly felt like an Umling for the first time, and I knew I had made the right decision when I chose to be readopted into my biological family.

Ironically, I was the first of my parent's children that Stan had ever met. My father's military career had kept him away from his brother and sisters for much of his adult life, so most of their children had never met one another. I was one of the first of my generation in the family to break through the barrier of time and distance that had been built over the years. Actually, the fact that Stan had never met any of my brothers or sisters made it much easier for him to accept me as his cousin without reservation. From both of our perspectives, it was as if my adoption had never occurred. Fortunately, I had brought pictures of my brothers and sisters, and he shared with me pictures of his own family. It was very apparent from the pictures he showed me that I closely resembled several of his brothers and his father as well.

Michael really enjoyed the visit, too. He met and played with his second cousin, Doris, who was about his age. Like Michael, Doris was an only child at that time, and she rarely had friends or family to play with. Michael and Doris had such a good time together that Doris began crying when it was time for us to leave.

Stan's wife, Candice, was a charming and attractive woman, with short, dark, blonde hair, and soft features. She had a gregarious personality that was immediately likeable. At first, our conversation was quite superficial, but Candice soon revealed that her life had been touched by adoption as well. Candice was a birth mother. She had given birth to a son before she met Stan. At that time in her life, she had no confidence in herself and no aspirations for her future. She also knew that the man who had fathered her son would never marry her. She didn't want to relinquish her child, but she also didn't want to deprive him of a happy childhood and a good future. During her pregnancy, she confided in a friend, who was the head of a private adoption service in Georgia and a well-known figure in the adoption industry. During the course of her pregnancy, this friend earned her trust, and Candice eventually agreed to allow the woman to adopt her son.

Although Candice agreed to relinquish her son, she still wanted to be a part of his life. Her friend encouraged her to pursue an "open adoption," which would allow Candice to retain visitation rights with her son after the placement. Since her friend was the adopting parent and a leader in the adoption field, Candice faithfully followed her friend's recommendations. Candice even presented to me her copy of the contract that she signed, which clearly stipulated that Candice was to have specific visitation rights throughout his childhood. However, within a year after her friend obtained custody of Candice's son, the woman suddenly moved away. Candice was never notified that her friend was moving and was never given her new address and phone number. She eventually tracked the adoptive mother down in North Carolina, but only after several years had passed. By this point in her son's life, Candice was afraid to take any formal action to restore her visitation rights.  She didn't know if her son would accept contact, and she didn't want her actions to damage his relationship with the only family he had known.  Still, she often wondered what her son was like and how he might feel about her.  Like virtually every birth mother and adoptee, she had no way to know.  I did my best to encourage Candice to pursue her legal rights to restore contact with her son.  In one sense, Candice's loss was more like a kidnapping than a placement, and it seemed even more unconscionable because a leader and advocate in the adoption field had perpetrated it.

To celebrate Stan's birthday and my first face-to-face reunion with my birth family, we went to a local Mexican restaurant for lunch.  After our meal, we returned to Stan's house, took some final pictures and parted company.  My first physical reunion was as rewarding as it was successful.  It wasn't overly emotional, but I never expected it to be.  After all, I had been in contact with my new family for several months before I started to meet them.  However, throughout our introduction, I never felt uncomfortable, as I had initially feared that I might.  The experience only heightened my anticipation of the impending reunion with my parents in November.  It also helped confirm in my mind that I had made the right choice in deciding to rejoin my biological family.  For the first time in my life, I felt truly complete, and I knew in my mind that I would not be haunted by hindsight over my decision—regardless of how the rest of my reunion and reintegration transpired.

***** *****

As Thanksgiving Day approached, I became increasingly nervous about my reunion trip.  I wanted everything to be just right.  My readoption petition was entering the final stages, and I didn't want to disappoint my parents at my first face-to-face meeting with them.  All the necessary arrangements had been made.  We had collected some small gifts for my parents, a new fishing pole for my father (with his extensive disabilities, fishing was the only recreational activity my father could still enjoy), and Barb had cross-stitched a small pillow for my mother that read simply:

Mom and Dad<br>
David<br>
Reunited<br>
November 25, 1998<br>
One Chapter Ends<br>
And a New One Begins.

I also brought along the photo album I had taken to New England during my search, which I intended to leave with my parents so they would always have some pictures from my past.

At 10:45 a.m. on Wednesday, November 25, we boarded a flight from Atlanta to Dallas. Once on the ground in Dallas, we picked up a rental car and headed south on I-35 towards Killeen. We stopped briefly in Waco to buy a dozen red roses for my mother, before we continued on our way. The holiday traffic was heavy, and it was nearly 6:00 p.m. before we reached the outskirts of Killeen. Since it was getting late, we decided to grab a quick meal before going on to my parent's house.

I believe I aged at least three years over the course of our trip to Killeen. At least, that's how my nerves made me feel. It's hard to describe the mixed feelings of excitement, anticipation, and fear that I felt when meeting my parents for the first time as an adult. In one sense, I already knew them. I had talked with them many times on the phone, and I knew what they looked like from the pictures they had sent. However, I had never felt the touch of their hands in all my life. In that sense, my parents were still virtual strangers, even though their blood coursed through my veins. I already knew that they accepted me as their son, but something in my mind reminded me acutely of just how fragile and untested my relationship with them was. By the end of our journey, I was exhausted from the trip and emotional stress.

Darkness was beginning to fall, as I pulled into the driveway of my parent's home. My mother had left the front porch light on and was keeping a watchful eye on the street for our arrival. I don't think I ever felt as nervous in my life as I did walking up the steps to the front door—not even when I watched Barb walk down the aisle at our wedding. I had the bouquet of roses in my hand, Barb was carrying the pillow for my mother, and Michael struggled to walk with the fishing pole for my father. Thinking back on it now, we must have appeared to be a rather odd-looking procession, as we marched up to the front landing. It must've looked like we were rehearsing for roles as the three wise men in a Christmas play.

I knocked on the screen door, and my mother yelled excitedly from the kitchen for us to come in. My father was sitting in the living room watching television. He got up from the chair as quickly as he could manage, given his disabilities, to greet us as we walked through the front door. He leaned into his crutches as he made his way across the room. My heart was pounding so hard that I thought it could be heard across the room. I froze momentarily, as I saw my mother approach me from the kitchen. I had waited so long—all my life—for this moment, and now that it was here, I really didn't know what to say or do. Fortunately, Barb gave me a subtle nudge, and I walked up to my mother, handed her the flowers, and gently wrapped my arms around her. As she pulled closer, I whispered in her ear, "I've missed you for so many years. I just can't believe this is finally happening. I love you, Mom." With those words, I could feel her squeeze me tighter. As our cheeks met momentarily, I felt the warmth of her silent tears. Finally, the hard part was over, and my reunion was complete.

I hugged my mother for what seemed like an eternity then turned to my father. Although age and war injuries had weakened his legs, his arms were as strong as steel. I don't believe I've ever been hugged so hard. My father was not very talkative. He had difficulties speaking, due to several strokes he had suffered in the past. He also had great difficulties remembering events and people from the past. After we hugged, he looked me in the eyes and struggled to say, "I hope we don't disappoint you, son."

His concern further alleviated my own fears. I just gave him a reassuring smile and said, "Once I knew that you accepted me, there was no way that I could be disappointed in you. I'm just eternally grateful that I have the chance to know you."

Although our initial introduction was brief, it was one of the highlights of my search. The last of my anxieties quickly faded away, and my heart surged with joy and contentment. I knew my life was now complete in every way that I had always wanted it to be. For the first time in my living memory, I truly knew how it felt to be part of a loving family. I was finally back where I always belonged.

We presented our gifts to my parents and unloaded our luggage from the car. My mother gave us a quick tour of their home and showed us the bedroom we would be using for the weekend. She seemed to have an inexhaustible supply of energy and was eager to talk. By the time we had become settled, Michael's fatigue from the long trip was becoming apparent. Barb got him ready for bed, as I sat down at the kitchen table to chat with my parents. Within a few minutes, Michael emerged from the bedroom, dressed in his pajamas. He ran up to me for his customary goodnight hug and kiss. However, I stopped him short and whispered in his ear to give his grandmother and grandfather a surprise hug and kiss first. He shyly approached my mother as she was talking and gave her a hug and peck on the cheek. Then he walked around to the back of the table towards my father. I'll never forget the scene that unfolded, when my father gave Michael his first goodnight hug and kiss.

While there were many aspects of my childhood upbringing that I didn't want to perpetuate as a parent, the one that stood out foremost in my mind was my adoptive family's lack of demonstrative affection. Hugs and kisses were very rarely given and were almost exclusively reserved for family reunions. Even then, affection was not expressed or received very enthusiastically. To help reverse that pattern, I had always made a conscious effort to tell my son frequently that I loved him, and I always gave him a hug and kiss at night before he went to bed. I wanted to make sure that my son would never have to wonder if I truly loved him. I also wanted to make it fun and comfortable for him to give me hugs and kisses. So, I had developed a habit of making a funny noise almost every time he gave me a kiss. After he kissed me, I would shake my head furiously from side to side and make a silly blubbering sound with my cheeks. I don't know where or how I learned to do it, as it was never done by anyone in my adoptive family. At any rate, I did it often because it always made Michael smile. To my amazement, my father instinctively did the exact same thing after receiving his first kiss from Michael, even though he had never seen me do it! Michael's eyes lit up, and he smiled from cheek to cheek when he saw my father make the same silly noise that he had heard me make so many times before. By the look on his face alone, I could tell that Michael instantly knew that the man he had just kissed was his real grandfather.

After Michael went to bed, we all talked and laughed for hours. My mother had a good sense of humor and laughed a lot, just as I always did. I showed my parents the pictures in the album I brought and talked about my past, while my parents shared with me many stories of my brothers and sisters. It felt odd to see pictures of my brothers and sisters as children and to not recognize who they were, but I was reassured by the fact that Michael would never experience those feelings. Even if I had lost my childhood with my biological family, Michael would carry the memories of his childhood experiences with them all his life. That knowledge alone made me realize how much I had truly accomplished by my search. I now had the rest of my life to build the relationship with my family that I had always wanted, and I couldn't wait to begin.

We awoke early Thanksgiving morning and made our preparations for the trip across town to Carolyn's house. Carolyn had bought a new house earlier in the year and with Mom's help, she had been redecorating it, room by room. As I discovered from all the work they had done, Carolyn and my mother had an innate talent for interior decorating. In fact, my mother had made many of the decorations that adorned her home.

Unfortunately, Carolyn was not the most affectionate or gregarious person in the family. She was very independent and had little contact or interaction with the rest of my brothers and sisters. She seemed accepting during my early telephone and e-mail conversations with her, even though she grew gradually more indifferent as time passed. Actually, my return to the family was not a surprise to her. She had accidentally learned about my adoption in early 1991.

Carolyn's husband, Billy, was an Army tank commander during the Persian Gulf War. When he was called to Saudi Arabia during Operation Desert Shield, Billy was forced to leave Carolyn behind in Killeen to care for their three children, one of which was his teenage son from a previous marriage. Carolyn did her best to treat Billy's teenage son as her own, but the boy refused to accept Carolyn's relationship with Billy, and he rebelled against her. Once Billy was gone, the child became uncontrollable and did everything in his power to make Carolyn's life difficult. After months of effort, Carolyn eventually decided that she could no longer care for the boy, so she called Mom for advice. Carolyn felt that her only option was to send Billy's son back to his biological mother. However, Mom became distraught at the thought of losing one of her grandchildren. She had already accepted Billy's son as part of her family, and she didn't want to lose "another" child. My mother then explained how she had given up one of Carolyn's brothers for adoption and that her decision had haunted her all her life. Mom advised Carolyn to do everything in her power to make the relationship work, because she didn't want her own daughter to live with the regret she had to bear. When I first talked to her, Carolyn told me that she thought about searching for me when she learned about my adoption, but she later decided against it. She had no information from which to begin a search, and she didn't want to reopen Mom's wounds without any hope for success.

Although Carolyn knew for years that I was out there somewhere, she was the least enthusiastic or excited about my return. Perhaps she was just hiding her real feelings, as she had a history of doing. On the other hand, her nonchalance about it all might just be an indication that she had expected me to turn up sooner or later. Whatever her real reasons were, I knew that she would be the most difficult person in the family with whom to establish a meaningful relationship. It would take several years and a number of failed efforts before I could eventually understand why.

When we arrived at her home, Carolyn was busy preparing a salad and vegetable tray. As I had expected, she reacted to our introduction with little emotion. She chose to wave from the kitchen rather than engage in an emotional display. However, she was generally pleasant and responsive, even though she rarely initiated a conversation. She did give us a tour of her home, which was a source of her pride and self-esteem.

I noticed the physical similarities between Carolyn and me the second I saw her face. We shared many facial features in common, including the Umling nose. However, we also shared a curious behavior pattern that I noticed immediately, when I realized how she was sitting at the kitchen counter. I have always had an uncommon way of crossing my legs whenever I sit down. Most men I know usually cross their legs by resting the ankle of their raised leg *on top* of the opposing knee. While I can cross my legs that way, I find it uncomfortable over long periods of time. My customary manner has always been to rest my raised leg on the seat of the chair with my ankle tucked *underneath* my other leg. Although I have known few, if any, men or women who cross their legs that way, Carolyn was doing the same thing when I first met her. Regardless of how she really felt about me, we still shared many characteristics in common.

After our tour of Carolyn's house, we sat down together for our Thanksgiving dinner. The more we talked the more comfortable and talkative Carolyn appeared to become. Later that evening, Carolyn and Billy led us on a tour of the traditional Fort Hood holiday lights display along the shores of Belton Lake. She also allowed Michael to spend the night at her house, so he could play with his new cousins, Aaron and John-John. Michael later wrote in his first grade school Journal about the night he spent with his cousins and how much fun he had meeting them. That made the trip doubly rewarding for me. Not only had I been able to connect with my family and my roots, but Michael did as well.

All in all, I was satisfied with my first visit with my parents and sister, Carolyn. It was by no means a fairy-tale reunion, but it was rewarding to me nonetheless. After all, I never expected my life to feel like a fairy tale. As I boarded our plane in Dallas for our return trip on Sunday, I began to feel the strength of the bond that had formed between my parents and me. Now more than ever before, I was intimately aware of what I had lost by virtue of my adoption. I couldn't turn back time and recapture the childhood memories I never experienced. Instead of feeling that I had the rest of my life to get to know them, I realized how little time remained to build a meaningful relationship with them to ease the pain of my loss. Every moment I had to spend with them or to talk with them was precious, and I didn't want to waste a single one. For now, I consoled myself with the fact that I at least had a chance to know them. Six months earlier, I couldn't have even said that. By the time we landed in Atlanta, I had made up my mind that I was going to meet as many of my relatives as I could. What was once only a dream was now an achievable ambition. I was not going to let it escape from my grasp this time around.

## *Desperately Seeking Sabrina*

During the months following my reunion with my parents, I made an intensive effort to meet as many of my biological relatives as I could. The next trip we took was to Shreveport, Louisiana to visit my father's younger brother, Eddie, and his family. Many of my relatives had said that I strongly resembled Uncle Eddie and that I even sounded like him over the telephone. We first visited him on January 15, 1999 and met his wife, Rose; his son, Steve; his daughter, Cindy; and their respective children. Barb and I both had to admit that the resemblance was striking and even extended to several of his children, as we had initially recognized when we met his son, Stan, in Alpharetta. Aunt Rose was an unbridled fountain of energy, and Uncle Eddie was a lighthearted prankster. When a person entered a room where he and others were having a casual conversation, he was fond of playfully saying, "Shhhh—Here he comes."

My "twin" sister, Kathy and her family stopped by our house for a two-day visit during their move from Utica, New York to Houston, Texas. Kathy's husband, Dale, had been transferred to the Houston office of his employer, and our house happened to be a convenient stop along the way. I can honestly say I have never enjoyed meeting anyone as much as I enjoyed meeting Kathy. We hit it off from the moment we met. It was as if we'd never been separated. Kathy was outgoing and fun loving–a stark contrast to Carolyn, who she resembled very closely. Kathy wore her heart on her sleeve which, to some in the family, was considered a sign of weakness or naiveté. To me, it was a breath of fresh air. With Kathy, I discovered a large part of the true personality I hid away from view for many years. She made me realize how much a part of the Umling family I always was even though I never knew them. Although her visit lasted only two days, we were actually able to finish each other's remarks before she left. In the years that passed since our first meeting on January 27, 1999, we visited Kathy numerous times, and she visited us on several other occasions. I even spent my 37th birthday with her and my parents at her new home in the Houston area. After they later moved to Shreveport, Louisiana, Michael spent a few weeks with Kathy and her two children during several of his summer vacations and came to know two of his cousins well.

I then planned what would become the grandest of my early reunion excursions. I decided to travel back to my father's childhood home, Ellwood City,

Pennsylvania.  Although all of my biological grandparents had died many years earlier, I wanted to visit their graves and see where they had lived.  I also wanted to meet Aunt Peg, who had helped me with my initial genealogical research on the Umling family, and Aunt Betty, who lived two hours northwest of Ellwood City in Willoughby, Ohio.  As an added benefit, Aunt Betty received an invitation to a retirement party for one of my distant cousins at the Ellwood City Saxon's Club the evening following our planned arrival.  She asked me if we would like to attend as her guests.  My grandfather was a former officer in the Ellwood City Saxon's Club, and my father was a former member as well, so I eagerly accepted. Not only would the retirement party give me a chance to meet dozens of relatives all at one time, but it would also give me my first exposure to my cultural heritage, including homemade Saxon dishes and ceremonial traditions.  We only had a three-day weekend to spend in the area, but we made the most of it.  With everything I had to look forward to, I never anticipated that it would eventually lead me on another search.

We left Anniston for Ellwood City on March 26, 1999.  I had planned to drive straight through to the Pittsburgh area, but as luck would have it, our rental car broke down in central West Virginia.  As a result, we had to spend the night at a local motel and truck stop until the rental car company could provide us with a replacement car the next morning.  By the time we reached Ellwood City, it was already early in the afternoon.  We tried to find Aunt Peg's house from the directions she gave us, but we got hopelessly lost.  I called her from a store on Main Street then waited for her to meet us at a local restaurant down the street.

When she arrived, we sat together at the restaurant and chatted for a while over soft drinks and a snack.  Both Aunt Peg and Aunt Betty shared my deep interest in our family heritage and Saxon culture, so I always had plenty to talk about with both of them.  Aunt Peg always took whatever life gave her and made the best of it.  Like many of my relatives, she possessed a strong will and determination to overcome any adversity she faced.  Her sense of independence and self-confidence were admirable and indomitable.

After talking about the family for half an hour, Aunt Peg led us to the Locust Grove Cemetery on a nearby hill.  Once there, she showed me the Umling family plot, where my grandparents were buried along with my uncle Bill and two of their other children who died at very young ages, Kate (who died at the age of 4) and Mary Ann (who died at birth).  It was an emotional experience for me to stand before my grandfather's grave knowing that I could have met him as a child had I not been adopted.  My mother had told me about the time they visited my grandfather, about a year before his death, and how he sang to Carolyn in

German as he bounced her on his knee. I would never know what that scene was like. I would never be able to hear the sound of his voice echoing in my memory. Pictures or stories simply can't replace those experiences and memories. The loss I experienced from my adoption was never more apparent to me than it was at that moment.

We spent about an hour at the cemetery, before returning to Aunt Peg's house. The retirement party was scheduled to start in a couple of hours, so we had some time to talk. I met two of my cousins, Kathy and Deloris, as well as Deloris' twin daughters, Danielle and Desiree. Michael played with the two girls, while the rest of us became better acquainted. Just as we were preparing to leave for the reunion party, Aunt Betty and Uncle Walter arrived from Willoughby. Aunt Betty impressed me as a sensitive, caring, and generous person. Uncle Walter was sincere and outspoken. I sensed immediately that I could always know where I stood with him. I appreciated that quality in him, as it reassured me that his concern for my family and me was genuine. Together, they made a good pair, and I felt comfortable with them from the start. We have remained close to them ever since. After a brief introduction, it was time to head off to the Saxon's Club.

Our evening at the retirement party was intense, to say the least. I met nearly a dozen blood relatives and many more long-time friends of my father's family. I can't even remember all of their names or even all the wonderful stories I heard, but I truly wish that I could. The food was fantastic, and we managed to discover a few traditional Saxon dishes that we wanted to prepare at home. I was especially pleased to find a large picture frame in the hallway outside the main meeting room containing individual photos of past club members. In it, I found pictures of my father and grandfather as they appeared in their youths. For the first time, I could clearly see the similarities between them and me at similar ages. I also admired the old Saxon shields that lined the tops of the walls around the main meeting room. I later learned that each major Saxon village in Transylvania had its own shield or coat of arms that residents often carried with them on their travels as tokens of community pride. Being part of a community in Transylvania meant something important to the Saxons, and I could sense the depth of that meaning by just standing in that meeting room admiring the decorative and colorful shields.

We stayed at the party as long as we could, but it was soon getting late, and Michael was growing visibly tired. Aunt Peg's house didn't have enough extra room for us to stay with her. So, we followed Aunt Betty and Uncle Walter back to their home in Ohio, where we spent that night and the rest of our stay in the area. By the time we arrived in Willoughby, it was very late, and we all went straight to bed. It had been a long but rewarding day.

The next morning, Uncle Walter left home early to pick up their older daughter, Linda, who lived in Cleveland's west end. Linda had been seriously injured as a child, when she was struck by an automobile. She experienced difficulty walking after the accident, so she never learned to drive. Since Michael was excited to see the big lake, Aunt Betty decided to drive us down to the lakeshore for a view of Lake Erie. We had taken Michael to beaches on the Atlantic Ocean and the Gulf of Mexico on many occasions, so he had a hard time believing that the expansive Lake Erie was really only a lake. On our way back to the house, Aunt Betty made a quick detour to show us President Garfield's homestead in nearby Mentor. By the time we got home, Uncle Walter had returned with Linda.

My cousin, Linda, is a wonderfully energetic and enthusiastic woman. She also has a well-known talent for storytelling. She had a particular interest in my story and my feelings about it. I told her all about my search and what I had learned about my adoption. I told her how wonderful it felt to find my biological family and discover how many of my family's physical and behavioral traits I inherited, including the Umling nose and temper. In fact, I had been so embarrassed about my childhood temper, that I had avoided discussing it, until I was specifically asked by several relatives if I had a fiery temper as a child.

Linda chuckled at my embarrassment about the Umling temper. As a life-long member of the family, she knew it intimately. She had seen many of her relatives exhibit it in all its various forms, and she even acknowledged that she had difficulties controlling it as a child. But, unlike me, she grew up in an environment in which that behavior pattern was understood and accepted, so she had a much more positive insight into it.

"I can understand why the notorious Umling temper might not be the most attractive feature a child can possess." Linda explained with a reassuring smile. "But that's because a child doesn't understand how to govern it and apply it in a positive way. I had the same problem with my temper when I was young. However, as I grew older, I learned to control it. Eventually, it evolved in me and became the source of my determination. Instead of just letting anger and frustration control my actions, I learned how to redirect my feelings into a motivating force that gives me the courage and strength I needed to overcome adversities. At some point in our lives, all of us learn how to do it. The Umling temper isn't necessarily a bad influence, as long as you learn how to make it a positive force in your life."

Her explanation nearly knocked me off my feet! Like Linda, I had channeled the childhood frustrations I felt as an adoptee trapped in a troubled family environment into an unyielding determination to find my biological family. The more I thought about it, the more I realized that Linda's insights also helped explain how I managed to avoid repeating my suicide attempt. For some reason, my will to survive was stronger than the destructive tendencies of my own self-recrimination. Perhaps I had instinctively redirected my anger at my self-hatred rather than myself. For whatever reason, I was driven from that day forward to overcome my anxieties and depression and to seek help when I knew I needed it. For the first time in my life, I had discovered strength in the one personality trait that always made me feel inferior and set me apart from the rest of my adoptive family.

As we talked, Linda became gradually more comfortable talking about herself. It was then that she revealed the source of her interest in my adoption. Linda's life, like my own, had been touched by adoption. In fact, Linda had placed her only daughter for adoption, and she had often thought of trying to find her.

Linda had married early in life, just after she completed high school. Her husband, Brian, was a social recluse with few ambitions in life. He seldom worked, and he was inclined to spend lots of time with his parents. Brian also was an alcoholic with violent and abusive tendencies. The early years of their marriage were difficult, and their finances were often stretched to the breaking point. Aunt Betty and Uncle Walter wanted to help, but Linda was always determined to make it on her own.

Within a couple of years, Linda became pregnant and gave birth to a baby girl on June 20, 1973. They decided to name her Sabrina. Unfortunately, the pregnancy occurred at a turbulent time in their relationship, and Linda soon realized that it would not last. They were already discussing divorce when Sabrina was born. Brian and his parents pressured Linda to place Sabrina for adoption. Linda never wanted to give up her newborn child, but she knew it would be difficult for her to raise the baby alone, and she knew that Brian would never provide any financial support. Reluctantly, Linda agreed to relinquish Sabrina, in the hope that she would receive a better life through adoption. Roughly three weeks after Sabrina's birth, Linda and Brian both signed the adoption papers. In less than a year, they were divorced.

Linda struggled for weeks to find a way to explain her actions to her parents. She believed that they would be disappointed with her. Sabrina was the only grandchild they would ever have. Linda never had any other children, and her younger sister, Janet, never had any children of her own. When she finally broke the news, it was devastating for the entire family. But Aunt Betty and Uncle Walter knew how painful the decision was for Linda, and they rallied to her support. Nevertheless, Aunt Betty told me that, for years after the adoption, she studied the face of every baby that crossed her path hoping that she would recognize one of them as the granddaughter she had lost. She never did.

Linda had thought about searching for her daughter on many occasions, but she couldn't bring herself to do it. First of all, she feared that Sabrina would reject her, which I now recognized to be as common a fear among birth parents as it is among adoptees. It is a common emotional gift bestowed by closed record adoptions. Linda loved her daughter so much that rejection would hurt worse than the original loss. Second, Linda felt it was inappropriate for her to interfere in her daughter's adoptive family relationship just to satisfy her own personal desire to know her. However, when Linda saw how much I resembled my father and other members of my family, she had to wonder if Sabrina would resemble her, too. I offered to help her search, but Linda wanted to think more about it first.

As Linda and I finished our long conversation, her sister, Janet, arrived for a brief visit. Janet worked as a dispatcher for the Willoughby Hills Police Department, and she had a tight second shift work schedule. Consequently, she couldn't stay long, but she wanted a chance to meet us. After Janet left, we gathered in the living room and watched some old family movies that Aunt Betty and Uncle Walter had filmed over the years. Although there was no sound, I was able to see a few brief images of my grandfather.

Aunt Betty also showed me a file she had kept containing old family papers and documents. It included my grandfather's baptismal record and his passport to America issued in 1921. I wrote down as many notes of the names and dates contained on those documents as I could. I knew that the information would prove useful in my genealogical research. When we had finished going through the file, Aunt Betty presented me with a copy of a book on the history of the Transylvanian Saxons. I've read it cover-to-cover at least twice since then, and I'll probably read it again. She also gave me a picture of my grandfather and grandmother taken on their wedding day in November 1922. I treasure that picture as one of the greatest gifts I received from my search and reunion. It still hangs on a wall in our bedroom.

After an early supper, Uncle Walter and I drove Linda back to her apartment. Before we left, I urged her to let me know if she wanted my help locating her daughter. I wanted more than anything else to help ease her pain. She promised to call me, if she decided she wanted to try. I wanted to spend more time talking about it with her, but we needed to leave for Alabama early in the morning, so we couldn't stay very long.

The next morning, we arose early and packed our bags for the long trip home. While Barb was in the shower, I went down to the kitchen for breakfast. Aunt Betty was already awake and dressed waiting for us to join her. I could tell by the expression on her face that she wanted to discuss something important. While we were alone in the kitchen, she confided her feelings to me about Sabrina's adoption. She told me how much it hurt to lose her granddaughter. Aunt Betty had held Sabrina in her arms only once, but the bond she felt for the baby never waned. She couldn't be angry with Linda for doing what she thought was best for the child, but she wished there could been another way to overcome the difficult situation she had faced. As far as Aunt Betty was concerned, my reunion with the family was a miracle that gave her hope that Sabrina could actually be found. Like Linda, Aunt Betty never wanted to interfere with Sabrina's relationship with her adoptive family, but she desperately wanted to see her granddaughter again and hold her in her arms one more time—if for no other reason than to tell her how much she had been loved. She asked me to help her find her long lost granddaughter.

I truly felt honored by her request. It seemed like the perfect opportunity to return something important to the family that had given my life new meaning. I couldn't refuse. Before we left, I asked Aunt Betty to collect as much descriptive information about Sabrina as she could, and I would do my best to help locate her. After a brief breakfast and a reluctant goodbye, we began the thirteen-hour ride home. For me, the trip had been one of the most fulfilling aspects of my entire reunion. It helped me feel closer to my true heritage than I had ever felt before. In fact, I began devouring the Saxon history book on the way home.

Whenever I was driving on the trip home, my thoughts returned to the impending search for Sabrina. All of my search experience had been from the adoptee's point of view. Searching from the birth family's perspective can be considerably more difficult, especially when you have no clue as to who the adoptive family might be. The birth family has no authority to request placement records from the adoption to provide a starting point for the search. I also would be searching from a distance, as I didn't have the extra vacation time I would need to search the records in Ohio. However, succeeding was especially important to me. I didn't want to let my biological family down on the first opportunity I was given to help them. Perhaps Aunt Betty was right, I consoled myself, privately. If there was a specific reason for my adoption and successful reunion, maybe this was it. Maybe—just maybe—this search would be the redemption I wanted for everything that had happened to me. At least, if it wasn't my destiny in life, perhaps I could make it my special contribution to my birth family. I was determined to find Sabrina, but I also knew I would need a lot of luck and a lot of help.

It was nearly a month after my weekend trip to Pennsylvania and Ohio before I received the basic information I needed to begin searching for Sabrina. Unfortunately, I was given very little information from which to work. All I knew was Sabrina's original birth name, her birthday and place of birth, her presumed date of placement (Aunt Betty wasn't sure of the exact date), and a basic physical description of her from Aunt Betty's memory along with a few birth photos. Aunt Betty had heard that Sabrina's adoptive parents were from the nearby city of Mentor, Ohio, but she knew nothing about them that would help me identify who they were. Armed with this information, I began placing Sabrina's descriptive information on the Internet. However, to have any realistic chance of success at all, I needed some help from my fellow adoptees on the Adoptee's Internet Mailing List.

To my surprise, our first break emerged only three days after I first posted Sabrina's information. An adoptee from Ohio sent me a message stating that she had access to records from her own search that might help us identify Sabrina's adoptive name. Apparently, she had acquired a listing of birth dates and locations for adoptive children born in the early 1970s, including the year that Sabrina was born and placed for adoption. When the adoptee researched her records, she discovered that only one adoptive child was born on June 20, 1973 at Lake County General Hospital. That child's adoptive name was Cheryl J. Hascomb. In addition, the record showed that the adoptive family's place of residence was Mentor, OH. The information was a perfect match, but I needed to be certain.

Armed with this information, I contacted Laura the next day. She, too, was born in Ohio and had considerable experience working on Ohio adoptee cases. I gave her the information and asked for her help confirming Sabrina's possible adoptive name. It took Laura less than 24 hours to research her records and confirm the find. The Sabrina we sought was indeed renamed Cheryl J. Hascomb! The search for Sabrina ended only eight days after it began. However, Laura could not establish a current phone number or mailing address for Cheryl. The available records showed that she had moved around quite a bit, but may be residing in western Ohio. Cheryl had recently used a telephone number that was listed under the name of her adoptive grandfather, who lived in Kenton, Ohio. The records also showed that she was using a street address in the nearby town of Bellefontaine around the same time. Unfortunately, Laura could give us no more definitive information on Cheryl's location.

We knew we were very close to locating her, but we needed one last piece of information—a current telephone number or mailing address. Laura knew that Cheryl didn't have a telephone service account, so contacting her by phone was out of the question. I couldn't be certain where she was living, and I didn't want to leave an awkward message for her with members of her adoptive family. I had no way to know how they would react if they somehow learned or deduced who I really was. My experiences with my own adoptive family had taught me to err on the side of caution. It would also be difficult to explain why we were calling her from Alabama, if we were forced to leave a message. Finally, I didn't want to be introducing myself to her in the company of her adoptive family. From my experience with first contact, the best chances of success could be achieved only through direct and private communication with the adoptee or birth parent.

I decided that the best way to locate her was to call her grandfather's home and ask for Cheryl's current mailing address. However, I needed a good excuse to request her address. Although I knew she wasn't married, I had no way of knowing whether or not she currently had a boyfriend. I didn't feel comfortable making the call myself. After all, a strange man asking for a single woman's mailing address would draw immediate suspicion from her adoptive family, especially if she did have a current boyfriend. I decided that it would attract less suspicion if Barb made the call. Fortunately, Barb's voice sounded quite youthful over the phone. I suggested that Barb pretend that she was an old high school friend of Cheryl's, who needed her current mailing address to send her a wedding invitation. It seemed like a simple, casual, and innocent excuse, and at nearly 26 years of age, Cheryl was certainly old enough to have lost touch with her friends from school.

When Barb called later that evening, an older woman answered the phone. She asked first to speak with Cheryl, but she wasn't living there. Barb then explained who she was, using the story I had contrived. According to Barb, the woman hesitated a moment, before giving her a mailing address. The address was a post office box in Mount Victory, Ohio, roughly ten miles south of Kenton.

I called both Aunt Betty and Linda the following morning with the news. We had located Sabrina and had obtained her current mailing address. They were both understandably shocked by how quickly the search was resolved. If not for the assistance of an adoptee in Ohio, the search might have required years to complete. At the time, Linda wasn't sure she was ready for first contact. But I reminded her that the timing really wasn't within her exclusive control. For all we knew, Sabrina might be actively searching for Linda, and she could receive a phone call out of the blue at any time, just as my own mother had. Once Linda realized that she had a better chance to prepare herself as long as we were initiating first contact, she gave me her permission to write the letter.

I spent most of that evening struggling to write Sabrina's first contact letter. I basically decided to write the letter I would want to have received if my birth family had contacted me first. I explained that I was her biological cousin and that I, too, had been placed for adoption. I told her how much her mother loved her and the reasons why she was placed for adoption. I also told her how I was received when I first contacted our biological family and that I knew her mother and grandparents would accept her. All she needed to do was call. Most importantly, however, I made sure to tell her that her biological family did not want to harm or interfere with her relationship with her adoptive family and that they too would be accepted by her birth relatives. I also told her that her biological relatives would not pressure her for a relationship. If she didn't feel comfortable meeting us, she only needed to tell us so, and we would respect her wishes. The final letter was between five and seven pages long. I dropped it in the mail on May 4, 1999.

Two days later, I received two phone messages from Cheryl—one at work and another at home. She had received my letter, and she wanted to talk. Once again, I called Aunt Betty and Linda with the news. I even played the message I had received at home, so they could hear Sabrina's voice for the first time. Both were overcome by tears, when they heard the message. It was a dream come true for them. They suggested that I return her call and establish a time when Linda could talk to Sabrina for the first time.

That evening, I called the number Cheryl had left in her message. It was her grandfather's telephone number. However, the person who answered my call was her adoptive mother, Madge. At first, I was nervous when I learned who was talking to me. However, she quickly put my mind at ease. She was not at all opposed to our search for Cheryl. In fact, she told me that Cheryl had decided only recently to search for her birth mother, and Madge had agreed to help. What's more, Madge even expressed interest in knowing Cheryl's biological family. When she adopted Cheryl, the caseworker had told Madge that Cheryl's birth mother truly loved her and wanted the best for her. Madge had never hidden that fact from Cheryl, and the knowledge of her birth mother's true feelings for her was a motivating factor in her decision to search.

Madge also told me that she had answered the phone when Barb called. She realized there was something peculiar about Barb's story, when she said she was an old high school friend of Cheryl. As it happened, Cheryl never finished high school, and she had no long-term friends who would have remembered her. However, Barb was so pleasant over the phone that she felt no threat from her, so she gave her the information she requested and waited to see what would become of it. Madge impressed me as an intuitive, intelligent, and self-confident woman. I apologized for the deception and explained why we tried to conceal our real identity and intent.

Unfortunately, Cheryl was at work when I returned her call. At that time, she worked on the second shift at a nearby Honda motorcycle plant. Madge asked me to call her after 11:00 a.m. the next day, as Cheryl had planned to be available at the house then to talk with me. I talked with Madge a while longer, before finally ending our conversation. Although we talked for less than an hour, I had developed a profound respect for Madge. She was totally supportive of Cheryl's desire to understand her roots and to know her birth family. To my relief, she confirmed in my mind that my expectations of my own adoptive mother had not been unreasonable. It was clear from the start that Cheryl's reunion would be successful in a way that mine never could.

The next day, I went home from work for lunch to call Cheryl. She was clearly excited to know that we had found her and was very interested in meeting her birth mother. Many of the feelings she expressed to me about her desire to know us were eerily familiar. Like me, Cheryl always felt a part of her was missing. Fortunately for her, the decision to search for her biological family was made easier by the fact that her adoptive mother had told her how much her birth mother had loved her.

I also learned that the reality of Cheryl's adoptive childhood did not live up to the public image of adoption. This realization was becoming far more commonplace than I had ever anticipated. It no longer surprised me to encounter a failed or improper adoption, as I had run across so many questionable practices throughout my search and reunion, including my own adoption. The prevalence of such irregularities raises additional questions in my mind about the full motivation behind closed adoptions and sealed records. Why is it that the adoption industry never publicly acknowledges that closed record adoptions also conveniently serve *their* interests in covering up mistakes and improprieties? That thought causes me to rephrase a quote I once heard attributed to Thomas Jefferson— "When people fear their government, it's called tyranny; when government fears its people, it's called accountability." I have taken the liberty to substitute the word "accountability" for Jefferson's "freedom." Either way, it is a principle that cleverly captures the perspective our founding fathers held when deciding how a responsible, democratic (or representative) system of government should work and how it should relate to the governed. Why else would government transparency be such an important issue in our society?

Although her earliest childhood years were good for Cheryl, her adoptive parents divorced before she was five years old. Madge remarried shortly thereafter, but her new husband suffered from a periodic drinking problem and was often abusive to Cheryl. He once beat Cheryl so severely that he broke her leg. At the age of fifteen, Cheryl ran away from home and lived on the streets for several days. Although she loved her adoptive mother and her grandfather, she could never tolerate her adoptive stepfather. Her stormy relationship with him had made her emotionally withdrawn and somewhat insecure. I could relate to that from my own childhood experiences. Madge tried to referee the relationship, but was trapped perilously in the middle of the situation unable to satisfy both her daughter and her husband. By the time Cheryl eventually decided to search for her birth family, her stepfather had been dead for several years. The letter I wrote to her was the fulfillment of her dreams, and she was ready to begin meeting her biological family.

Cheryl wanted to speak with her birth mother, but she wasn't sure how to approach her. Her quandary reminded me of my own first contact call to my birth mother. The only advice I could give her was the approach I had used. I told her to talk to her birth mother in the same way that she would to her prospective fiancé's parents when meeting them for the first time. I don't know if it was very comforting advice, but it must have helped. Cheryl spoke with Linda on the telephone for the first time the following Saturday, and they were formally reunited on Mother's Day, 1999.

As I anticipated after my first talk with Madge, Cheryl's reunion was a complete success. In fact, Cheryl, Madge, and her adoptive grandfather celebrated her 26th birthday at Aunt Betty and Uncle Walter's house in June. Linda and her parents developed a fond relationship with Cheryl's adoptive family that persisted for many years. When Cheryl was married on October 28, 2000, Uncle Walter walked her down the aisle with Linda, Aunt Betty, and Madge in attendance.  Linda and her parents were also able to be present for the birth of Cheryl's two sons and Aunt Betty was able to hold them in her arms, just as she had held Cheryl all those years ago.

As for me, I met Cheryl and the rest of her adoptive family for the first time in November 1999.  It was rewarding to see how well both families got along together and to realize how much Cheryl resembled Linda and her aunt Janet. She didn't have to tell me how it made her feel, as I understood it intimately from my own experience.  Although I didn't feel that I had played a major or pivotal role in the search for Sabrina/Cheryl, I was proud to have been involved in the process of restoring another piece of my birth family.  I was also comforted by the knowledge that it *was* possible for an adoptive family and a biological family to come together as one for the benefit of the adoptive child.  It made me realize just what my own adoptive family could have enjoyed, if they had simply opened their hearts and allowed it to happen.  I guess Cheryl's reunion will always give me cause to stop and think of what might have been.  It has always been difficult for me to just set aside missed opportunities in my mind, even though I know I can't change the outcome.

## *The Final Homecoming*

I believe it was shortly after our Thanksgiving 1998 reunion trip to Killeen that my mother first mentioned her aspirations of returning to New Hampshire. My father had difficulties with his mobility when the weather was good, but the summer heat in Texas made it impossible for him to get out of the house very often.  Both he and my mother wanted to return to New Hampshire, where they could spend more time outdoors and be closer to their long-time friends.  My mother also wanted to spend some time with her other children—Rose, Dave, and Bill—who were all living there at that time.  The news was a little disappointing to me at first.  After all, I had just met my parents for the first time, and they were talking about moving even farther away.  Given my work responsibilities and limited vacation time, I knew that I wouldn't be able to spend as much time as I wanted to with them, once they had moved.  However, I wanted whatever was best for my parents, and it was becoming clear that, after nearly five years, they were tired of living in Texas.

My parents' decision to move back to New Hampshire gave me cause to consider moving back to New England as well.  Most of Barb's family still lived in the Albany, NY area and southwestern Vermont, and throughout the years she had occasionally expressed her desire to live once again in or near her beloved

Vermont. Although we referred to ourselves as economic refugees from New England, we always clung to the hope that we could someday return to the mountains we knew and revel once again in the glory of their autumn colors. Fall was always my favorite season in northern New England, and although autumn colors do eventually descend into the mountains of Alabama, they are never as brilliant. While northern New England winters can be notoriously brutal and tedious at times, we also missed our traditional white Christmases. However, our return was always dependent on our financial health, the cost of relocating, and the availability of well-paying jobs.

By the end of 1998, Barb and I had lived in the south for more than seven years, and we were beginning to feel that we might have finally achieved the financial boost we had hoped to gain when we made the decision to move in 1991. The only real reason that we hadn't considered moving back to New England sooner was my long-standing resistance to live anywhere near my adoptive family. I had learned to appreciate my distance and independence from them long before I decided to search for my biological family. However, my perspective had changed significantly, since my reunion and readoption, and Barb and I both agreed that our son would benefit from some knowledge of his New England roots. We also knew that it would be beneficial for him to spend more quality time with our respective families. It would certainly be beneficial to me. I had lost so much over the years, that I dearly wanted the opportunity to know my parents and family better. I also feared that my father's advanced age, medical history, and declining condition would leave me with very little quality time to spend with him. The only problem was that there were very few career advancement opportunities for me in New Hampshire and Vermont, which I knew that I needed to help offset the impact of relocating to a significantly higher cost market.

In late January 1999, I began calling some of my old regional planning colleagues and friends in New Hampshire and Vermont to inquire about job opportunities in the area. Kim, my former executive director at the Lakes Region Planning Commission, told me about a couple of executive directorships that were opening in New Hampshire. One was at the Strafford Regional Planning Commission in Dover, NH. That position immediately attracted my attention, because my two half-brothers, Dave and Bill Conner, lived in the immediate area, and my mother was talking about moving to Rochester, which was located immediately north of Dover. The position would also put me in the seacoast area where I was born, which was well removed from the normal stomping grounds of my adoptive family.

Ironically, the second position was at the Precision Valley Regional Planning Commission in Granville, NH. The agency had the distinct benefits of serving communities in two states–Vermont and New Hampshire (which made the agency somewhat unique in the regional planning field)–and it was located almost exactly halfway between Arlington, VT (where Barb's parents lived) and the NH seacoast, where my parents were planning to locate. On the other hand, the agency was located in the Connecticut River Valley and very close to the area where I lived throughout my childhood. My adoptive mother had long since moved away, and I hadn't spent any significant time in the area since 1985. But I was still a little cautious about the reactions that people who knew me as a child would have to my new name and family association. I had struggled so hard over the years to become a better and more self-confident person that I was somewhat hesitant to live in such close proximity to the childhood memories and experiences that had been the bane of my existence. How would it make me feel to live in that area again? How would my childhood friends and acquaintances react to me? Would they understand? Would they blame me for the damage that my search and subsequent readoption had caused to my adoptive family? Then again, perhaps the experience would be the best way for me to confront and finish slaying the dragons from my past. By taking the job and succeeding, I might finally be able to overcome in my mind the childhood insecurities that had haunted me for so many years. I at least knew that housing would be more affordable in the Precision Valley region than along the seacoast.

Normally, executive director jobs did not open frequently. They are among the most stable and coveted professional positions in the regional planning field. The fact that two such positions out of a total of only nine regional agencies in the state were open at the same time was an incredible opportunity. I certainly didn't feel that I could take either opportunity lightly, if I sincerely wanted a chance to get a promotion and live closer to my new family. After a couple of weeks of careful thought and consideration, I decided to apply for both positions and let fate decide. Would I end up living in the area where I was born or where I grew up? Perhaps I wouldn't be selected for either job or perhaps I would be given a choice. My life experiences had taught me that blind chance was a temperamental companion. It had taken my life to the depth of despair and the height of joy. I had no idea where it would lead me now. New Hampshire's influence on my life had always been as unpredictable as its weather.

Roughly one month later, I received a call from the Precision Valley Regional Planning Commission. They asked me to interview for their position. I had heard no response from the Strafford Regional Planning Commission, so I called them before arranging a date for my interview at the other agency. If I was going to make a trip all the way to New Hampshire, I wanted to interview for both positions during the same trip. Although Strafford's search for a new executive director was proceeding at a much slower pace than Precision Valley's, they also wanted to interview me, nonetheless.

Secure in the knowledge that I was a serious candidate for both positions, I made arrangements for my first trip back to New Hampshire, since my final adoptee search in 1998. My sister, Rose, offered to pick me up at the Manchester airport. She lived in nearby Derry and was equally eager to meet me in person. She also encouraged me to stay with her during my trip. I also made arrangements to meet my brothers Dave and Bill following my interview at the Strafford Regional Planning Commission.

On the evening of April 8, 1999, I boarded a plane in Birmingham for my flight to New Hampshire. When I arrived, Rose and her husband, Rick, met me at the airport. Rose spotted me right away because I looked so much like my father and younger brother, Tim. As the eldest sibling, Rose was the one that all of my brothers and sisters respected most. She was, in effect, the surrogate mother hen of the roost, just as her mother had been within her own family. Her self-assurance and determination were the foundation of her stature within the family, and it commanded my immediate respect. Yet, her emotional fortitude was tempered by strong doses of empathy and sentimentality which served as the source of her deep and heartfelt concern for all of her brothers and sisters. Her husband, Rick, was very intelligent, perceptive, and rational—traits nurtured by his extensive former military service. His qualities appealed to my analytical and reflective nature. I enjoyed my early conversations with them both, and they did their utmost to make me feel welcome during my stay with them.

I interviewed for the two positions the following day. I felt confident of my professional capabilities based on my twelve years of professional experience and my intimate knowledge of New Hampshire—especially the Precision Valley area. I also recognized that my status as a native of the state would be an asset to both agencies. All of the regional planning commissions in New Hampshire at that time were headed by executives from other states. I enjoyed interviewing for both positions, and I was convinced that the staffs of both agencies were competent and professional. After I finished my interview with the Strafford Regional Planning Commission that afternoon, I drove north to the nearby town of Milton, where my brother, Dave, and his family lived.

Dave lived with his long-time girlfriend, Leeann. Although they had never married, they had one daughter together, Nicole, and Leeann's three older children from a previous relationship—Ryan, Ronny, and Breanna. Dave was considered the family prankster. He had a natural sense of humor and a fun-loving spirit. His rugged, tough-man appearance and persona masked a sensitive and generous heart. Although Dave had lived most of his adult life in the seacoast area of New Hampshire, he exhibited a worldliness that I hadn't discovered in my other brothers or sisters. He was resourceful and intuitive. As teenagers, both Dave and Bill had hitchhiked across the country, although Dave spent considerably more time on the road than Bill did. Dave was also a good storyteller, and I loved listening to his tales of the road. They reminded me of my childhood dreams of running away. Had I grown up as part of my biological family, I might have been inspired to follow him on his traveling adventures. After all, my wife has always felt I needed more spontaneity in my life.

Dave's long-time girlfriend, Leeann, was a proud, well-mannered, and friendly woman. Although she was quiet at times, she had a good sense of humor that I found to be very compatible with my own. Of course, she was bound to have a good sense of humor after spending as much time as she had with Dave. They had been together for nearly ten years, and they seemed as well suited to one another as any married couple could be.

Shortly after I met Dave and his family, we were joined by Rose, Rick, and their daughter, Sheena. Once we were all together at Dave's house, we walked across the street to a family restaurant for a pleasant supper and lively conversation. It was a wonderful experience to hear the childhood tales Dave and Rose had to tell. They focused on the most pleasant of their childhood memories and adventures. However, I would eventually learn that not all of their early experiences were so pleasant. These unpleasant childhood experiences contributed to some unresolved jealousies and animosities between the Conner and Umling children that would later prove to be eerily similar to the rift that formed between the adoptive and natural children in my adoptive family. Although I had never shared their experiences (and perhaps because of that), they treated me with greater affection and respect than I had ever received from my adoptive family. By the time we finished our meal and parted company, I was truly looking forward to the times I might have to spend with them, if I was able to land one of the job opportunities. I spent that night at Dave's house, as he had planned a family cookout the next day.

Unfortunately, the weather was too cold on Saturday to eat outdoors, but Dave still cooked the meal on his grill. As he prepared the meal, my other brother, Bill, arrived with his family. Of the three Conner children, Bill had led the hardest life. As I would quickly discover, Bill was the one who was most affected by the problems in my biological family. He had many unresolved and bitter feelings about his childhood, with which I could easily relate. His father's accidental death also bothered Bill greatly, because it had occurred before he was born and before Bill learned that he looked so much like his father. When I first talked to him, I could sense that he understood my lifelong desire to know my biological parents at a deeper and more personal level than the rest of my brothers and sisters. However, he also knew that he would never have the opportunity to know his biological father that I was given to know my own. I believe that knowledge only made it harder for Bill to accept the loss of his own father.

Unfortunately, Bill had never sought counseling for his emotional turmoil, as I had done in the past, so it still affected his attitudes and behavior. Despite his unresolved feelings of resentment towards the Umling side of the family, Bill willingly gave me a chance to establish my own rapport with him. Perhaps he could relate to the stories I had told him about my own childhood experiences. Whatever his reasons for the acceptance he gave me, I was appreciative of it. For I soon discovered that, beneath his troubled exterior, he possessed a heart of gold, and he was always willing to lend his help or a kind word whenever it was needed. His darker side was often revealed after a few beers.

Once again, we had a good time getting to know one another. We played a few round-robin games of horseshoes and basketball. I had never played horseshoes before, but I enjoyed it immensely. After the picnic, I said my goodbyes to my brothers and returned to Rose's house in preparation for my return trip home the next morning. That night, Rose and I spent hours talking about my reunion and my feelings about rejoining the family. I couldn't help but feel overwhelmed by the kindness the Conners had shown me. Although my new family clearly had its own problems, I was grateful to be a meaningful part of it.

On April 19, ten days after my interviews, I received a job offer from the Precision Valley Regional Planning Commission. The time to make a decision had arrived. First, I called the Strafford Regional Planning Commission to determine the status of their search process. Unfortunately, their process would not conclude until late May or early June, which meant that I had to make a decision on the Precision Valley job well before I would know the outcome of the Strafford position. I thought carefully about the offer for two days before accepting it and resigning my position at East Alabama on April 21, 1999. I was scheduled to start work in my new position on June 1.

Once I had made the decision to accept the Precision Valley job, my wife and I began our preparations for the move. Given the high cost of living in New Hampshire, it was imperative for us to sell our house in Oxford before buying a new home in the Granville area. We simply couldn't afford to make payments on both a new house in New Hampshire and our current home in Alabama. Our mortgage commitments on the Oxford house would also be a significant impediment on our eligibility for affordable financing in New Hampshire. Barb was concerned about our ability to sell the house quickly because one of the two local military installations in the Anniston area, Fort McClellan, was scheduled for closure at the end of September. The resulting impact of that base closure on the local economy and housing market was expected to be significant. However, the local real estate agent we hired was confident that our house was marketable and likely to sell before the impacts from the base closure were felt. Barb and I spent the rest of April and all of May making final improvements to the house to increase our chances of selling it quickly.

Just before my final day of work in Anniston, I received a call from my brother, Dave. He and Leeann had finally decided to get married, and he wanted to ask me if I would be willing to serve as his Best Man at his wedding on September 18. I was stunned by his request, but honored to have been asked. At first, I asked him if Bill might not be a more appropriate Best Man, since they had grown up together. I certainly didn't want to be unappreciative of his request, but I also didn't want to become a source of contention between my two brothers. I was learning that there were enough sources of resentment between the Conners and Umlings for me to risk adding to them. Dave quickly reassured me that he had asked Bill first, but he didn't feel comfortable in the role. In fact, Bill had suggested that Dave ask me. How could I possibly refuse such a generous request? I eagerly accepted.

As the end of May approached, it was becoming apparent that our house would not sell before I had to begin work in Granville. I was not too concerned though, as we were receiving a steady stream of prospective buyers. However, we had to face a decision about how to handle my relocation. I had to be in Granville, NH on June 1. Unfortunately, Barb had not had an opportunity to begin applying for jobs in the Granville area. For a number of reasons, we decided that she needed to maintain her current job in the Anniston area until the house sold. First of all, we needed her income to cover our monthly expenses. Second, we needed someone in Anniston to maintain and watch the house until it sold and then to sign the sales agreement and contract, once a buyer was found. Finally, the only way we could afford the transition without sacrificing the savings we needed to cover our moving expenses was for me to find an inexpensive room to rent for myself in Granville until we could sell the house. With the high cost of living in New Hampshire, the cost of an apartment for all of us would have been more than we could afford. For the time being, our temporary separation was necessary, but neither of us felt it would last for long. Surely, our house in Oxford would sell. With that thought in mind, I packed my belongings, and on May 29, after celebrating Barb's birthday, I began my trip north to New Hampshire.

The trip to Granville was more than 1,400 miles by highway from Oxford. To help manage my travel expenses, I made arrangements to visit my remaining half-brother, John Gary Umling, along the way. Gary, as he preferred to be called, lived in the Washington, DC area of Maryland, which was roughly the halfway point on my trip. The opportunity to meet him also had a special significance for me. Gary was my father's son by his previous wife Maggie. When my father divorced her to marry my mother, Maggie refused him any contact with his son. Like me, Gary grew up without ever knowing our father. What's more, I would be the first of my other brothers and sisters to meet him. Although they had always known that Gary existed, none of them had ever met him before. As a result, Gary and I shared an additional bond beyond our blood relationship. Neither of us ever knew our father or the rest of our family. Although I could only spend part of one day with him, I was especially excited to finally meet him.

Like many of my other siblings, especially Kathy, Gary was very open and expressive. We talked at length about our feelings and reactions to the family as outsiders. Gary was also going through a painful divorce, and he talked at length about the impacts it had on him. His honesty and sincerity were admirable qualities. I also met his two sons, Kyle and Gary. Ironically, Kyle closely resembled my son both in age and appearance. I only wished that I could have spent more time with John Gary, but my work schedule would not permit it, and I had another long drive before me.

When I arrived in New Hampshire, I had not yet found a place to live. I had made arrangements to stay in a hotel in nearby Riverdale, VT, until I could secure more comfortable and affordable temporary accommodations. However, my first destination was Derry to spend another day with Rose, before beginning my new job. I wanted a day to relax from my trip with my sister before reporting to work.

The realities of my new job hit me in the face like an Arctic blast in the dead of winter. First of all, three former staff persons had recently resigned on the heels of the former executive director, and several other remaining employees were disgruntled over personality conflicts. In fact, the personality conflicts within the office had been festering for years and only rose to the surface when the outgoing executive director promoted one of the competing employees within a week of leaving. One additional planner had been seeking another job during the time that I was being considered for my position.

Additionally, on my third day on the job, I had to attend a meeting with a representative at the Vermont Agency of Community Affairs regarding a petition by one of the agency's four Vermont towns to withdraw from the Precision Valley Regional Planning Commission and join a neighboring region. I soon learned that my counterpart at the neighboring agency had met with the outgoing town, at the request of a town councilman, while it was still a member of our region without our knowledge. As I later learned, this councilman was disgruntled with the commission because he was denied appointment as the executive director of our agency when my predecessor was hired. That town councilman had also organized the movement within the town council to withdraw, despite the fact that the town's planning commission opposed it.

As if that wasn't enough, the fiscal year for the regional planning commission was coming to a close at the end of the month, and the agency had to absorb a $2,500 loss. One of the agency's traditional partners in Vermont had refused to pay the commission for work it had requested because a written contract had not been signed for the project, even though the work had been done. That amount might not seem like a lot, but regional planning commissions are non-profit entities, and any shortfall in revenues can make a big difference on the fiscal year balance sheet. The director of the defaulting partner was also embroiled in a battle of words and ideologies between two competing chambers of commerce serving communities in the region that disrupted the Precision Valley's administration of a state-funded cooperative venture between the two chambers. The battle threatened to delay work on the project and had political repercussions for similar programs across the state.

The list of problems I faced did not stop there. Our agency was involved in a contentious public hearing regarding a state development permit for a convenience store in one of our Vermont towns. The issues surrounding the project were so controversial for the tiny hamlet that it divided the town council and the town planning commission, both of which expected our agency to support their respective positions. As it happened, this town had withdrawn from its former region to become a member of our region in 1991 because the former regional planning commission had taken a stance against the town council on a similar development application. It certainly didn't help matters to learn that the governor's office was also trying to intervene in the debate. Finally, our commission had a member of its board of directors who had been fired many years ago and was constantly trying to keep our agency from expanding its planning services to member communities.

Clearly, I had my work cut out for me from the very start. I embarked on an aggressive effort to hire new planners to replace the outgoing staff. I even conducted several meetings with the remaining staff to air, discuss, and resolve the lingering personality conflicts and encourage them to work together for the benefit of the agency. To lighten the tension between competing staff members, we called them our "come-to-Jesus meetings." I also began a tour of the region to meet with every one of the region's remaining 29 town and city councils to introduce myself, reinforce their confidence in the agency, and offer our services to them. Finally, I carefully reviewed all of our projects for the coming year to make sure that we had signed contracts for every service we had agreed to provide.

The time required to undertake these efforts was staggering. During my first six months on the job, I had logged over 170 hours of overtime, not including the time I donated to the agency by reporting to work early each day. However, the hard work and dedication was generating positive results. The agency was fully staffed by the middle of August, and all of the employees I inherited decided to remain with the commission. I had actually managed to convince one of our larger towns to resume paying dues to the commission after dropping its sponsorship of the region many years ago, and a former member town in New Hampshire sought to rejoin our region. Even our revenue shortfall from the defaulted contract was soon erased. What appeared at first blush to be a questionable career move was gradually turning out to be a modest success story.

As for my readoption and name change, I was surprised to find that my new co-workers and work associates were completely supportive, just as all my former colleagues in Anniston had been. In fact, one of the commission's board members was a long-time friend of my adoptive family, and even he was comfortable with my decision. When the local newspaper in Granville learned about my search and readoption, they decided to do a sidebar story about it as part of their article on my appointment as the new executive director of the regional planning commission. However, the reactions of the people with whom I worked professionally would not be the real test of my acceptance. The real test would come at the hands of the people I grew up with in North Georgetown. I knew that if they could accept what I had done, then anyone could.

Actually, I was not at all confident that my childhood friends would accept the actions I had taken regarding my readoption. That's why I waited until mid-September before making my first attempt to explain it to them. The person I decided to approach first was Terry Spaulding. Terry was one of the kids I first met at the North Georgetown village school. His parents were good friends with my adoptive parents during my early childhood years, but they later had a disagreement when I was about eleven years old that ended their close relationship. While they never became enemies, I never really understood the reasons for the "falling out" that occurred. Fortunately, it never affected my friendship with Terry. We remained friends through elementary school even though I started spending more of my time with Greg Dobbins. After our first year of high school, we started riding different buses and attending different classes, so I began to lose contact with him. However, I knew I could trust him to be honest with me about his personal impressions and to keep the issue from becoming a public spectacle within the community.

One Sunday afternoon in September, I decided to visit his home in Barrington, Vermont, which was directly across the Connecticut River from Georgetown. I had contacted Terry's father several weeks earlier to get his telephone number and arrange the visit. When I met him for the first time in over twenty years, I couldn't believe how little his appearance had changed. We exchanged pleasantries when we met, then I gave him my business card. When his eyes caught the name, he didn't know what to say or ask, but he looked up at me with a puzzled expression. I suggested that we sit down for a while, so I could explain the reasons for the strange name on my card.

For the next hour or so, I explained the various paths my life had taken, since I left North Georgetown in 1980. He had known that I was an adoptee, but he never knew about the problems that developed within my adoptive family or how those incidents affected me. I never talked about that to anyone, because, for most of my childhood, I felt that I was largely responsible for them. So, I naturally didn't want to discuss them. Besides, I thought no one would believe or understand my perspectives on it, and it wasn't the kind of thing people openly talked about in a small town.

Terry listened attentively as I explained everything, including my counseling, the gradual disintegration of my relationship with my adoptive family, and my eventual search for my biological family. I even showed him photographs of my birth relatives, so he could see how closely I resembled them. All the while, I watched his expressions and reactions to everything I said, hoping to understand what he was thinking or how he would respond to my story. However, he just sat there listening calmly without even raising an eyebrow. He just wasn't an excitable person. That was the personality trait I was depending on by seeking his reactions.

When I finally finished, I asked him what his thoughts were. His response caught me by surprise. "Well, we all knew that your adoptive mother was a bit strange," he casually replied. "That's why everyone just tip-toed around her. No one wanted to get on her bad side."

"What? I'm not sure I understand what you mean."

Terry looked away silently into empty space for a moment before his eyes focused again on me. "Do you remember when Andy died?" He was referring to his baby brother, who was born with leukemia and died when he was only a few years old. I could remember hearing about it as a child, but I couldn't recall when it occurred, and I didn't know the specific circumstances surrounding it that caused him to ask me about it.

"Yeah, I think I can remember hearing about it," I replied. "But I never knew all the details. Didn't he survive for a number of years?"

"Yes, he died when he was three years old. It happened not long after your adoptive mother lost her own son. When Andy died, it really hurt my mother, even though she had known for some time that it was going to happen. She had always prayed for him to go into remission when he began to outlive his original life expectancy. The loss always hit her hardest when she went to church on Sundays. In fact, she was crying one Sunday after the services, when Ellen approached my mother to offer her condolences. However, what she said really hurt my mother's feelings more. She said that it was okay that Andy died, because she had lost her own son. Several other members of the church heard her say that and felt it was a rather inappropriate and selfish thing to say. Ellen never apologized. That's when my mother stopped speaking to her. I guess your parents figured out how everyone felt about it, because they stopped coming to church shortly after that."

"Oh my God," I replied. "I never knew anything about that. My adoptive parents always told us that they stopped going to the church because the demands of farming were too great on my father's time, and they didn't like the new minister."

"Well, I don't know this for a fact, but I imagine they didn't like the new minister because he might have said something to her about it. But it was a small town and no one was going to make a big issue of it. I think most people just kept their distance for a while, until it passed. You know—for the sake of the community. I know your adoptive mother said some strange or inappropriate things to other people in town, but that's the incident I remember most."

I was truly stunned by Terry's revelation. In a way, it made me feel more confident that some of the people in North Georgetown might have known some aspects of my adoptive family's odd behavior well enough to understand and accept my decision to be readopted by my birth family. But, in another sense, it was disappointing. It made me realize that I never had to keep it all to myself as long as I did. If I had sensed that other people seemed to suspect problems with my adoptive family, I might have been able to talk about it years earlier with someone, perhaps the minister. Suddenly, I felt as though I had cheated myself from the emotional security I desperately wanted and needed all those years ago. I guess that's why people say that hindsight is always 20-20.

Terry and I continued our conversation for another hour. He told me how everyone who stayed in the community after high school was still living and working in the area. In fact, one of the bullies we both disliked in school had become the president of the bank his father founded. It was a small bank in a small town, but, from what Terry said, his "prestigious" position had clearly gone to his head. Even Terry chuckled at that.

Although I didn't want to live in North Georgetown again, I was glad I went to see Terry. His understanding and acceptance of my new identity was exactly the vindication my long-tormented conscience needed. It reassured me that I would not have to second-guess my decision to rejoin my biological family. I have made many mistakes in my life, but that was not one of them. Once I completely and fully accepted that conclusion, I knew I could become a whole person again. New Hampshire might still possess the remaining secrets surrounding my initial adoption, but neither the state nor my adoptive family would ever control my life again. The demons from my past were finally exorcised. That was the true peace of mind I had earned from all my search efforts.

My return to New Hampshire not only carried me to the pinnacle of my planning career and helped me release many of my childhood anxieties once and for all, it also gave me an opportunity to enjoy some pleasant experiences with my newly discovered biological family and my in-laws. I spent virtually every weekend with members of my birth family or my wife's parents. I joined Rose and her family on a trip to Salem, Massachusetts to tour the House of Seven Gables and all the Salem witch trial sites. I finally met my full brother, Tim and his wife (my former adoptive cousin), in late June, along with several of my mother's immediate relatives. Unfortunately, the Woodward family was not very close-knit, so some of them were harder to get to know than my father's side of the family. My mother still resented much of her childhood treatment within the family and refused to talk about them or spend much time with them. Still, I met as many of them as I could.

I spent most of my weekends with my brother, Dave, and sister, Rose. They both had plenty of room in their homes, which made it more comfortable for me to spend occasional nights with them. Whenever we got together, we always had a good time. Dave especially enjoyed family outings, such as cookouts, trips to the local arcades, playing horseshoes, and other outdoor activities. One Saturday in late July, Dave, Bill, Rose, their families, and I all met at a picnic area in the White Mountains that had been a traditional family reunion site for the Woodwards. We had a huge picnic and went swimming, very briefly, in the icy-cold Swift River. Although I could never relive my childhood with them, I will always treasure the memory of my weekend trips to visit my brothers and sister. Those experiences gave me something to look forward to every week, which made it easier for me to confront the most difficult and trying aspects of my new job. I don't know if I would have survived that job as comfortably and confidently as I did without them.

My parents didn't arrive in New Hampshire until August 11. It felt wonderful to see them again for the first time since my 37th birthday, six months earlier. For the first few weeks after their arrival, they lived with Rose, until they could find a home of their own in the Rochester area. They eventually found a rental home on the city's north side, only a few miles south of Dave's home in Milton. Once they were settled in their new home, I started spending my weekends with them. By then, it was time for Dave's wedding.

Dave and Leeann were married in an elegant stone church, built in the early 1800s. The service was a simple, but beautiful affair. I felt honored to stand at the altar with both of my brothers. After the ceremony, the wedding party shifted to a reception hall in Rochester. As the Groom's Best Man, I had the responsibility of giving a speech before the first toast. It was an ominous responsibility, as I had only known my brother and sister-in-law for a year. Most of the friends and family attending the wedding had known them for many years. What could I possibly say to a room full of family and long-time friends that would be appropriate to the occasion? However, the night before the wedding, I finally decided what to say. At the appointed time, I stood up, champagne glass in hand and began my speech.

"First of all, I want to say what an honor it is for me to be here on this special occasion. I know that most of you are aware of my situation and the reasons why I never had the opportunity to know the Bride and Groom as well as all of you do. Unfortunately, that means that I can't stand here and regale you with humorous stories from the past about my brother..." I hesitated for a moment and assumed a thoughtful pose and expression, as if I had suddenly become aware of a startling revelation. Then, I turned to Dave and said, "So, *that's* why you asked me to be your Best Man." My comment immediately lightened the atmosphere. I then went on to say how much it meant to me to find my brother and how much I looked forward to the memories I would share with them throughout the rest of my life. I ended my brief speech with a toast to the Bride and Groom, and I wished them all the happiness that their lives together could bring.

The times I spent with my family over the month following the wedding were among the most enjoyable and rewarding of my reunion. My mother introduced me to many of her long-time friends, including Jacki McNiel and Mary Meeks. Jacki had been one of my mother's closest friends over the years. My father took me on a tour of the U.S.S. Albacore, a mothballed naval submarine that was on permanent display in Portsmouth. After he retired from the Air Force, my father worked for several years on similar subs at the Portsmouth Naval Shipyard. He even gave me a tour of the shipyard itself and showed me some of the buildings where he had worked when I was just a child.

My parents even showed me two of the homes in Rochester and New Durham where they once lived. They also told me that, in the late 1980s, they had lived in a house in downtown Sanbornville, NH, right across the street from the Wakefield Town Hall. That historical tidbit was immediately significant to me, because the town of Wakefield was a member of the Lakes Region Planning Commission during the time that I worked there in the late 1980s. In fact, I had spent the better part of a week in the Wakefield Town Hall during March 1988 researching residential property tax cards as part of a regional housing study that the commission was preparing for the state. At that time, a surprise spring snowstorm had dumped about a foot of snow on the region, and a large number of the parking spaces around the town hall were buried under piles of snow that had been plowed from the adjoining streets and sidewalks. Since I normally didn't arrive at the town hall until all of the few remaining parking spaces had been taken, I had to park in front of a house across the street from the town hall. Ironically, I was parking right in front of the house in which my biological parents were living at the time! Had they seen me parking there, they might have mistaken me for my brother, Tim. In fact, under the right circumstances, I could have been accidentally reunited with my birth family in March 1988, a full ten years earlier!

One week after my parents showed me where they had lived, they came to visit me in Granville, and I gave them a tour of the area where I was raised. I showed them the old family farm in North Georgetown, the village school, and many of the other significant places from my childhood years. Revisiting the places from my past with them felt a little eerie, but it left me with a wonderfully fulfilling sense of closure to my childhood memories. In a sense, the trip was a fitting catharsis for me, as I believe it was for my mother, as well. It seemed to give her a small, but valuable piece of my past, which she had all but lost by virtue of my adoption.

However, by mid-October, our fortunes began to change. On the afternoon of October 18, I left work to visit my parents for the weekend, as had become my routine. Everything was fine, until I was awakened early the next morning by my mother. My father had fallen on his way to the bathroom, and she was unable to help him get up. She knew that something was wrong, and she needed me to drive him to the Veteran's Hospital in Manchester. At first, I suggested an ambulance which I knew would be faster, and I thought they might carry with them much of the medical equipment they would need to start treating him along the way. But my father adamantly refused, so we had no choice but to help him into my car and transport him to Manchester, which was an hour's drive from their home in Rochester. I struggled to keep him conscious throughout the trip.

Soon after we arrived at the hospital, our worst fears were confirmed. My father had suffered his third stroke. The doctors had managed to stabilize his condition, and they were preparing to transfer him to a larger facility in Boston. He remained at the Boston hospital for nearly a week, before they finally released him. Although the stroke had damaged his spirit, he managed to gradually recover most of his mobility in the following weeks. The only visible effects were a slight reduction in his ability to speak and a loss of dexterity on his left side. Had I not been there to drive him to the hospital when I did, his condition might have been much worse.

At the same time, I was beginning to realize that our house in Oxford was not going to sell as quickly as we had hoped. Although Barb and Michael had managed to visit me in New Hampshire for a week at the end of August and I called them every night, we had been separated for months. When Fort McClellan officially closed on September 30, we were no longer receiving any prospective buyers. We desperately considered as many alternatives as we could. Unfortunately, when the housing market collapsed, the rental market went with it. At the prevailing rental prices in the post-Fort McClellan housing market, we couldn't even afford to cover our monthly mortgage costs by renting it. As a result, we decided that renting the house was not a viable option. Besides, we couldn't afford to buy a replacement home in Granville until we were able to sell the house in Oxford. Every option we explored was going to leave us with a substantial financial loss that we couldn't afford to bear.

In an ironic twist of fate, I learned that the East Alabama Regional Planning and Development Commission had been unable to fill my old position. Some of my former co-workers and friends kept bumping into my wife and son around town, so they knew we were experiencing difficulties with our transition. Several of them asked me to consider returning. In fact, I also received a couple of telephone calls from local officials in East Alabama with whom I had worked closely. They, too, implored me to consider returning. Given the financial problems we were facing, I felt I had no choice but to seriously consider returning to Alabama. No matter how much I benefited from and enjoyed the time I was able to spend with my biological family, my first priority was to my wife and son. I couldn't abandon them, and I couldn't force them to face a significantly lower standard of living simply because I wanted to be nearer to our families. I held out as long as I could, hoping against all odds that the situation would change. However, by Thanksgiving, my decision was clear. I couldn't spend the entire winter apart from my family waiting to see if the Anniston housing market would recover in the spring.

On December 1, 1999, the six-month anniversary date of my employment at Precision Valley, I submitted my formal resignation as the agency's executive director. It was a heart-wrenching decision, but I knew that it was best for all involved. I needed to be with my wife and son again. My family gave me a wonderful going away party in mid-December. My co-workers at Precision Valley did the same during the following week. Then, in the frigid early morning hours of December 18, I regretfully packed my personal belongings into my car and headed south. My final New Hampshire homecoming was over, nearly seven months after it began.

Once again, I found myself working with my friends at East Alabama. Although I wished I hadn't been separated from my wife and son for so long, I will never regret the time I spent in New Hampshire. It helped bring me closer to my new family, and it made me realize that I had the ability to be an executive director. In fact, I felt more comfortable with my life than I ever had before. I continued to visit, entertain, and communicate with all my new relatives as well as the remaining members of my adoptive family who accepted my new life. I also researched my family's genealogy in whatever spare time I had remaining. I didn't know where my life would lead from there, but I was comfortable and relieved with the direction it was taking. All I could say for certain is that it would never be the same again. The familiarity I had with that life-long growth pattern was reassuring. Perhaps there's just no better way to end my own story than with that thought.

## *Afterthoughts*

Shortly after I returned to Oxford, I began writing the story you have just read, while all the details remained fresh in my mind. I wanted to document for my son everything that had happened and preserve the story in the hope that it would inspire or help other adoptees who may consider searching. I have read and learned of many adoption stories throughout my life—even before my own search. All of them focus on the stories of their searches and reunions, but very few of them explain in any meaningful detail how the shrouding of the adoptee's birth heritage influenced his or her essential self-image or affected the adoptive family relationship. Those consequential aspects of closed-record adoption were very important to me and my personal growth, so I felt a need to reveal and explain them. These were my primary motivations to write this story.

However, I couldn't bring myself to publish the story after it was initially completed in late 2000. I felt it would embarrass my adoptive mother and cause her more pain. After all, the truth is rarely sensitive to your ego. Perhaps that is why it is often so difficult for many people to face. To be honest, I must admit that some aspects of the story still feel embarrassing to me.

Although I could hope that my adoptive sisters might eventually read it, I couldn't be sure that they were ready to think critically and honestly about the problems we shared during our childhood—much less discuss them openly. I'm the kind of person who now feels compelled to do that. I felt certain they still buried the uncomfortable truth about our past deep in the dark recesses of their minds and pretended that it never happened. After all, they made it quite clear that I was dead to them. All I could actually expect to accomplish by publishing the story was to make them even angrier with me than they already were. Anger and resentment were always difficult feelings for my adoptive family to bear, much less resolve. Although more than two years had passed since my reunion and readoption, I concluded that the wounds were simply too fresh and raw, and the publishing of my story would only make that situation worse.

When the book was finished, I shared copies of it with my new family. It gave them the details of my past that they never knew and helped them understand my reasons for searching. They found great comfort and satisfaction in that. Otherwise, the story, along with the documentation I compiled during my exhaustive search, remained in boxes for many years, like so many of the plans I have written during my career.

As time passed, my relationship with my biological family gradually evolved into a pattern of normalcy—which is a difficult term for a person with my family experiences to define. The excitement and novelty of the initial reunions gradually waned and more natural, relaxed, and genuine relationships emerged. That is what should be expected of a normal family. We are simply no model of a perfect family, nor would we have been, if I had never been placed for adoption.

By 2005, I had spent enough quality time with all of my immediate family and many extended family members that we all gained a thorough understanding of each other. I now know all the individual traits and characteristics that we have in common as well as those that make us different. There is simply no room for misperceptions or false pretenses anymore. Simply put, I learned what they were really like when they were not trying to make a good first impression. As with any large family, I have stronger relationships with those siblings and relatives that share the most in common with me and less intense relationships with those who are most different. In many ways, I am as close to Aunt Betty and her family as I am to my own mother and siblings. My family still has its own disagreements and unresolved problems, but they have not altered my standing within it, nor would they be substantively different if I had never been relinquished or never returned. This is what I refer to as a pattern of normalcy.

I cannot assert to you that the acceptance I received from my birth family has given me a new or renewed implicit sense of trust in close interpersonal relationships. This is a problem or a deficiency in emotional security that I find many, if not most, adoptees share. I will eagerly admit that I allowed myself to have high expectations in the potential long-term strength and quality of my relationships with each new family member I met, based on the initial reception

I received. I believe that such hopeful expectations are typical in the early stages of any intimate interpersonal relationships that begin better than initially anticipated. In some cases, that investment of trust was rewarded; in other cases, it wasn't. At least I didn't force them to have any relationship with me that they didn't genuinely want to have.

However, time and the growing familiarity that naturally comes with it, gradually tempers your perceptions and adjusts your expectations accordingly. This process of "assimilation" invariably occurred within my birth family, as I gained more experience and understanding from my routine interactions with them. I'm sure they came to understand me better in the same way. What I can honestly say about the integrity of my own interactions with them is that I was no longer trying to mold myself into someone or something that I *wasn't* just to earn their acceptance and affections. The greater self-assurance that I carefully built and honed over the years now outweighs the negative self-image I internalized during my youth, and it allows me to more comfortably accept who I really am and should be. It may be a lifelong recovery process that I will never fully complete, but I can be confident that I am not unique or alone in that respect.

While the vast majority of my current relationships with my biological relatives are positive, some were not successful. It is never easy to mend the emotional distance that time and separation create. Many people cling to the belief that "absence makes the heart grow fonder," and perhaps it does initially work that way—especially if a strong and close relationship has been established *before* the separation occurs. I think it usually depends on how long and how complete the separation is. Obviously, the longing that makes the heart grow fonder for a missing person cannot automatically occur in the case of a closed adoption. The sudden knowledge that a person you never knew is genetically related to you is not always an effective catalyst upon which to forge a sincere or lasting emotional attachment.

For example, I was never able to establish a successful or meaningful brother-sister relationship with my youngest sister, Carolyn. She was fiercely independent and carried with her a number of scars and skeletons from the past that affected her relationships with most of the family. Of all my brothers and sisters, I believe Carolyn had achieved the most in life, if success can be truly measured in monetary terms. To her, the career she had achieved and the material wealth she accumulated were her primary sources of pride, and she seemed to be offended by anyone she perceived as a potential challenge to her perceived status. That appears to be her competitive nature. Carolyn had become comfortable with her self-image as the most successful member of her family, and I believe she eventually viewed my education, professional career, and income as an unwelcomed challenge to her self-image. My mother said that her attitude towards me began to change when she first saw a picture of me wearing a suit and tie.

The picture I had sent was a family portrait we had taken for a recent Christmas, and the only reason I was wearing a suit for it was that we had the picture taken during work hours, and I had to come straight to the studio from the office. Personally, I never felt comfortable wearing suits because they always made me feel like I was wearing a costume. I was raised in rural poverty and never owned or wore a suit until I was in college. To me, it was something I *had* to wear for the work I did, in order to project the required professional image. It meant nothing more to me than that, and I would always shed my suit as soon as I got home from work and return to my casual clothes—which, as my wife would freely attest, could hardly be considered stylish by anybody's standard. During the coldest months, I still wear the same style of plaid, flannel work shirts I wore as a child.

However, that incidental picture, Carolyn's insecurities, and her growing realization of my career and standard of living caused her to perceive me as a threat to her self-image and stature within the family. Over time, she became resentful of the efforts my supporting family members made to encourage her to accept me as her brother. In the end, she simply couldn't, and she eventually took the position that I was not a legitimate member of her family because I did not grow up with them. She would insult me when I tried to contact her and became resentful of everyone's efforts to accept me as part of her family. It seemed sadly ironic to be treated that way by the only sibling who knew for many years that I had been lost to adoption. Her attitude and behavior reminded me of someone from my past.

In that regard, she impressed me as the "Daphne" of my birth family. Daphne never truly accepted me as her brother because I wasn't born into her family. To her, I was a source of division and envy. On the other hand, my biological sister, Carolyn, wouldn't accept me as a legitimate member of her family because I didn't grow up within it. Here again was the age-old adoptee dilemma. What family could I legitimately feel a part of? Who has the absolute right to decide that for me? Should my relinquishment and adoption—actions that I did not request, instigate, or control—make me an illegitimate member of *both* my adoptive and birth families? How can I reconcile this adoption process dilemma and honestly feel that it was done in my best interest?

Therein lays the inherent and basic philosophical conundrum and unintended consequence of the adoption process that is caused by closed records and the permanent veil of secrecy that it creates. Because of Daphne's and Carolyn's insecurities and jealousies, I could not develop any meaningful, positive, or lasting family relationship with either of them. However, if the process had allowed my biological family to know me, then Carolyn might not have been able to contend that I was illegitimate. Of my seven biological brothers and sisters, she remains the only one who summarily rejected me. It didn't matter much to the rest of my siblings because she refused to communicate with many of them as well. My relationships with my remaining brothers and sisters have become as normal as any relationships they have with each other, given the unresolved, long-standing animosities between the Conners and Umlings and the geographical distances between us.

The evolution of my relationship with my birth family may not sound like a fairy-tale ending to my search, reunion, and readoption, but I believe it is an honest and objective assessment. It is important for all searching adoptees to understand that a successful reunion does not necessarily mean that it will always feel like a fairy tale. But I believe that even a normal relationship is truly better and emotionally healthier than living with unanswered questions and empty hopes. At least that is my experience and my assessment. I would never choose to reverse everything that transpired and go back to the person that I was.

***** *****

I continued to work for the East Alabama Regional Planning and Development Commission for another four-and-a-half years, after I returned to the job in January 2000. In December 2003, my father's health began to deteriorate significantly, and he was eventually diagnosed with terminal cancer. Responding to my desire to spend what time I could with him and Barb's and my shared desire to bring Michael closer to his extended families and eventually place him in a better high school environment, I accepted a new job in Southern Maryland (where my brother John Gary lived) in 2004. That new job placed me in charge of a county planning department with a staff of 26 (which would eventually grow to 30) and gave me a substantial raise that I could never achieve in Alabama. The day I received the job offer I called my mother in New Hampshire to let her know we would finally be moving closer to them. As soon as I finished giving her the good news, she told me that my father had passed away earlier that morning. At least I was able to spend five days with him in the month before he died, and I could be satisfied that I had six precious years to know him.

Our experiences living in the Washington, DC metropolitan area—a major, rapidly growing, urbanized area that was unfamiliar to both of us—eventually led me to regret leaving the rural areas I had served throughout my career. Barb and I both found it difficult to adapt to the intensely urban environment into which we had moved. The noise and traffic we experienced on a daily basis was overwhelming and unsettling. The almost compulsive obsession with material wealth and image that we saw displayed conspicuously throughout the greater Washington society was as pretentious and suffocating as it was appalling. The inflated cost of living quickly consumed most of the pay increase we received. I struggled to reconcile the realities of how the modern business world actually worked with the traditional, rural core values that I internalized through my upbringing and could now more comfortably accept. We had spent so much time living in relatively isolated rural areas and small cities that we weren't adequately prepared for the lifestyle changes we would encounter or the demands they would place on us.

I also became increasingly bored with the routine and repetitive nature of my planning work and disillusioned by the evolution of the profession in a more politically biased and urban-design-oriented direction. The different essential needs and issues of the rural areas I had served for so much of my career have become increasingly lost to an urban-focused profession. Over time, I began to feel as though I was a victim of my own education and experiences. We desperately needed some relief from it all.

In the final analysis, it didn't matter that I had learned how to work effectively in and plan for urban areas. It didn't matter that I could truly appreciate a few aspects of urban life. It also didn't matter that I was driven into the outside world by the persistent cajoling of my adoptive parents and the insecurities I harbored from my failed childhood. I eventually came to the inevitable conclusion that I was naturally inclined to live in the rural mountain environment I grew to know from my childhood *despite* the negative feelings I internalized from it. I guess Water Cronkite said it best, "That's the way it is." Just because a cat loves to eat fish does not necessarily mean it can learn to live more happily, comfortably, or successfully in the ocean. I needed a lifestyle and environment that satisfied *most* of my basic needs—not just a few. Some urban dwellers truly appreciate a rural setting and enjoy vacationing there, even though they would never desire to give up their cherished urban lifestyle to live in it. I came to the conclusion that I was inherently the opposite kind of person—and always would be.

Eventually, Barb and I responded to the stress and incongruities of a truly modern urban lifestyle by escaping to the rural hinterlands of the Appalachian Mountains—with which we were intimately familiar and to which we were repeatedly drawn. We used many of those trips to seek a place that could give us some meaningful prospects for a more suitable and comfortable retirement. In October 2006, we eventually found that place in Pendleton County, West Virginia. It was a great relief for me to realize that I could finally separate the guilt and resentment I felt growing up in my adoptive family from the true affinity I had for our traditional, rural farm environment enough to pursue that lifestyle in my retirement. In all honesty, that is the lifestyle that best suits me and my core values.

This was an important revelation in my ongoing efforts to understand who I truly was. However, it was not acquired through the quality of my relationship with my birth family. It was my determination to search for answers to the unresolved questions about my hidden past and the deeper understanding of my nature I had gained from it that helped me separate the positive and negative feelings from my upbringing and finally understand their subtle influences on me. That understanding ultimately made it easier for me to *accept* who I really am, and it helped me resolve the constant struggle I faced by my forced transition into the outside modern world. It is also the best evidence I can offer to prove that I have outgrown the constricting anxieties from my past, and it continues to be one of the greatest personal benefits I received from the entire search and reunion process.

Viewed in that context, the overall quality of my current relationships with individual members of my birth family (regardless of how they may be judged) should not be considered the *primary* benefit I obtained, but an *added* benefit. The ultimate goal was to become a healthier and more complete and secure person. Regardless of how, after reading my story, anyone chooses to judge my actions, it would be inconceivable to suggest that they did not ultimately make me a better and more self-confident person than I was when I first left home.

In October 2007, I landed what I conceived to be a pre-retirement job as the city planner for Cumberland, MD. This job placed us within a comfortable driving distance to our Pendleton County retirement property and was far less stressful than my previous job in Charles County. It also didn't require that I wear a suit. We began constructing our retirement home on our Pendleton County property in early 2010 and are just now finishing it as I edit and update this story.

In the process of moving into the area, we were repeatedly asked why we accepted a reduction in income to come here from the Washington, DC area, where so many of their children flee to find the jobs and opportunities for advancement that have become increasingly scarce in the Cumberland economy. While explaining our decision, my adoption story would invariably be told again and again. Repeated local interest in that adventure caused me to resurrect the book I had written and consider editing and updating it. I undertook that effort in 2014—nearly seven years after moving to the area and a full sixteen years after my search was completed. In the process, I learned that virtually all of my adoptive family's remaining prior generations had passed away during the intervening years. Between 2002 and 2013, my adoptive mother, grandmother, Aunt Karen, and Great-Aunt Sue all had died. My adoptive sisters were scattered. There were now fewer reasons to withhold publishing it.

***** *****

Now that I am 52 years old, I occasionally take time to sit on the front porch of our Pendleton County retirement house and admire our sweeping view of the majestic, forested Appalachian Mountain ridgelines that ripple rhythmically across the landscape—like ocean waves. As the serenity of that view gradually unclutters my mind and helps me put my thoughts into perspective, I often find myself reflecting upon the various lives I have led. Based on the medical history I gained through my adoptee search, I know full well that I have fewer years to live. I know of no males in my biological family who have lived to be 90, and the gradual impacts of age on my health and vitality give me no assurance that I will be the first.

That's okay with me, because I can now look forward to living the remainder of my life in the adopted home of my choosing unfettered by the frightful ghosts and insecurities of my past. As I told our friends when we purchased our retirement property, my gravestone goes up with the house. Perhaps I just don't fear death as much as some people do. I faced it early in my life. I realize that, if I had been successful in my 1979 suicide attempt, my life could have ended when I was only seventeen years old. As far as I'm concerned, I've been living on borrowed time for the past 35 years.

However, as I contemplate the full measure of my past, I am reminded of many memories of my childhood on the farm—both good and bad; my college and early adult years—when I struggled to make sense of it all and discover who I really was; and my eventual reunion with my biological family—which gave me the acceptance and perspective I needed to sort it all out and resolve the difficult questions that always nagged and haunted me. At first blush, my story seems quite unusual and bizarre, given all the dramatic changes and personal discoveries I experienced over the years. When I put all those pieces together and contemplate the complete picture that the puzzle forms, I find that the person I truly am isn't dictated by one family or experience but a mish-mash of them all. It's as though someone threw a bunch of random ingredients into a blender, turned it on, and ended up with a reasonably satisfying drink completely by chance. I guess you could call me a curious, marginally successful mongrel of life.

That thought makes me chuckle because I have spent my entire professional career advising people of the need to *plan* for a successful future—as though it was something you could know in advance and achieve by following a thoughtfully predetermined course. All the while, it appears that I stumbled into it with absolutely no idea of where I was heading or what I would face next. Perhaps that explains why so many of the plans I and most other planners write eventually end up collecting dust on a shelf.

For example, do you know how many professionally prepared local government comprehensive plans adopted in the years *immediately* prior to 2007 accurately predicted the so-called "Great Recession" of 2007-2009 and understood or addressed the impacts it would have on their respective governments and their long-range goals? After all, that recession was so severe that many local governments (and states) teetered on the edge of fiscal insolvency for years after most economists declared that it had ended and several large cities actually filed for bankruptcy protection. While planners can't be expected to anticipate everything, any economic and fiscal crisis of that magnitude has a significant impact on a community's most basic planning priorities and its capacity to implement its plan in a timely manner. Yet, many professional planners today insist that communities should follow their adopted comprehensive plans religiously, as though any failure to do so might cause a calamity of the same magnitude. Although I have asked this question of many of the most conceited planning colleagues I know, I have yet to identify even one that managed to account for it. Obviously, planning for the future is not the precise and reliable science that many professionals frequently and arrogantly assert it to be.

My experiences have taught me that there is something inherently intriguing and mystical about the random patterns of our lives that fiendishly defies our understanding and deliberate intent. No matter how carefully or determinedly we chart the course we wish to take in life, reality still refuses to accept our basic assumptions and limited understanding of it. As I said earlier, all great theories are great in theory, but not necessarily in reality. I think that is a fundamental truth. There is always something out there in the mist—like the next mountain in the distance that is beyond our view—we can't fully understand or comprehend that inevitably alters our course and leads us in an unanticipated new direction. Life often appears to be well ordered and follows basic rules, but we never seem to know them all. It's almost as though life is a perpetual design-build project that requires frequent adjustment to our best laid plans and theories. Just ask any physicist or cosmologist.

Then again, if we *could* suddenly illuminate and resolve all of the subtle mysteries in life, how boring might it ultimately become? If you always know how to win the game before you even start, how long would you really want to play? I guess it's really the fact that you *can't* know the outcome in advance that makes the challenge of pursing it more enticing and rewarding. I also feel it exerts a humbling influence that is periodically necessary to keep our egos in check. We seem to need some unanswerable questions to ponder in order to instill in us a sense of wonder about the future that will inspire us to new heights and make life worth living. After all, isn't that why the proverbial bear went over the mountain? Perhaps that is also why ghost stories, the Loch Ness Monster, Bigfoot, alien abductions, and other legends remain ingrained in our social conscience, despite the persistent lack of any objectively verifiable evidence to prove their existence.

I often think that our endless pursuit of answers to the mysteries that defy our understanding may be the spice of life that makes the cold, hard realities of living easier to accept and bear. It's the constant struggle to resolve the unanswered questions and overcome the adversities in our paths that makes our successes so sweet and gratifying—just as it makes our failures so frustrating. Even so, you have to fight and persevere to succeed. Random luck will only carry you so far. If your life is not giving you the meaning you want from it, then you'd better work to give it meaning. I just can't promise you that your efforts will always be rewarded. Sometimes, you may not even recognize the reward. Perhaps you have to look more closely to find it. All I can say is that you are far less likely to achieve the satisfaction you desire from life, if you don't even try. The answers you seek in life are not actively searching for your questions.

Perhaps the real value in planning is that it helps you make better or more considered course changes along the way, rather than dictating or predetermining the entire path. At least, that's how I have come to see it, and it seems perfectly justified by the lessons I've learned from the various lives I've lived. You can never know it all in advance, no matter how smart you may think you are, so you had better be prepared to face and strategically navigate the unexpected and unavoidable whims of life. Even then, random chance can intervene again and force you to alter your plans. Never arrogantly assume you have absolute control over all the moving pieces of our complex, intertwined lives. That's exactly how I approached my adoptee search, and I would advise all searching adoptees and birth parents to think of it that way. Furthermore, now that I am at the end of my professional planning career, I hope these thoughts will help the younger planners I leave behind temper their own attitudes about and expectations of the plans they will write and put their work aspirations into proper perspective.

As I contemplate the random puzzle pieces that made my own picture complete, I can now accept and appreciate the fondest memories I have of my childhood life on the farm; the strong attachment I have to the rural environment in which I was raised; and the core values of hard work and integrity I internalized from our traditional, self-reliant lifestyle. At the same time, I can better understand and appreciate the adversities I faced—as I struggled to overcome my own insecurities and the challenges of our marginal and meager living. My frequent struggles to overcome them gave me a strong determination to combat my self-hatred and succeed in my adult life. I couldn't have completed my adoptee search without it.

I also appreciate the understanding and unconditional acceptance I received from my wife and biological family, which allowed me to feel more confident about myself and realize that I could be a person worthy of such love and affection. Even the painful pieces tossed at me along the way that never seemed to fit helped mold and polish the final picture. *All* of these influences were necessary and essential for me to understand and accept who I am and should be. They all had a meaningful purpose and role in defining who I am, even if I couldn't fully understand or accept it at the time. You should always be appreciative of whatever you have in life—good or bad, because those are the only resources you have to use in building the future you seek.

While it may seem, even to me, that my life was a wild roller coaster ride, I'm sure that (if you really think carefully about it) most people experience dramatic and traumatic ups and downs, highs and lows that impact their lives and inevitably shape what they become. The differences are most apparent in the overall balance of the elements, not in the breadth or quality of the individual experiences. If there's some inherent truth to that thought, perhaps my lives were simply more different than they were unusual or bizarre, after all.

While many readers might presume that I oppose adoption from the experiences I have recounted and the reactions I had to them, nothing could be further from the truth. I freely recognize that there will always be circumstances where some form of adoption is needed to provide a home and family for children who would otherwise have none. Cases of severe child abuse, gross neglect, and even child abandonment are well documented in our society and seem to grow with each passing year. Some children lose their entire biological families to tragedy, such as natural disasters, house fires, airline accidents, automobile accidents, and murder. It would be patently stupid of me to ignore all of that. Certainly, anyone with half a brain would agree that adoption is infinitely preferable to an institutional childhood or a life on the streets. Hopefully, no one would believe me to be too arrogant to understand and accept that. However, the mere fact that adoption is necessary in our society does not mean that the manner in which it is currently conducted is the only or most appropriate way it could or should be conducted. Furthermore, I simply do not feel that a child's family background, medical history, or cultural heritage *must* be sacrificed in order to give a child a proper home or an adoptive family.

Our society and legal system appear to treat adoption as an either-or scenario. An adoptive child can either be part of his adoptive family or his biological family, not both. To me, that is a severely narrow, ignorant, arrogant, and inherently indefensible point of view. Our society benefits from *more* essential and meaningful connections between people, not fewer. What would the word "community" mean if that was not a truism? I believe that we need to consider a middle ground, where the adoptee has a meaningful opportunity and the inherent *right* to know and benefit from *both* of the major influences in his or her life—adoptive *and* biological—just as I have done. As I suggested earlier, if an adoptee's blood lineage and cultural heritage is so insignificant that it could be casually erased and replaced by a paper one—as the current adoption process would have you believe—then why do so many people today spend so much time, energy and money researching their own family genealogies? Should a person's true blood lineage and cultural heritage only be legitimately important to those who have not been adopted? If you treasure and value the knowledge of your family's lineage, be thankful that you are not an adoptee.

As recently as 1998, voters in Oregon passed a new law (Measure 58) to give adult adoptees access to their original birth certificates, essentially opening previously sealed adoption records. However, before the new law was put into effect, a lawsuit was filed to block it by a group of adoption professionals representing birth mothers who did not want their identities known by the children they had placed for adoption. The appeal significantly delayed implementation of the law. One or more of the birth mothers were rape victims and feared that the child they bore from the rape would track them down and make it easier for their rapists to find them. Although the plaintiffs in the case were primarily concerned that opening previously sealed adoption records would violate their confidentiality, no such promise or guaranty has ever been proffered by the adoption process. In fact, every closed record law I have studied provides opportunities, under specific conditions, for adoptees to petition the court to unseal their adoption records.

Although I have met and known literally hundreds of adoptees who have searched or are searching for their birth parents, I have never heard any of them say that they would *force* their biological parents to accept them, nor would they even wish to contact a father who had conceived them by rape. Even my own second cousin, Cheryl (Sabrina), showed no interest in pursuing a relationship with her biological father, once her birth mother explained what he had done. For most adoptees, searching is not about rebuilding broken families or replacing their adoptive families. Searching is about understanding our heritages and discovering who our blood relatives might be. (If you don't want to blindly marry a blood relative, that information might be important to know.) It usually stems from a desire to recognize and understand the reflection in the mirror. Virtually *anyone* would be naturally curious about that at some point in his or her life. In my case, it went much further than that, but my circumstances were far from typical. The absolute severing of my birth family's connection to me and the permanent sealing of my adoption records gave my adoptive mother the expectation that she was taking complete ownership of me—which was a sense of possession that she took to the extreme, regardless of how real it was or how much control she had over it.

I acknowledge that many adoptees may never choose to search. However, is the fact that some adoptees do not want to search any legitimate reason to deny those who do want or *need* (due to serious medical conditions) to find their biological roots of their right to search? Allowing me to search for my biological family does not force any other adoptee to search, if he or she chooses not to do so. Perhaps some adoptees who wish to arbitrarily deny the right to search for those adoptees desiring to do so are actually afraid that open records will make it more difficult for them to resist the temptation to search, which for them may be a choice or decision they would prefer not to face.

There is also the concern raised in Oregon about opening adoption records in cases where an adoptee was conceived by rape. Actually, if a convicted rapist really wanted to know the name or identity of his victim (assuming that information isn't already known), all he would have to do is access the court records or media coverage of the trial, from which he cannot be barred access. I see no reason why giving an adoptee access to his or her own birth records would make it any easier for a rapist to identify or find his victim. Besides, the evidence from my search and thousands of others each year makes it clear that adoptees can, with a lot of time, effort, and money, find their biological parents anyway. If I were a birth mother who had been raped, I think I would want my child to find me first, rather than my rapist. Who knows what an unrepentant rapist might manipulate the victim's child into doing for him? Finally, it is important to understand that only a very small percentage of adoptees are the product of a rape. In all of my contacts with adoptees, I have yet to meet one, even though I know they exist.

Another argument against open records raised by birth mothers in Oregon and, coincidentally, by religious conservatives, is that open records will lead to higher incidents of abortion. The argument here is that birth mothers who fear the negative social stigma associated with an out-of-wedlock birth will choose abortion over adoption, if they realize that their confidentiality will not be protected by the adoption process. If that line of reasoning is valid, perhaps the assurance that adoption records will remain permanently sealed will entice more women to have out-of-wedlock or extramarital pregnancies because it creates a secretive process for them to conveniently and secretly dispose of their unwanted child. Of course, any admission that more mothers have extramarital sex or don't choose abortion *because* of sealed adoption records may say far more about the frustrations and struggles of religious leaders to effectively advance or promote their moral values than it does about the social impact of open records.

Furthermore, I must reiterate that the adoption process *does not* guarantee a birth mother's privacy. If it did, then every birth parent that has ever been found (now numbering in the thousands annually) would be able to sue his or her respective state for breach of contract. Also, it is hard for me to believe, with the number, frequency, and percentage of out-of-wedlock births that occur in today's society, that an out-of-wedlock birth carries such a negative stigma that birth mothers would suddenly flood abortion clinics to avoid an open record adoption. If it does, then I would prefer to treat the problem, not the symptom.

It is also important to understand that adoption records in many states did not begin to be sealed by law until the 1930s. Prior to then, all adoption records were open. In fact, Kansas never changed its laws to seal adoption records. The first state to close adoption records was Minnesota in 1917. Oregon did not begin sealing its adoption records until 1957. Alabama became the last state to seal adoption records in 1991. Are we to honestly believe that changes in the abortion rate since the 1930s can be directly attributed to the sealing of adoption records? If so, then it would appear that the sealing of adoption records has caused *more* abortions over time, not fewer. What about the states that never sealed their adoption records or did so only in recent years? I may be a bit naive about many things, but I believe that changes in the abortion rate over the last century were driven more by court decisions legalizing abortions and the corresponding growth of abortion clinics than by changes in the laws regarding adoption records.

Access to information about one's true genetic lineage and medical history should be viewed and treated as a civil rights issue. Why? If for no other reason than the withholding of that information from adoptees separates one class of citizens in this society from the rest and subjects them to different limitations on their fundamental rights. After all, those who have not been adopted cannot be legally denied by the state access to basic information about themselves. The law restricting access to that information applies *only* and *exclusively* to adoptees, even though it provides no substantive or necessary public benefit to society. It also makes adoptees the only class of citizens in society that can have one of their basic, fundamental privacy rights (access to basic public records about themselves) procedurally stripped away by the state as a child, never again to be restored as an adult. My background information was made the exclusive property of the state and the courts long before I had any legal right to object. Control of information regarding one's true identity, medical history, and lineage is, to me, a civil rights issue, for all the same *reasons* (although not to the same *degree*) as suffrage was to women or freedom was to slaves.

To further reinforce my point, consider a recent bill (House Bill 286) that was introduced before the General Assembly of North Carolina during its 1999 session. At first blush, the bill appeared to assist adoptees searching to find their biological families. It would have established a public registry for adoptees and birth families to post and exchange search information. However, the bill also sought to make it a Class I felony for an adoptee to access sealed information in any form *outside* of the public registry. In essence, that bill (had it passed into law) could have made me guilty of a major crime for having conducted my own adoptee search. Although my search involved the use of public records that any non-adoptee could use for genealogical research, the bill considered by the North Carolina Legislature could be interpreted in a way that would make it illegal for an adoptee to use them in much the same vein. What public benefit does a law like that really serve? Do we really need laws to punish adoptees because they want to know their genetic and medical backgrounds? Would it really make the streets of Charlotte or Raleigh safer to know that some adoptee will not be slinking around in the dark of night trying to discover where he came from?

As far as those who object to open record adoptions on moral or religious grounds are concerned, I would like to recommend some additional Bible study, specifically on the story of Moses. After all, he would appear to be the earliest recorded adoptee, even if his placement wasn't officially processed as such by the Egyptian government. However, he was effectively adopted by the reigning King of Egypt, which was about as close to official government sanction as it could get. I find it quite interesting that, according to the Bible, God eventually made Moses aware of his biological roots and that awareness was part of His plan to lead the Hebrews out of their enslavement (at the hands of his adoptive father) and into the Promised Land. I find it even more ironic that, out of all the people alive during Moses' time, God would choose him—the world's earliest recorded adoptee—to receive the Ten Commandments, one of which explicitly says, "Honor thy father and thy mother..." If God thought that open adoption records might lead to higher incidents of abortion, do you really think that He would have led Moses to find his biological mother? Furthermore, what do you think God was really saying when He gave that particular Commandment to an adoptee?

As far as I'm concerned, I don't feel that I did anything wrong or immoral in searching for my biological family. I feel that my reunion with them has had only positive benefits for all of us, even as it became the undoing of my adoptive family relationship. For what it's worth, I never intended or asked for that to happen, and if I had, I wouldn't have continued to communicate with the only members of that family who accepted me for who I really am. I do not resent being an adoptee, and I am not opposed to adoption, per se. I just don't like being treated or judged differently because of it. Moreover, I am disappointed that our wonderful system of government cannot seem to find a way to legitimize open adoptions as the preferred process. After all, adoption is primarily intended to *benefit* the adoptee, not deny the adoptee access to his medical history. Does an adoptive family really have to *own* an adoptee in order to make that child an equal part of its family? Why can't we use the adoption process to give a needy child a *second* family that can provide a supportive, nurturing environment that the child's biological parents or family might not otherwise be able to provide on their own? Isn't that the emotional (fairy tale) happy ending that we would truly desire for every unwanted or abandoned child? That's what I hope that adoption in this country can eventually become.

On October 1, 2000, as I was writing this story, Alabama became only the third state in the union to enact a law (after Oregon and Tennessee) that allowed adult adoptees to access information about their birth records, essentially re-opening sealed adoption records. After all the criticisms I have heard from people across the country about Alabama's historic record on civil rights, I am proud to say that Alabama became one of the undisputed leaders in this country in recognizing the basic civil rights of adult adoptees. Oddly enough, it occurred with little disruption in the normal course of events. There were no reported incidents of mass rioting, looting, or moral decay. As far as I know, no waiting lines formed at the few abortion clinics that existed around the state, nor did the new law become the topic of any church sermons. In fact, the sun rose and set that day, just as it has throughout recorded history. I can safely report that it continues to do so today a full fourteen years after the law went into effect.

According to the American Adoption Congress, which supports and actively promotes open record adoption laws, a total of only nine states had enacted open record laws by 2014. They are Alabama, Alaska, Colorado, Kansas, Maine, New Jersey, New Hampshire, Oregon, and Tennessee. As I noted earlier, adoption files were *never* closed in Kansas, and they were only closed in Alabama after 1990. When New Hampshire finally opened its records in 2005, I obtained a copy of my original (unamended) birth certificate—the most basic record I was denied throughout my search. Although it would have confirmed my birth mother's name, it bore an incorrect home address that she used when I was born. Fortunately, I corrected all of the lies (both by the state and my mother) when I amended my birth certificate as part of my 1998 readoption process. I had to argue with the Portsmouth city clerk to amend it, and she had to be further instructed by the NH Department of Health and Human Services before she would correct and release it. That amended birth certificate remains the only fully truthful one of the three I possess. I still keep the original birth certificate I received from the Portsmouth city clerk as a spoil of war and a vindication of my search efforts.

Although nine states now have open adoption records, an additional seven (Connecticut, Delaware, Illinois, Massachusetts, Montana, Ohio, and Vermont) have adopted some limited open record laws with specific restrictions. The restrictions usually relate to adoption records that were finalized before a certain year or adoptions where a birth parent has specifically requested that the files remain sealed. Again, what specific benefit do those restrictions serve? If only nine states have fully recognized basic adoptee rights by 2014, I feel we have a long way to go.

I only hope that those of you who read my story will gain from it a broader perspective on the adoption process and what it really means for many people affected by it. Obviously, I don't speak for all adoptees (and would never pretend to), but my experiences are not as unique as most adoption professionals would have you believe. Just look at how the adoption process impacted my own adoptive and biological families. In my case, those impacts went far beyond simple questions and curiosity. My adoptive father was always fond of saying, "Before you judge someone, you should walk a mile in his shoes." That should be especially true of those who advocate for laws that create a second class of citizens or deny legal equality to a small segment of the population. I truly hope the North Carolina legislature hears and understands my words. If adoption is truly intended to benefit the children, please make sure that it respects *all* of their needs, both as children *and* as future independent adults. If there is to be a true meaning for the bizarre life I have led, I believe that is it. It is also the moral I would like to offer for my own life story.

www.ingramcontent.com/pod-product-compliance
Lightning Source LLC
Chambersburg PA
CBHW061959280526
45787CB00005B/1922